The Fight Of My Life Is Wrapped Up In My Father

Involve fathers are God's antidote against youth

REBELLION

© Copyright 2013 Drexel Deal

All Rights Reserved

ISBN #: 13-9780615885506

No part of this publication may be reproduced, stored in a retrieval system or transmitted in any form or by any means without the prior written permission of the author.

DISCLAIMER:

- Some names and identifying details have been changed to protect the privacy of individuals.

- Although the author and publisher have made every effort to ensure that the information in this book was correct at press time, the author and publisher do not assume and hereby disclaim any liability to any party for any loss, damage, or disruption caused by errors or omissions, whether such errors or omissions result from negligence, accident, or any other cause.

Acknowledgments

First of all, I would like to thank the almighty God for his amazing power to save and deliver us from anything, and from out of everything. I'm what I am today, and I'm where I am today because of your grace and tender mercy toward me. I thank you for a second lease on life, for a second chance to do it the right way and that is your way which is always right. As you say in your word, "Whoever offers praise glorifies me; and to him who orders his conduct aright I will show the salvation of God." Psalms 50: 23 NKJV.

I would also like to express my deepest gratitude and appreciation to the many people who made this book possible. To all those whom I was fortunate to have interviewed, many thanks go out to you. To those who allowed me to quote their words I am eternally in your debt.

To my Editor, Natalie Ballard, thank you for taking on a novice like me. For putting up with my rewrites, and not to mention my strong Bahamian dialect that is often found in my writings.

Special thanks to Dr. D. Paul Riley, who has been a mentor and father figure in my life. I thank God for directing me to you, for you saw in me what so many others missed. You brought out in me what others couldn't, and you believed in me when I didn't even believe in myself. You didn't only inspire me with your words, but you supported me in just about all of my undertakings. I know that the path I'm on now is because of you.

Special thanks go out to Lenore Armstrong, thank you for being there and for your help.

Special thanks also goes out to Raquel Davis, and my nephew Leon Strachan Jr., for jumping in and assisting me at the last minute. It helped me to appreciate, that help is never far away in our family. Many thanks go out to you all.

To my mother, Angela and my sisters Vanessa and Mellissa, thank you for your support in my darkest hour. I'm sorry for the hurt and pain that I put you all through. I can now see that when I wrecked my life I did the same to you all. I love you guys, stay strong and let's continue to move on together.

To my son Lowell, you continue to teach me each day what it means to be a father. You're the best son any father could ever ask for. I'm proud of you, and I will always love you. To my nieces and nephews I thank God for you all, and my commitment is to support you as I would support my son.
To my aunts Pearlene and Paula the back bone of our family, I and others could never thank you enough for fighting for us before we were even born. You two are real soldiers, and I salute you from the bottom of my heart. Aunt Pearlene: you've taught me how to fight for one's family. Aunt Paula: you've taught me how to give unselfishly to one's family. Together you two have moved mountains that once stood in our way. I know that we don't say it much, but you gals are truly appreciated.
To my other family members, thank you for your support over the years. To my cousins Otis, Ricardo, JJ and Jamie I'm proud of you guys, continue to stand firm and don't forget together we stand stronger.
To Cheryl Williams Forbes from New York, thank you for being a friend and a second mother.
To Kimberly Rolle-Gibson in the Berry islands, thank you for being a friend.
To Norman, you're the true definition of what a true friend is all about. May you do well in your new life, and I'm proud of your turn around.
I humbly beg forgiveness for not mentioning all those who have supported me in word and deed over the 17 years of my blindness. Your names are just too numerous to mention but thank you and may God richly bless you all.
Special thanks also go out to those who financially assisted me, in making this book a reality through their kind donations such as: Mr. Marlon Johnson from BTC, Mr. Robert Baker from Bahamas Industrial Maintenance LTD., Bishop Laish Boyd from The Anglican Diocese. The Bahamas Alliance for the Blind, and the Disabled Persons' Organization.
Not to mention my cousin and little brother, Mr. Jamain Carey and his wife Anastasia. Who are the proprietors of CareyScape Depot. From The Royal Bahamas Police Force, Mr. Ellison Greenslade our Commissioner of Police, and Mr. Felix Stubbs from IBM. Not to mention my good friends Mr. Jamaal Farquharson, a long with Mr. Vance McKenzie and his wife Kenya proprietors of Baha Retreat.

Table of Contents

Acknowledgments..2
Table of Contents..4
Preface..5
Introduction..11
Chapter 1:　The Robbery 15
Chapter 2:　Almost Burned Alive..................................32
Chapter 3:　The Unwanted Child...................................53
Chapter 4:　My Quiet and Angry Years.........................75
Chapter 5:　My Eruption in School................................95
Chapter 6:　Kicked Out Of School...............................110
Chapter 7:　From Idle to Criminal................................128
Chapter 8:　A Close Call..145
Chapter 9:　Landing in the Hawks' Nest......................158
Chapter 10: From A Youngster to a Monster................175
Chapter 11:　The Ultimate Lesson from Prison..................190
Chapter 12: The Birth of the Rebellions.......................203
Chapter 13: When Underdogs Unite.............................223
Chapter 14: The Ultimate Bahamian Cultural Expression....250
Chapter 15: The War within..268
Epilog: 286
Appendix...288

Preface
The Dream

"All our dreams can come true, if we have the courage to pursue them." —Walt Disney

"I'm disappointed in you," said Judge Banks.
"I know. I'm disappointed in myself," says Will Smith, with his head hanging down toward the ground in shame.
Judge Banks just looked at him in silence, with deep disappointment in his eyes. He then said, "There's a book I read several weeks ago. I can't remember the name of the author, but the book is called, *"The Fight of My Life is Wrapped Up in My Father."* Son, I want you to read this book."
I now sat up with rapt attention as I watched The Fresh Prince of Bell-Air. What started out as simple entertainment was now becoming educational. Being a book lover, I wondered why Judge Banks wants Will to read this particular book. I reasoned to myself, if a street-smart brother from Philly could benefit from that book, then I better read it too. I hoped that Judge Banks would repeat the book's title once more.
Will Smith slowly raised his head and said, "Okay," believing that he's getting off the hook easily just by agreeing to read a book. He began to say, "So I guess . . ."
But the judge firmly cuts him off and said, "I will decide your punishment later. Once you have read the book, then we can meet to discuss it further."

Disappointed, Will said with a defeated gesture, "Okay, okay."
Now there's a look on Will's face as if he's almost forgotten something. He asked, "So what's the name of that book again?"

I'm really tuned in this time, and I have my paper and pen ready in hand.
My heart skipped a beat as Judge Banks slowly repeats the name again, this time putting emphasis on each word: ***"The Fight of My Life is Wrapped Up in My Father."***

Relief washed over me once I had captured the title. Like a kid in a candy store, I squealed with delight for this was my lucky day. I have the name of the book! Looking down at what I had written, I couldn't believe my good fortune. This is how I've stumbled across some of the best books in my collection.

Now back to The Fresh Prince. I didn't know what Will Smith had done this time, but I knew one thing Judge Banks was really ticked off with him. However, I knew something else as well; I was going to finish reading this book before Will. What made this book even more valuable to me is that it had been recommended by my favorite TV comedy show. As I pondered over the title that would soon be added to my collection, from out of nowhere somebody or something hit me really hard, bringing me out of my dream.

I woke up dazed and disoriented. I couldn't see a thing around me, because everything was in total darkness. I knew that I was not at home. This was not my room and I was not lying in my own bed. Instead of panicking, I just lie still on the bed and allowed my ears to tell me where I was. Most of all, I wanted to know who in the world hit me. I was ready for a fight now. Here I was enjoying the best dream of my life and someone had the audacity to wake me up from it; this had better be good.

I lie there trying to sense who else was in the room with me, because if it was an intruder then this was going to be an all-out fight. Even though I was totally blind and couldn't see a thing, yet this was in the early morning hours, which meant it was still dark. If someone was in here with me, then he was just as blind as I am. But I also had something else up my sleeve—the element of shock and surprise. Whoever it was, they wouldn't be expecting a fight from a blind person.

At first, the only thing that was audible was my own heart frantically pounding away in my chest. As I tried to figure out what was going on, I slowly took in several deep breaths, trying to make it sound as if I was still asleep. More importantly, I wanted to get my heartbeat under control and keep this person off guard, and in doing so maybe I could sense where they were in the room. My remaining senses were now working in overdrive as they bounced from wall to wall in an attempt to pinpoint and honed in on my target. There was no doubt in my mind that someone was in here with me, because that hit was just too hard to be mistaken for something else. Within seconds, my heartbeat was under control, but I had yet to sense any movement and I still didn't know where I was.

After a few more seconds of lying there, taking in the quietness of the early morning hours, my memory slowly began to come back to me. I could hear the distant sounds of the sea waves as they made their way in and splashed on the shore. I smell the fresh fragrant scent of the ocean breeze as it gently blew against the curtains at the windows. But the sound of the curtain flapping in the wind was the only sound coming from within the room other than that, it was quiet.

I could neither hear nor sense the presence of anyone else in the room with me. This was one of the first things I learned after becoming blind: everything and everyone has a presence, right down to the light coming from a simple light bulb. However, the only sound was that of the sea breeze gently blowing through the windows, and so I relaxed but remained motionless, taking in everything with my senses.

I never knew that sleeping by the sea could be so delightfully invigorating for the mind and body. Lying here taking in the various sounds and scent of the sea was like a dream of its own. No wonder millions of tourists flock to our shores each year. It's not just the sun, sand, and sea I believe they come for, but it's the tranquil serenity of it all. It's just a shame that I never recognized it before the loss of my sight. It was about that time that it all came back to me, where I was, and why I was not in my own bed.

I was on one of the small inhabited islands of The Bahamas, called Bimini, which is pronounced bim-mi-nee. I was in route home to Nassau, which was my reason for being on this small but majestic island. The island of Bimini is just seven miles long and less than a mile wide. It is approximately 120 miles off Nassau, the capital of The Bahamas, and is the closest point in The Bahamas to the mainland of the United States, located a mere 50 miles from Florida. The population of this northernmost island is 1,600.

The island is rich in history, and was a favorite getaway spot for the American journalist and best-selling author Ernest Hemingway, as well as Adam Clayton Powell, Jr., the first African American Congressman, and the late civil rights leader Dr. Martin Luther King, Jr.* I had spent the last two weeks of 2002 in Cat Cay, which is another smaller, privately owned island just eight miles off Bimini. I had visited my mother Angela whom everyone called Angie, and my Aunt Paula, both of whom had been working on this tropical paradise for the past four months. [1]

While on Cat Cay, I had met Pastor Rolle, who is a native of Bimini. It was then that I asked him if he could set up a speaking engagement for me on the island to address students at the public all-age school there. Pastor Rolle not only arranged the speaking engagement for the public school, but also lined me up to speak to the only two private schools on the island as well as one of the local churches. At that time, I had been totally blind for six years and seven months. I lost my sight in a foiled armed robbery attempt just two days after my 21st birthday in 1996. I was shot four times at close range with a 12-gauge shotgun. One of those shots hit me in my head which resulted in me being totally blind.

For the past two years, I had been speaking to various private and public schools in Nassau making students aware of the dangers of gang violence and of the short-term payment of crime. Through the aid of Toastmasters and many others, I was able to take the mess of my life and craft a stern but compelling message for our youths, using my life as a warning of the permanent consequences that can result from a life of crime and gang violence.

---

*appendix

A relative of Pastor Arthur Rolle, who was not on the island at the time, owned the house that I was staying in on Bimini. This meant that I was by myself, and so everything was quiet throughout the entire house. Now that I was aware of why I was sleeping in this strange bed, I was still trying to figure out who or what in the world hit me. Even as I pondered this, I felt no physical pain, which was strange to me because it was a very hard hit. As I lie there quiet and still, I got this weird sensation or revelation as some would call it. I realized that the hit that woke me, was not external rather it was internal. As I've said before, I felt no pain, but there was a slight throbbing that was fading away within me. It was as if someone took a sledgehammer and swung it with both hands to hit a 500-pound brass church bell. What woke me was not the sound, because there was no sound. Rather it was the vibration from the hit, which woke me up and caused me to feel this throbbing on the inside.

I lied there in bed still and quiet, trying to wrap my mind around what I had just experienced. I asked myself, "What manner of thing is this that goes around hitting people inwardly?"

Then I remembered the dream, which was a welcome distraction from the inward knock. Now, one must appreciate that I do not remember 90% of my dreams, and if I do, it is days later when something happens that triggers the memory of such. So to be able to remember this dream shortly after waking up was most gratifying, especially because I had the name of a book I most definitely wanted. I slowly rolled out of bed, located my digital recorder, and recorded the title of the book from my dream. I know that I have a good memory, but this book sounded too serious to be trusted to memory alone. As the Chinese proverb goes, "Better a light ink pen than the strongest memory." I guess in my case it would probably read, "Better your recorder than your memory." As I lie back down, I couldn't believe my good fortune. Not only was I able to remember my dream, but I also got a book title as well.

In the year 2000, I had spent more than $600 on audio books alone. The reason I remembered the amount so clearly is because my bookstore of choice, Logos Book Store, had a promotion going on at the time. Any customer who spent more than $500 in a year on book purchases could win a $50 gift certificate. It goes without saying; I won the gift certificate.

As soon as I got back to Nassau, I set about locating the book by placing a call to Logos, asking them to find the book for me online. I didn't have the name of an author to give them, nor the ISBN number for the book to make their search easier. None-the-less, the young lady at the store said that she would call me back in a few minutes when she found it, and also tell me the cost to land it in Nassau. The long and the short of it is this. When she called back, she told me that the book didn't exist, at least not by that title. When I told her how I came across the name of the book, she adjusted her search terms but nothing came up even close.

I hung up the phone, feeling a bit disappointed and frustrated at the same time. I knew that I remembered the correct name of the book, and had even taken immediate steps to record the title just to make sure I didn't forget it. Moreover, it sounded like a logical title of a book to me; even the young lady herself said so. So why couldn't I find it? Better yet, why in the world couldn't the bookstore clerk find it? The answer came to me as clear as the bell vibration that woke me up on the island of Bimini: "The book doesn't exist because you haven't written it yet."

INTRODUCTION

"Sometimes the best way to understand something of value is to study its absence." —Richard Carlson, PhD.

This book is a study of the negative aftermath of the absentee father. Growing up without a father, I now realize through my interviews with many former gang members and harden criminals, that we all shared a common bond of neglect, rejection and fatherlessness.

Therefore, in our quest to be loved, accepted and appreciated we created a world of our own. Looking back, I can now better appreciate that we never chose to join a gang, rather we just chose to be a part of a more loving family. Whose home just happened to be the streets, and the way we showed our love and support of each other was through violence.

This is a project that has been in the making for more than ten years. The book is written in such a way, that parents, young adults and teenagers can understand and relate to. It's gripping, vividly graphic, and dramatic as I relate the brutality and savagery of gang life. The interviews are with many former gang members, gang leaders, drug dealers, and former death row inmates. Even though some of these individuals were from rival gangs, yet we were able to put aside our differences, for we had come to realize that our backgrounds and home conditions were quite similar. Each interviewee brings the picture into clearer focus, and at the bottom of this picture, just one thing stands out: Absentee Fathers.

There's no doubt in my mind, that the gangs were our feeble attempt to replace our fathers. So what was it the gang provided for us that we were unable to get from our homes? Why are gang members so loyal to their gang and each other? What is it that attracts a young person to join a gang, or to get involved in a life of crime? Why were we so fascinated with guns, and the senseless violence we inflicted on each other? Even though we had this strong bond of unity, and the gang was the family we always wanted, yet one day without warning, my gang exploded in a deadly internal war. I now found myself desperately fighting for my life against friends, and a leader who was not only violent, ruthless, and brutal, but more strategically clever about the cold art of war.

Through my interviews with him, I would also learn that he once put out an execution order on my life. The result of which led to me being shot, after dodging and running from a hail of bullets. When he revealed to me what save my life on that night, it makes the hair on the back of my neck stand up. He helped me to appreciate, that I was not lucky on that night I was shot, but rather I was saved by a higher power for such a time as this. As he himself said, "I'm glad the way the whole thing gone, because that means you have a bigger purpose what you're serving now, and I have a bigger purpose why the Lord choose to still let me be here."

We will sit down with this mysterious individual, as he and I go head to head once again. With our differences way behind us, we will look back on our lives to discover how we went from youngsters to monsters. By revealing how easy it was for us to stumble into a life of crime, and eventually becoming hardcore gangsters and remorseless predators.

This individual goes by the street name 'Scrooge'. He is one who prefers to lurk behind in the shadows, to be heard of but not seen, to have his presence felt without being present. Scrooge is a clever and charismatic person, with the communication skills of a politician, the military intelligence of a four-star general and the leadership skills of a President of a fortune 500 Company.

Yet one would never guess that he was a gangster, much less the leader of the most notorious street gang in The Bahamas. One former high ranking police officer once described him as, *"A calm person with a beautiful smile."*

When one combines these unique skills together with his violent nature, you don't just end up with a gang leader, but the godfather of street gangs in The Bahamas. Who took the concept from the home, and built the largest street gang in our country. By taking thirteen seemingly unpretentious young men, and grew them into thousands and one of the largest gangs in the Caribbean, the 'Rebellion Raiders'.

Scrooge himself said, *"I came from as low as one could come, with no mother and no father. So in return I build a family for myself and these fellas were a part of my family. So I had to look out for them, as if I was looking out for my children."*

He reveals how the 'Rebellions' came about, how they went from the under dogs, to become the top dogs in the gang world. One will see that the answer to our gang and crime problems, are found in those conditions which brought about the Rebellions and many other gangs. We will also look at what brought the Rebellions crashing down, which was the result of a furious internal war between him and me. Not to mention other interviews with social experts such as police officers, educators, youth pastors, psychologists, and even a former member of parliament who all helped to bring the solutions to our social ills into clearer focus. Even though each interviewee experiences, back ground and level of education are all different, yet their advice and input are supportive of each other.

No two interviews were conducted together, and some were even conducted years apart. Yet one would often discover throughout this book, a high ranking police official's insight being the same ones shared by a gangster. It truly brings the scripture alive when it states in Deuteronomy 19: 15 *"by the mouth of two or three witnesses the matter shall be established." NKJV.*

We will uncover and learn together how our children's hopes, dreams, and futures are all tightly wrapped up in us as fathers. While this book is geared towards fathers, yet it is a must read especially for single mothers. In fact I was raised by a single mother, and in my country more than 70% of children are born outside of marriage each year. So what does a mother do when her son tells her, that he has chosen crime as a career? How can a single mother steer her child away from gangs and a life of crime, which so often leads to imprisonment or an early death?

What does a mother do when her child gives her money that she knows he didn't work for? To top it off, things are rough at home, the telephone is off, the cupboard is bare, and she is behind on her bills. How does a parent become a willing party to their child's death?

More importantly, those of us who were once involved in a life of crime and were considered monsters, we will retrace our steps and answer three important questions. First, how did we become what we were? As we all are aware, no child is born a gangster or a criminal; we were just as cute, adorable, and cuddly as any newborn baby. So what went wrong? How did I and so many others stumbled into a life of crime, and grew into monsters?

Secondly, how did we make that change and exit a world of violence, criminality and tyranny and live to talk about it? What you will find out is this: somebody intervened in each of our lives. So what did they say to us to get us thinking differently? While not all of us made it out, there are a few who are still in the trenches so to speak. Therefore you will be provided, with up to the minute intelligence on the mindset of today's youth.

Third and most importantly, we will cut to the chase and answer the real questions. How can we now prevent others from getting into such self-defeating and destructive lifestyles? How can we better strengthen families and communities to become resistant to such negative social trends?

The central theme of this book is prevention. Is it not better to prevent a crime, rather than talk about how well we can solve it? Isn't it far better to prevent the development of a monster, rather than talk about how well we can capture and cage such a monster?

In order to make this book practical to the challenges our youths face today, we will begin by looking at what were my home conditions growing up, as well as my behavioral problems at school and how I entered a life of crime and eventually joining a notorious street gang.

In spite of being both emotionally deficient and physically disfigured, after the shooting which left me blind, I can honestly say I have no regrets about my disability, for I know of too many close friends and acquaintances who didn't survive the streets. It was due to the loss of my physical sight, which enabled me to save something much greater, that being my life. As it states in Matthew 5:29, *"For it is more profitable for you that one of your members perish, than for your whole body to be cast into hell." NKJV*.

Chapter 1
THE ROBBERY

"Robbery always claims the life of the robber—this is what happens to anyone who lives by violence." —Proverbs 1:19

Violence is rather a strange phenomenon that can be compared to fire, and once out of control it's loyal to no one, not even to the person who started it. For those of us who lived by violence; we were also consumed by it. We once prevailed and conquered our foes by it, and in return for our reward, it conquered us. One day you are its accomplice as the perpetrator, and the next day you are its victim.

Yet this was my life before losing my sight, I was committed to the street game of gangbanging. This also meant that anything goes in my world, especially when it came to making a dollar. As a hard-core gangster I came up from the bottom committing petty crimes; now I'm at the top of this game and my crimes are much bigger. I earned every letter in my street name, Raw Deal, by shooting first and shooting again just for the fun of it. I had a simple philosophy when it came to the streets—actually it wasn't mine; I borrowed it from my father. He once told me, "If you're going to fight, hit first, and hit hard." Therefore, I was always on the offence. I hit first, never allowing anyone to throw the first blow.

As a result I was invited to become a member, of the largest and the most dangerous street gang in The Bahamas, called the Rebellion Raiders. I joined the Rebellions at the age of sixteen and committed myself to the gang so much so by the age of nineteen, I was one of its top generals. I robbed, stabbed and shot my way to the top. It wasn't long before the leader of the Rebellions and I was at odds with each other. It climaxed in a deadly shootout, ending with both of us being shot. This led to a rift in the gang. What followed next was a furious internal war. After the dust had settled, more Rebellions were shot and killed like never before at the hands of our very own.

Now at the age of 21, this is my wretched life, it's either shoot or be shot, kill or be killed, and my biggest threat comes from within my own gang. I know that this is the life I have chosen for myself, so now I have to ride with it or be run over by it, which I know would eventually happen one day. But right now, I'm determined to ride this out of control freight train to my grave.

Yet deep down within I want to be out of this suicidal game, even though I want out, but I don't know how to get out. To make matters worse, it's hard to walk away from this lifestyle, especially when you have shot so many people. Was I now going to say to my victims, "Hey, the game is over and I'm moving on with my life?" You have to be kidding; these guys want to only know that I'm dead.

They could care less if I had changed my life and was trying to do the right thing. It was for this reason I was always strapped, and was now pulling the trigger no longer to prove myself but rather I was doing it out of fear. The bravery was long gone; instead, it had been replaced with a sense of survival, and it's for this reason I seriously hated my life.

I had just shot an innocent fella the other night during a simple petty street armed robbery. This individual wanted to purchase a handgun, and I just happened to have had a 9 with a broken firing pin. After giving me his cash for the gun, I then pulled the 9 from my waistband and handed it to him. He checked out the 9 for a few seconds. I told him, "The gun is empty. I don't sell loaded guns for my safety and yours."

He looked the gun over and, satisfied with his purchase, he then stuffed it into the waistband of his pants. He was now ready for action. As a matter of fact, he even stood taller. It's amazing how one can get a sense of confidence just by having a gun in your waistband.

At this stage, I'm already ahead of the game, because the gun didn't work and I had his cash. But I wasn't ready to let go of that weapon yet; besides, there's three other people I wanted to sell this 9 to. I produced another 9 from my waistband and said to him in a gruff voice, "Give me my gun back." I could tell by the look on his face that he was stunned, for he just stood there for a second or two looking at the gun in my hand. I guess he was trying to figure out if I was serious. A street armed robbery always seems at first as if it's a joke, and I'm speaking from my own personal experience of being robbed as a teenager. The gun I held on him was also a 9, but this one was chrome and much bigger. This weapon was my main gun, for this baby has never let me down. I even dubbed her the 'Dog Killer', due to the many times I had used it in drive-by shootings in a rival gang community - the Hoyas Bull Dogs. This fella was still there staring at the gun in my hand and unable to move, so I pointed the muzzle at his waist. This time I shouted my request to him. "Give me my flipping gun!"

He jumped slightly as he came out of his trance, and this was where everything got messy. Moving with lightning speed, he drew the gun from his waistband and then point it at me muzzle first as if he was going to shoot. That was when I snapped, because I had seen this movie before, which was on the night I was shot by a fellow Rebellion. I had forgotten that the gun in his hand was unloaded, and didn't even work. I pulled the trigger twice hitting him in the hand holding the gun, and to his left side. The gun flew out of his hand and landed on the ground next to my right foot.

He quickly turned around and ran to his car [which was a small Honda CRX.] Once inside he started up the engine to make his escape. As he fumbled with the shift trying to find the reverse gear, I could tell that it was a standard shift vehicle. I was now in a full-blown anger and I didn't understand why, especially since I had the upper hand. I retrieved the gun from the ground and took two quick steps toward his vehicle. He was now reversing away so I fired two quick shots into the hood of his car.

Disgusted with myself for losing my cool, I turned around and quickly walked to my girlfriend's vehicle, which I was driving. With both guns now firmly secured in the waistband of my pants, I got behind the steering wheel of the car. At first, everything was quiet as I started up the vehicle and began to make my way out of the area.

Then I heard a voice coming from the backseat. "Deal, tell me you didn't shoot him?"

The person who had asked the question was Ryan 'Whitey' Woods. He was a top general in the Rebellions. Whitey was slimly built and stood about six foot one. His street name resulted from his fair complexion. It might have been his childhood nickname, but it was now his street name and he was respected throughout the island. His signature weapon of choice was the .357 magnum revolver, and it was Whitey who had set up this little street robbery.

In the back passenger seat to Whitey's left was Dolan, my top dog and right-hand man. Dolan was like a pit bull: he didn't talk much, but he was ruthless and vicious as they come. He had a long scar on the left side of his face. It made him look even more menacing, and caused one to think twice before saying or doing anything out of the way.

In the front passenger seat with me was my girlfriend Jackie, who was Dolan's older sister. Jackie was older than I was, and she was also the first female gangster that I had ever dated.

This was Jackie's third time witnessing me shoot someone, and during one of those shooting she was actually driving. I was now starting to wonder, which one of us were enjoying these shootings more? Truth be told, I think that she enjoyed it more than I did, because she was always talkative and excited after each shooting.

When Jackie and I were dating I was at the top of my street fame. Even though I only stood about 5ft. 9in., and weighed in around 175lbs, yet my street presence was much larger. I've always taken pride in my body, for I've always been lean and fit. I have broad shoulders, which was my reward for consistently doing pushups.

I'm the first to admit that I'm no prince charming; in fact I'm far from it. My face has always been spotted with acne from my teenage years. Not to mention I have one of those noses that demands attention, a gift from my bio dad. Yet for some strange reason, females have always been attracted to me, and it was usually they who made the first move.

I guess it's because I don't carry myself like some street ragamuffin, for my hair is always kept trim and I'm always well groom. For I never leave home with my pants hanging below my hips, for there's always a belt around my waist. In fact a belt is a necessary component of my daily wardrobe, for without it I cannot be strapped.

I'm just an ordinary looking young black male; and if you don't know me you would never suspect me of being a gangster. In fact not just any gangster, but someone capable of committing and ordering unspeakable horrors.

I'm a naturally quiet person and don't go looking for trouble. In truth I don't have to, because trouble always seems to find me. A former girlfriend name Latoya once told me, "By looking at you one would never guess that you could hurt a fly. But Oh, if people only knew."

Not only was I quiet, but I was also shy about making eye contact with anyone. Latoya often said to me: "You always look innocent, incapable of doing anything violent."

When one look at it carefully, she was indeed right. For I was always innocent, doesn't the law states that one is presume innocent until proven guilty?

As I was driving away from the shooting, I thought to myself, "I couldn't believe that I shot him either. It was a simple little street robbery. I had probably done this hundreds of time without ever firing a single shot. Yet I just shot someone for nothing.

The shooting itself didn't bother me; I've shot too many people for that. What bothered me most was the fact that I lost control; I lost my cool. I had always prided myself on being the calm one, the steady hand. I was the one who was always in control.

In fact I patterned my outward demeanor, after the FBI special agent Fox Mulder from the hit American TV series The X-Files. Who was always calm, expressionless, emotionless but effective at his job. Yet I'd just done the unthinkable—I panicked, and in so doing, I needlessly shot someone. To make matters worse, he probably knew my name. Hell, this was a dumb shooting. These were the ones I hated the most, because if charged before the courts, these were the most difficult cases to win.

My thoughts were interrupted by Whitey, as he repeated his question. "Deal, tell me you didn't shoot him?"

Shoots, I had forgotten about him. I had even forgotten that there were others in here with me. "Yeah, I shot him," I calmly replied.

Whitey sighed, and then slouched back in the soft black leather seat of Jackie's German made Ford Mercury. Batman has his Batmobile for catching thugs and bandits; well, Jackie's vehicle was our Gangstermobile for every sort of violent crime. The color was a dark navy blue that could pass for black at night, all of the windows were blacked out and the interior was also black.

Whitey then said in a low voice, "I told him who you were, just in case he had any funny (underhanded) ideas of trying to swing you."

There was a deep silence that engulfed the vehicle as we all thought about the implication of Whitey's words. This meant that I was no doubt going to be arrested for attempted murder, and in all likelihood, remanded to prison. There's nothing worse than a dumb, stupid crime, and this was most definitely one of them.

However, Jackie broke the silence by saying, "For a man who was shot, he sure moved pretty fast."

Then she asked, "Did you'll see how quickly he got into his car and drove away?"

Everyone laughed and added their own two cents about the incident, but I couldn't join in on their conversation, because I had too much mental chatter going on in my own head.

I was still angry with myself for losing control. This was the first time that such a thing had happened, and I hoped that it never happened again. I dropped Dolan and Whitey off, and it wasn't until I was home that I remembered that I didn't share the money from the robbery with them. It was four hundred dollars. Divided four ways, this meant that my take would only be one hundred dollars. Therefore, I was going to prison just for one hundred dollars. Oh, I just hate a dumb shooting!

However, two days later Whitey sent word to me. "The fella you shot the other night told the police he didn't know who shot him. But he's telling his boys on the block that he's going to kill you."

From the pit of my stomach, I let loose with a hearty laugh. It was more out of relief than anything else. I was thankful to this fella for helping me dodge an attempted murder and possibly an armed robbery charge. I just had to admire his spirit though, so from one gangster to another, I gave him a silent salute of respect, by saying inwardly, "Yeah, dog, yeah you ready."

On the other hand about killing me—well, he better join the line with others who wished to do the same. It would be a cold day in hell, for him or anyone else to creep up and shoot me simply because, I was always locked and loaded ready to fire at the drop of a hat. Whoever shoots me no doubt caught me with my weapon on safety. The man who would kill me must have nerves of steel, because I'm determined to go down shooting to my death.

It's A Dog Eat Lion Game

"Criminals do not die by the hands of the law. They die by the hands of other men." —George Bernard Shaw

Ever since joining the gang, I always knew that my life span was going to be a short one. Heck, I didn't even expect to see the age of 21. Yet here I am, alive and well to fight another day. Do you know what's so sad about all of this? I knew that I was going to die violently because of the life that I was living. But if the truth be told, I just didn't care. My thing was this, 'we all have to exit this world one day, so why not exit it with a bang?' Besides, if you asked me it's a lot quicker to go out that way. So if I didn't care about my life, then what makes you think that I would care about another's life?

My life is long gone, and I have already accepted my faith. In fact, I'm already having nightmares of being gunned down by my two worse enemies, namely Franz a fellow Rebellion. The next one was Die a rival gang leader, who would go on to be dubbed The Bahamas top gangster

However, here's the worse part about all of this, how do you defend against a person who is ready to die? How do you defend against a person who don't fear being sent to prison for life? How do you defend against a person who has nothing to lose? It's like trying to defend against a suicide bomber, who has no problem going out in a glorified bang.

I had also discovered something strange but true. The fact is, all gangsters live in dog years. We come up fast in terms of making a name for ourselves, but, once our names have been established on the streets, we are on our way out. When you have developed a serious street reputation, then you begin to live on borrowed time. Often enough the person to cut you down will be someone younger than you, who is more vicious and has something to prove. The truth is, it is the younger inexperience gangsters who often cut down the older original gangsters. The best way for this young thug to prove himself to others, is to simply cut down an established gangster.

Thus, this cruel cycle of senseless violence repeats itself, with the younger being more vicious and rootless than his predecessor. It's the dog, who kills the lion, and once he has killed the lion, he's no longer a dog; he's now a lion himself. Yet this is nothing new. Once upon a time, there was a young unknown shepherd boy by the name of David. Who cut down the elite, battle-tested warrior Goliath, and just like that, David became an instant hero. Some thousands of years after his death, David is still best known for killing Goliath. I too would take a similar path to the top in the gang world, for my quick rise to the top was as a result of shooting the leader of my gang.

The gang that I'm a part of was best known for its unity. But right now, it was quickly disintegrating, not from forces without, but from within. We were turning our guns on each other. I had already survived two such encounters that could've been fatal. Instead, both times I just limped away with a shot to my left leg. I wonder how unlucky can one leg be, to be hit twice with a .357 magnum. But who's complaining? My left leg is as good as ever and I'm alive to fight another day.

I have also discovered that it's essential to have nine lives like a cat when one is in a gang, because every one of them will be needed. If I was going down a checklist, this would've been the first thing checked on my list. However, I was using up mine too quickly. It was as if they were soda pops I was going through. As a matter of fact, I was using them up even before I joined the gang, and it would only accelerate once I joined up with the Rebellions.

How many close encounters with death can one person survive? At the age of 21, I had surpassed more than 10 such close encounters with death, which began when I was but 5 years of age. This enemy who has been hotly pursuing me for more than 16 years has no shame to his game at all. At least with me there were certain things I would've never done, and knowingly hurt a child was just one of them.

What Makes Armed Robbers So Dangerous

"One who has a deaden conscience can never live within the confinements of the law."

I was patiently waiting for the arrival of an armored vehicle that I had been watching for two and a half months. Tonight was the night that I was going to make my move. The reason I had watched them for so long, because there was a particular time of the month that I wanted to pull off this armed robbery. I guess that every businessperson might agree that sales are much better at the end of the month, largely in part because of government payday. One of the local food store giants owned the armored vehicle that I was watching. Two of the store's daytime security officers, both armed with shotguns, operated the armored vehicle. They would normally pick up the deposit bags from the store's ten different locations and then make one final deposit to the bank.

The part I hated most about this type of armed robbery was the wait that could sometimes be nerve-racking. There are just so many things that could go wrong. Suppose my intended target sees me —who, by the way are armed with their own guns, or someone else sees me and calls the police.

For me the hardest part about committing any armed robbery is getting started. It is that decision to act right then, or to get the ball rolling. But, once you've engaged your target, everything is a blur; that is just how quickly it happens.

As I lie in wait for my target, I'm nervous, afraid, hyped up, and my mind is filled with second guesses. It is a feeling that never leaves you regardless of how many armed robberies you have already committed. You are always afraid. I could understand why some fellas take drugs just before their crimes: because they need something to help them quiet their minds. However, I don't do drugs nor do I drink alcohol, but the thing that gets me high like a kite is a crime well done. Then there's the scent of freshly fired gunpowder, or the sounds of the empty bullet casings hitting the ground as they are ejected each time I pull the trigger. These two things never fail to get me high; the truth is I'm seriously addicted to violence.

There is another dangerous component to armed robberies, one that I could never understand. I noticed some time ago that with each robbery I committed there was an intense out of control anger that gripped me. It was as if I was there to get something that was inherently mine, and I came to take it by force. I've heard many stories directly from individuals about how they just burst into stores with their guns drawn. They would be shouting at people, gun butting them sometimes for no reason at all. One individual told me that he ran into a store and jump kicked a fella who just stood there. The only reason he was kicked is that he was there.

It's as if once you've overridden your conscience of going through with the act, it is replaced with anger and a level of brutality that is usually reserved for when you are fighting for your life. This, to me, is what makes armed robberies so dangerous—because the slightest provocation or any sudden movement by anyone could lead to them being shot or killed. It is always an extremely delicate and dicey situation, because the armed robber is pulling the trigger out of fear more than anything else.

As with many of my past criminal offenses, I stumbled across this armored vehicle night deposit routine. There is an actual term that the police use for this: "crimes of opportunity."

Some months prior to this, I had been riding past a bank with a friend named Norman. I noticed a male get out of a vehicle, bend down to tie his shoelace, get up, and look around him. Then he took a sealed package out of a paper bag that he was carrying in his hand, and quickly dropped it into a night deposit drop box. I couldn't believe my eyes. I said to Norman in amazement, "Did you see that just now?"

Norman said, "See what?"

I pointed to the man, who was now heading back to his vehicle, and said, "Homeboy just made a cash deposit."
I looked at the time and made note of the day of the week. Then I said to Norman, "I'll be back here next week, about a half an hour earlier, looking out for him to see if he would do the same thing again."
Norman asked me, "If he comes back next week and do the same thing again, what are you going to do?"
Never taking my eyes off the individual who was now in his vehicle, I calmly said, "we gon' rob him." We continued on our way to wherever we were going.
The following week on the same day but about an hour earlier, I was there by myself watching in the distance with my binoculars—that's right, my binoculars. I was one who truly believed in investing in his tools. Before the loss of my sight, I had a bulletproof vest, synchronized walkie-talkie, and eight handguns in my possession. As they say, a man is only as good as his tools. Even though I was hiding some two blocks away from the bank, I could see everything as if I was standing just a few feet away.
Some forty-five minutes later, the same vehicle from last week pulled up. This time I was able to see the company's name, painted on the side of the vehicle. Then the same guy from last week got out with a bag in his hand, and casually approached the deposit box. He bent down as if to tie his shoelaces, and covertly looked to the left and to the right. Then he got up and took a good look around him, and in a flash, he made his deposit. I smiled and said, "I gat ya, buddy."
I couldn't believe how easy he was making this. I looked at the other vehicles closely to make sure that another vehicle, which may just have some off duty police officers in it, wasn't following him. But to my surprise, this chap was working alone. I removed the binoculars from my eyes and wondered, how stupid can this person be. Who in the world was advising him? This wasn't a small company whose vehicle he was driving, but for goodness sake; they were taunting me to rob them. He came back on the same day of the week, around the same time and driving the same vehicle.

The following week, again on the same day and time, I made my move. When he came out of his vehicle and did that little trick, pretending as if he was tying his shoelace, as he was getting up from his survey of the area, I was already there waiting on him with my gun in my hand. I crept up on him from his blind side; he never even saw or heard me coming. With my gun firmly pressed against his lower back, I shouted at him, "Give me the bag!"

He spun around and his eyes widened with fear, when he saw me standing there wearing a mask and holding a gun in my hand. I could tell by the expression on his face that his worst fear was now a reality. I always liked this particular part of an armed robbery; the shouting, it always psyches you up but spooks the victim out. He slowly began to back away from me. I pointed at the bag in his hand and shouted again, "Give me the flipping bag!"

He handed the bag over to me. Correction: he threw the bag at me. Like a football wide receiver, I caught it in midair, and in a flash, I was gone. I then dashed around the building to the back road, where Norman was waiting in his truck. He drove a blue solid Chevy Silverado 1500 series pickup truck, that was always kept sparkling clean. Norman pulled up alongside me and stopped, and like an athlete I dove onto the back bed of the truck without touching the sides. As soon as my body made contact with the flatbed of the truck, Norman pushed the pedal to the metal, and we took off with the sound of tires screaming and rubber burning—another successful one under my belt.   These were the armed robberies I favored, as opposed to running in stores and demanding money from people. This type of armed robbery took less time and was less confrontational. They were quick, simple, and easy. In less than ten seconds, the deed was usually done. Some bystanders didn't even realize what took place. However, at the same time it was riskier because the act itself was being committed in the open, so you never knew who was around or if an off-duty police officer was following them in a different vehicle. I had a simple motto for armed robberies that I borrowed from the Jamaican reggae artist Terror Fabulous. He said in one of his songs, "Gangster brandish his gun and get paid." Well, I guess today was payday for me, because I just brandished my gun and was paid.

The Take Down
"To do evil is like sport to a fool, but a man of understanding has wisdom." —Proverbs 10: 23
It was one of those beautiful, warm tropical evening, for we were in the heart of summer on the island. Yet the temperature wasn't that unbearable. The air was still and the humidity was high, but it was a perfect evening for an outdoor barbecue. However, on this night I had other plans in mind, plans that would prove to be more sinister. I could never have guessed that the events of this night would change my life forever. What I once considered the worst event of my life brought about an unbelievable change for the better. It was the Greek playwright Euripides who stated: *"There is in the worst of fortune the best of chances for a happy change."*
The year was 1996, and the date was July 5. It was a Friday night and I had just turned 21 two days prior, which, by the way, was a miracle unto itself. Due to the violent life I was living, this was a milestone and something worth celebrating. But on this beautiful summer evening, I was not in a celebratory mood. Rather, I was in a predatory mood and that was what I was doing: lying and waiting for my prey to arrive. The stakes were high for this would be the biggest armed robbery of my career. Either I walk away with more than one hundred thousand dollars or I'm carried away in a body bag. Tonight, this must go down. I had tried this on two different occasions with three other individuals, but for some reason or another, we were unable to pull it off. The bank's location did not offer a good, convenient, and secure hiding place, as opposed to the other bank months earlier. This bank was located right on a busy traffic light intersection, so I was across the road from the bank as opposed to being in its parking lot, because it had none. I improvised as best as I possibly could.
Even though the purse size of this take down should be much bigger, but for me, it was not the money that was my main motive; it was the challenge and the thrill where I got my kicks. Armed robbery to me was like a sport. To take on an armored vehicle with two armed security guards—it was like an athlete attending the Olympic Games. I was sending a direct challenge to our local law enforcement officers. Figure this one out; catch me if you can.

So on this beautiful summer evening I was in hiding, behind a three-foot wall in the yard of the Good Shepherd Funeral Home. Even though the temperature was warm and humid, I wore a green hooded jacket, with the hood already over my head. The color of my jacket really blends in nicely, with the surrounding tree hedges along the wall. The irony of my hiding place did not hit me until years later, but if I had died that night, at least I would've been right next to a funeral home.
I felt the sweat slowly trickling down my lower back, as I patiently wait for my target. As different vehicles pulled up to the traffic light, I could hear conversations going on in some of them. There was one that really caught my attention. It was a one-way argument between a boyfriend/girlfriend or husband/wife. I said "one-way" because the female was doing the arguing and the guy was trying to calm her down. She was accusing him of cheating, and he was there calmly saying, "It's not what you think."

      At that moment, I envied him and the problem he was facing. I wished that I was in his shoes, because his problems seemed far lighter than mine, especially in light of what I'm about to do. I was even tempted to put my head up just to have a look at the female, but I kept my head down, hidden and out of sight.
Listening to their argument made me aware of how empty my life was, and I hated the life I was living all the more. It was quite obvious to me this lady was deeply in love, for she was fighting for what she thought to be hers. Even though I was dating two females at the time, and stringing a third one along, yet I've yet to discover that kind of love. I guess this was why my favorite song was 'I wana be love', by the Jamaican reggae super star Buju Banton.
I was slowly coming to the realization that the females I was dating were more or less into my street rep [reputation], than they were actually into me. Did I mention already that I hated my life? Simply because it was empty. Yes I had the street fame, the guns and the girls but my life was still empty. I was bleeding and hemorrhaging on the inside, and only I alone knew. I was reaching out for something, in an attempt to add meaning to my life. Even though I didn't quite know what that something was, yet I was still reaching out for it.

I was like a blind man groping around in the dark, trying to find the light switch. However, when I found it and flicked the switch, nothing happened even though there was light I was still in darkness. This was how I felt about my life; I was alive but not living. I was physically present but emotionally absent. What was missing was not the absence of light around me; rather it was the absence of light within me.

What I was lacking was not outside of me; rather it was on the inside. Even though I knew all of the above to be true, yet I knew of something else to be true and it was more frightening. I knew that somehow I had cross an invisible line, from man to beast and into a world of monsters.

When the traffic light changed they drove off, taking their problems that I wish I had along with them. I shook my head in disbelief, here I am about to commit the biggest robbery of my criminal career, yet I'm being caught up in night time soap opera. I then focused my attention back on the task at hand, for I had a job to do.

It seemed as if I had been hiding here for hours, even though it had really been fewer than 45 minutes. I looked at my watch for the last time that night, and saw that the armored vehicle was running about 35 minutes late. I began to wonder if they were going to come at all that night. Had they picked up on anything during the two and a half months I had been watching them? If so, what did they notice? As these thoughts were going through my mind, I heard the unmistakable rumble of the diesel engine even before I saw it. There was my money truck; better late than never.

It was a gray armored truck that the guards were in, and the model was probably some 10 to 15 years old. Without a doubt this vehicle has serve its time, but I guess the store owners weren't finish with it as yet. Even though it was not impressive, none-the-less, it was still a tank on wheels.

As they settled in and parked, one of the guards got out from the back with his shotgun. He walked around to the front and surveyed the entire area. Satisfied that everything was clear, he then nodded his approval to the other guard, who was still in the vehicle. Upon getting the go-ahead, the other guard then opened his door, which was just opposite the night deposit box, and started to make his deposits. Yet I couldn't move because there were so many cars sitting at the red light.

I always knew there were going to be cars around, but I did not anticipate this many vehicles tonight. He was now putting the third bag in which represented three stores, which means he had seven more bags to go. It was during this time that the light changed to green, and the cars drove off the light.

I then made my move. I took the safety off my 9, and in a flash I sprang over the wall running toward the guards with my gun extended. The goal was to fire two shots in their direction, just to let them know that I meant business. I tried to squeeze the trigger as I ran, but nothing happened. Both of the guards had now caught sight of me, and I could see the looks of puzzlement on their faces.

Those looks said, "Is this really happening? Is this real what I'm seeing?"

Even though both of them were armed with shotguns, I had the element of surprise on my side. They were shocked, like a deer caught in the headlights of a vehicle, not knowing what to do. One of the guards finally realized that I was having problems firing my gun. I guess he saw the slight jerking of my hand as I attempted to fire my weapon. He started to bring up his gun, positioning himself to open fire on me. It was then that I discovered to my horror, in my haste in jumping over the wall, I had accidentally pushed the safety back on my weapon. So that's why this gun wouldn't fire.

The 9 I held in my hand was a mini one, with fifteen shots in the clip and one in the chamber. This was not my original plan. I had wanted to come out here with two guns in my hand so they could see and know right away that I was serious. However, I was unable to pick up my main 9, my 'Dog Killer'. So for this reason I planned to fire two shots in their direction to throw them off balance. The average person with a gun in his hand doesn't know how to react when under fire. It's human nature to instinctively look for cover, or simply run away.

Because this was my plan, I took on the riskiest role to be the first to make contact with the guards. I was to hold the lookout guard at gunpoint, and then Don, my backup man who was hiding across the street, would emerge and get the other guard to throw his gun under the truck. I would then get my guard to do the same. We would get one of them to fill the gym bag I had slung across my shoulder and then we would be on our way. Now the tables have turned in the guards' favor, for I had given up my element of surprise. It was gone because my gun didn't fire—this was now going to be a gun battle.

When I finally took the safety off my weapon again, I was in survival mode. I regretted not having that second 9, because all hell was about to break loose. I was going into this gun battle, without my 'cherish dog killer' in my hand. I wondered why I had loan it out anyway, but it was too late for that now. It was right at this moment, that I knew my life would never be the same again.

I focused first on the lookout guard, forgetting the one standing behind the driver's door. The lookout guard was centering his gun on me. I quickly drew a bead in his direction. I didn't need a perfect shot; I just needed to start firing the gun. I could always adjust my aim after each shot, until one of them took him down, and I had sufficient bullets for that.

When I fired, it was as if an explosion went off, because we both fired our weapons at the same time. I can say this because I heard only one shot rather than two gunshots. My world was immediately punched into total darkness, and I hit the ground hard with a thud. I heard when my gun clattered to the ground and slid away from me.

As soon as I was on the ground, I heard two additional gunshots rang out. Being on the receiving end of a 12-gauge shotgun blast is not a pleasant thing. The sound of those two shots alone was deafening. My body was rocked twice by the impact. It was as if I had been kicked, both times by someone wearing a huge steel-toe boot. I told myself, "Keep still and don't even move a finger, because if you do, you will be shot again." Those were my last thoughts, because after that I lost all consciousness.

This book consists not only of my stories of mistakes, rather it's all our stories of mistakes and heart aches. It's the plight of all of us who were rebelling, and kicking against the social messes we found ourselves in. Yet there are so many others who are not alive today, and I feel obligated in not allowing the lessons of their mistakes to lie in the grave with them.

It was the United States Senator, Al Franken, who stated, "Mistakes are a part of being human. Precious life lessons that can only be learned the hard way unless it's a fatal mistake, which, at least, others can learn from." I'm revealing all of those mistakes and more, sadly a lot of them are fatal. In an attempt to have these real life lessons obtained in blood, prevent the blood-shedding of so many others. These stories are ones that young people can understand and identify with. While at the same time empowering them, to make better decisions about their choice of friends, the proper use of their time and how one wrong move can be fatal. I guess the major question that we all have to ask ourselves at the end of the day would be: how could I and so many others have been prevented from becoming monsters? You be the judge.

I now extend my hand to you, and personally invite you to take a journey with me into the heartlands of innocence to menacing, from a youngster to a monster, and the making of a predator. I will safely walk you down the deserted and darkened street corners which were once my world of crime, gang violence and senseless murders.

It's a different world unto itself, one which could only be observed up close by invitation only. Together we will learn the motivation behind hard-core gangsters, and explore the minds of cold-blooded murderers. You will discover the way they think about their own lives, and why they are so remorseless about the taking of another's life. So, if you will, please journey with me as we discover together how the fight of our lives were wrapped up in our fathers.

Chapter 2
ALMOST BURNED ALIVE

"What's done to children, they will do to society." —Dr. Karl Menninger

As I look back over my childhood, it becomes clear that the events related below changed my young life forever. It didn't matter to me that we were poor, because everything I wanted and needed was in my family. However, our father would later move on with another woman, and his selfish actions would change all of our lives for the worse. I firmly believe that there's no gift more precious to a child than to grow up in a loving two-parent home. This is the key foundation of any civil society. This is the heartbeat of every economy—the contribution of the simple home consisting of a husband, a wife, and their children.

When we refuse to acknowledge this huge contribution by the home toward an orderly, productive, and peaceful society, then we all might as well start wearing bulletproof vests, because social problems will abound, violence will become a sport unto itself, and we all will live in fear of unloved children.

The Best Years of My Life

"When we are children we seldom think of the future. This innocence leaves us free to enjoy ourselves as few adults can. The day we fret about the future is the day we leave our childhood behind." Patrick Rothfuss author of 'The Name of the Wind'

One of my earliest childhood memories is of running from my mother, and it was an all-out run from her. It was as though I was running for my life, because if she caught me, I would be in some serious trouble. The year was 1979 and I was just four years of age. OPEC had just shocked the Western world with its second gas price hike within seven years. The popular songs then were "Le Freak" by Chic and the Village People released "Y.M.C.A.," their most popular song to date. But what did I care; I was only four years old and living life to the fullest each day!

As I ran, a rock tumbled past my foot on the ground. My mother had thrown it in her frustration to catch me. When I realized how close that rock came to me, my little feet just picked up speed. To use the Bahamian term, 'I was rolling.' My mother screamed, "Drexel, come here now!" 'Sorry, mummy, but I can't hear you', my mind is locked into escape mode, and my feet have taken over. Besides, I am not a fool. I know what's in store for me if she catches me.

I can't remember which one of my misdeeds I was running away from this time, but I knew one thing—I was having fun. So there was no way in this world I was going to let it come to an end. If I had to, I would run all day and into the evening. Usually during these times running away from my mother, I would often be caught by one of her sisters or her brothers, or just an older person in the community who was faster than I was.

They would bring me back to her and I would be kicking, screaming, and crying because I knew what was going to happen next. However, if I managed to escape their grip, I wouldn't come home until it was safe.

Safe, for me, meant waiting until my father came home. He was always mild and calm in dealing with me, unlike my mother, whose only answer for misbehavior was a belt. However, my father always talked to me. In my father's presence there was never a problem with my behavior, because I was daddy's little boy and everybody knew it. I always knew that I was loved by my father, and I loved him much more in return.

There is nothing greater that a boy can receive from his father, than to know that he is loved and accepted by him. As my mother told me later in life, "Your father really loved you. When he would come home from work, it was all about you." Even though we were poor, I never knew it. My earlier childhood memories were filled with love, laughter, and much fun.

The best years of my life were spent in a small, over the hill community called Montell Heights. The inner city communities in New Providence are referred to as the "over-the-hill" area. It is a term dating back from our time under colonial rule. There is a ridge of hills on the northern side of the island, which runs almost the entire length of New Providence. One time ago in our history, the white ruling minority lived on the northern side of the hills where the prime beachfront properties are, and the black majority resided over the hill on the southern side of the island. **

I was probably the most loved and popular kid within a two-block radius living in Montell Heights during that time. My mother allowed my hair to grow long, and there used to be arguments among the older neighborhood girls as to who was going to plait my hair on a given day.

I can remember clearly one day, after spending almost three hours getting my hair plaited, Altamese—who always looked out for me—had disapproved of how another one of the neighborhood girls had plaited my hair. Because of this, she loosed it all out and again for the next three hours, I was sitting down getting my hair plaited all over again. At times, I didn't mind because I was getting so much attention from the older neighborhood girls, but most times, I just wanted to be free to enjoy my playtime.

I spent the majority of my time outside. I was as adventurous a boy child as they come. Like any typical young boy, I craved the outdoors. There, I was alive and free with nature. There was always something new to try, like climbing fruit trees, catching butterflies and bees with my bare hands, and making wooden toys.

My days were always filled with activities, and my specialty was throwing things, which usually got me in a lot of hot water. I could remember my father purchasing for me a cherry red and chrome bicycle, with what we call a 'loaf of bread seat'. He had purchased the bike for fifty dollars from my uncle Trevor, who is my mother's youngest brother. That bicycle alone made me the most popular kid in our little community. Every chance I got I was riding that beauty.

There was never a dull moment growing up in Montell Heights. I had everything a child could ever want—a mother who took good care of the home, and a father who provided well for the home, one who was strong but gentle with his children. I also had an extended family who was deeply involved in my early upbringing, and a great small community that was safe for all to live in.

So how does a once adorable child with the cutest smile become a monster? How did I get to the point in my life where I attempted to take down an armored vehicle protected by two armed security guards? What are the social triggers that lead to delinquent behaviors within our youth?

My First Lesson about Friends

"Words are easy, like the wind; Faithful friends are hard to find." —William Shakespeare

One day, some kids from the neighborhood and I were outside playing under a sapodilla fruit tree, what we simply refer to locally as a dilly tree. Someone came up with the bright idea to hit the dillies [shorten for sapodilla] down with rocks. After a few unsuccessful tries with smaller rocks, I picked up the biggest rock that I could handle. With all of the strength in my little arm, I threw it at the nearest dilly in sight. It missed the dilly altogether, hit the trunk of the tree, and bounced back to the ground with a thump. Immediately, I heard a blood-curdling scream. I spun around in terror looking to see what's wrong, only to discover that it was my sister Vanessa, who was holding her head and screaming her lungs out.

I am older than Vanessa by more than a year and seven months. I stood there frozen in place just staring at her. What got my attention was the blood. I would always remember that because it was seeping through her little fingers. It was everywhere. Her screams were bringing some of the older neighbors out to investigate; they began to converge where we were under the dilly tree. The minute they saw Vanessa, who was still screaming and holding her head, they gasped and said, "Oh my God, who did this?" They took hold of Vanessa, and above her screams they kept shouting, "Who did this? Who did this?"

The neighborhood kids, who had witnessed everything and who were visibly shaken up over the whole ordeal, began to point their trembling fingers at me saying, "DD did it" (referring to me by my childhood nickname). One by one, my friends began to flee, but I couldn't move.

I stood there staring at my sister. I had never seen so much blood. I had never heard Vanessa scream like this before. I had never been so afraid in my entire life. Before I had a chance to register the enormity of my troubles, strong hands gripped me, and both my sister Vanessa and I were marched off in search of my mother, who by this time was coming to meet us, surrounded by some of my friends and the neighborhood kids who had fled earlier.

Then the beating marathon began. My mother started it. I believe she beat me that day more out of fear than anything else. Vanessa and I were then marched off to my grandmother, Leona Blossom Taylor-Johnson-Joseph whom everybody simply called 'mum'. She lived on Bell Road, the back street behind my family's house. After doctoring Vanessa's head and stopping the bleeding, mum then had her way with me. Boy, did I get it. I was beaten severely, and that was not the end of my problems.

When my father came home later that evening, before he could exit his vehicle, the same kids who delivered the news to my mother now were doing the same to my father. Even though I had received a beating from my mother and grandmother earlier, I don't remember them other than the knowledge that they had beaten me. The beating I will always remember was the one I got from my father. It was not as though it was worse than the earlier ones, but it was the first and the last time my father would beat me. This was the beating that everybody was waiting for.

There was a crowd of onlookers outside. Even though our door was closed, I could hear them chanting, "That's right, hit him again, oh, he needs that!" I couldn't see their faces, but I knew the sounds of their voices. The hurt I felt came not from my father's belt, but from what my friends were saying outside. These were people I played with each day, and they were saying things like, "Oh, he needed that a long time ago! Put it on him, hit him again! Oh, that's good for him!" I couldn't believe my ears. In just one day, I went from the most loved kid in the community to the most hated kid. This was ridiculous. I made an honest mistake; and now my friends had turned their backs on me. Some had even gone so far as to ensure that I got a good beating.

However, my sister Vanessa made a full recovery, and the very next day she was up and about, getting in my way again. What could I say; hard-headedness is just a part of our family.

Our Father Moves On Without Us

"The single biggest social problem in our society may be the growing absence of fathers from their children's homes, because it contributes to so many other social problems." — President Bill Clinton

When I was five years old, my father and mother split up. To be more accurate, my father walked out on us. When he left us, my mother was pregnant with her last child—my sister Melissa Shaquanya. We all just called her Quannie. I'm older than she is by five and a half years. Even though my mother and father had been together for more than five years, they never married. My mother says prior to giving birth to Vanessa and me, she never worked. It was only after she was a few weeks pregnant with Quannie did she get a job at Heastie's Restaurant and Bar, located on Carmichael and Bacardi Road. My mother worked as a waitress there; it was my father who brought home the lion's share of the income. He was employed as a maintenance worker in the engineer department at one of our local hotels.

When my father walked out on us, my mother was twenty-one years old with two young kids and weeks away from having her third. She was unskilled and uneducated. Except for the fact that she could read and write, she was otherwise unqualified for the real world.

To top it off, my father didn't go peacefully. One would think that when a man wants to leave his family, he would do so peacefully and somewhat decently. Rather he started telling family members and friends that my mother was not pregnant by him. "The child she is carrying is for her dark boyfriend. That baby is not mine. You just watch and see. It's not going to have my complexion."

It is really amazing to me today that the average man doesn't know how to end a relationship. Looking back now, it is almost laughable. Some months prior, one of my mother's younger sisters had given birth to a child belonging to my father. However, upon my sister's safe delivery, I guess he had to change his talk. He couldn't deny this one. As we say locally, my sister Quannie was "killing him." She was the spitting image of him, complexion and all. Nonetheless, my father had other plans and we were not included. As a matter of fact, he didn't want us around at all.

My mother told the following story. "I was awakened from my sleep one night by Quannie consistently crying, who was just a baby then. I didn't want to get up right then, for I had just fallen off to sleep. Anyway, I managed to pull myself out of the bed and as I was preparing a bottle for her, I heard the sounds of footsteps running from the side of our house and the neighbor's dogs started barking. Out of curiosity, I walked over to the glass door, shaking Quannie's made bottle in my hand. When I glanced through the glass door, there was a red, fiery glow coming from the side of the house.
I paused for a brief second with Quannie's bottle in my hand, trying to figure out what was going on. Why was the side of the house so bright with light and why did I hear footsteps running at this hour of the night? That was when it hit me. "Angie, the place is on fire."
"Quannie's bottle fell from my hand, and shattered when it hit the floor. I almost lost it. It was a fight to not lose control of myself. I knew that I couldn't afford to lose control then, because I had to look out for you all and get you'll to safety. I ran into the bedroom and quickly snatched up Quannie, woke up you and Vanessa, and ran across the street to our neighbor Raymond's house, screaming for help. Raymond, along with other neighbors was able to put out the fire." My mother then said to me, with tinges of both happiness and sorrow in her voice, "Thank goodness for Quannie's crying waking me up. If not, we all would've perished that night."
My father was arrested and questioned about the incident, but being a former police officer, he knew the system and was eventually released due to lack of evidence. My father served as a police officer before he had met my mother, but because of his short temper, he was expelled from the force. He had pulled his service revolver on his superior in a heated argument. According to my mother, the story he gave the police was that he was out fishing.
My mother would later explain to us when we were older, "Your father had never been out fishing, not once, during the five years that we were together." However, my mother learned many years later that Theresa, our stepmother, whom my father married after leaving my mother, had corroborated his story, which provided him with an alibi. She confessed to my mother that she lied for my father, and that it was not his first time doing such a thing. Apparently, he was paid eight hundred dollars by a shady businessman to burn down his company for insurance benefits.

However, my father ensured that my mother was left with nothing. He destroyed everything they had together. I don't know when it happened, whether it was after the fire or before, but he destroyed everything we owned by pouring paint over our stuff. We were left only with the clothing on our backs. I remember slowly walking through the place we had lived in together as a family, and stepping over some of my clothing, which were now covered with white paint.
As a child, I didn't understand it, and now as a father myself, I still don't understand it. Why did my father had to be so destructive? Why destroy everything that was ours? Why leave all of your kids with only the clothing on their backs? I could never understand why he tried to kill all of us, especially when it was his decision to move on. Why didn't he just leave us in peace and go on his merry way? How could a man even think about destroying his entire family just like that?
The problem was, according to my mother, that even though my father had moved on to another woman he still wanted to have her around, but this time as the other woman. He was still coming around seeking intimacy with my mother, but she stood her ground by not giving into him. I guess he figured since he couldn't lay and play with both of them, then the one who was putting up the most resistance had to go. That was my mother and us. It was mother Teresa who stated, "It is a poverty to decide that a child must die so that you may live as you wish."
However, our father was willing to kill an entire family, so that he could live and do as he pleased.

Our Young Lives Would Be Change Forever
"Over the past thirty years, the rise in violent crime parallels the rise in families abandoned by fathers." —Patrick F. Fagan Ph.D.
Due to the fire damage to the building, the landlord asked my mother to move. We had to stay with my grandmother, who lived behind us on the next street. These were really some rough years for us. My grandmother rented a two-bedroom place, with no electricity and no indoor plumbing. On top of that, there were five or six of my aunts and uncles living there, and some of my aunts were starting to have kids of their own.

Even though my mother worked as a waitress, her take home pay was not enough to support us all effectively. My mother shared a story with me once about those early days, after our father had left. It is a particular story that I have never forgotten. She began, "This day I had no money at all. Things were a bit slow at work and I was still trying to settle in at mum's place. To make matters worse, Quannie was out of baby food and was on her last diaper, which needed to be changed."

My mother continued, "My sister's boyfriend Willie, her children's father, had stopped by to visit. I was sitting down in the doorway of mum's house with Quannie on my lap. Willie was getting ready to enter by passing Quannie and I. He asked me, 'Angie, are you all right?' I said to him, 'Yes, Willie, I'm all right.' But as he was stepping inside the door to pass me, he quietly and quickly slipped something in my free hand. When Willie had walked off, I opened my hand to discover a twenty dollar note tightly balled up." My mother then said, this time with deep emotions in her voice, "That twenty dollars at that time meant the world to me. It wasn't much, but I made it stretch to purchase stuff for all three of you kids." Then she concluded, "As long as I live, I will never forget what Willie did, and I hope one day to be able to repay his kindness."

Willie was the first gangster I ever met. He was a law unto himself. He was dangerous, clever, and resourceful, but most of all, he was kind and gentle to us kids. We all loved Willie. It was said that Willie was once in a shootout with police officers and was wounded in his shoulder in the process. However, as the story goes, Willie never went to the hospital to seek medical treatment. Instead, he heated a knife over a fire and dug the bullet out of the wound himself. He was a legend in the Montell Heights area.

Even though we were just young kids at the time, my sister Vanessa and I knew what was going on. I was keenly aware of the deep longing for my father. When my father was released by the police for attempted arson, he drove through the corner where we once lived as a family together. As he pulled up in his red car, my aunt Shelly was trying to carry me back to my grandmother's place, but I broke free from her grip and ran to his vehicle. In spite of what everybody was saying about him, this was my father, my hero and the love of my life. There was no one that I idolized and wanted to be like more than him. Yet I would never forget that encounter with my father on that day. For some reason or another, I stopped short about three feet from his car door. I guess that I sensed that something was wrong; something was missing here. It had been days since I had seen him last, so even though I was happy to see him, I was still cautious. But it was quite evident that he wasn't happy to see me, because he just stared at me for a few seconds. Then he asked, "DD, are you all right?"
 I answered, "Yes sir."
There was no warmth in his voice, no twinkle in his eyes that said, "I'm glad to see you, too." It was as if I was seeing this man for the first time. He had this cold and chilling stare. There was no love there, no fondness, but a coldness that I'd never seen before in my father. He treated me as if I was just one of the neighborhood boys that he was trying to be polite to. My father then said to me, "You be a good boy now," and just like that, it was over, because he then turned around and drove away. I just stood there watching the back of his vehicle as he drove away, until it exited the corner. All the while, I pleaded in my heart for him to come back. I don't mean the stranger who had just been here, but the man I had come to adored and loved as my hero.
 I stood there for a long time, just looking out toward the end of the corner. I hoped that his car would return and everything would be made right. Deep down within myself, though, I knew that my father was gone for good, because the man who was just there—I knew he didn't love me anymore. How do some men do that? How can they just turn their love for their kids off like a water faucet? How could some fathers be so cold to their children because they are no longer involved with their children's mother? Is it any wonder why Dr. Karl Menninger stated close to fifty years ago, "What is done to children, they will do to society."

I hung my head down, looking at my toes as I twiddled them back and forward in the dirt. Tears started to well up in my eyes. I quickly lifted my head up and stared toward the end of the corner. I willed myself not to cry in the open. I willed myself to be strong. I could almost hear myself saying, "DD, don't cry," and I didn't. I did not cry at all. After it became obvious to me that my father wasn't coming back, I turned around and slowly walked toward mum's place with a heavy heart. As a young five-year-old boy, I could never imagine how my life would be changed forever from that day on. Looking back at it all now, I believe that my father's only purpose for coming around there that day was to announce by way of his presence, that he was out of the police's hands. He had beaten the system because he was once a part of it, so he was untouchable, and he wanted my mother to know that he was out.

In 1995 Patrick F. Fagan Ph.D. former president of the heritage foundation released a comprehensive and compelling study that was conducted to find out the source of violent crimes which was affecting the American way of life. The Heritage Foundation is a research and educational institution 'a think tank', which was founded in 1973. Based in Washington D. C. it is one of America's largest public policy research organizations, and is the most broadly supported 'think tank' institute in the US.

The findings of this detailed study were captured in a 25-page document entitled, 'The real root causes of violent crimes'. Throughout this book I would often refer to this study and their findings, for its findings were well received by the general public and policy makers. To obtain a complete copy of this study, one can visit the website of the Heritage Foundation at: www. heritage.org. However, Dr. Fagan stated, "The breakup of his parents' marriage during the first five years of his life places a child at high risk of becoming a juvenile delinquent."

If we are going to be, "The best little country in the world," as our present Prime Minister Perry Christie likes to say, then we must urgently address the cause of fatherless homes, and stabilize this bleeding ulcer that is pulling fathers away from their family and children.

When Our Father Left, Our Status Left As Well
"I cannot think of any need in childhood as strong as the need for a father's protection." —Sigmund Freud

After our father walked out on us, we never saw much of him. When my father left, everything left with him. His influence, protection, finances—they were all gone. Vanessa and I went from two little adorable kids in our local area to being just regular kids. Special favors and treatment were no longer extended to us, because our neighbors no longer had to work to gain our father's approval through us. I slowly began to discover that all in our neighborhood, family included were treating us differently. We were not being treated with any disrespect, but just differently from what we were accustomed to when our father was around. At the time, I didn't understand it.

Looking back, I now realize that when our father left, our status left as well. My father was a popular figure in our local community. He had a good job, his own car, and he was the life of the party. People loved him and by extension, we were also loved in return. However, when he left that all went with him. As a child growing up I began to notice, that children are treated differently by all in the community when their fathers are involved in their lives.

Yet this in itself is nothing new, even advertisers know that you could win over a parent by winning over the child. This is also Biblical because as Christians we gain our heavenly Father's approval and love, by first loving his only begotten son. As Jesus states: *"And he who loves Me will be loved by My Father, and I will love him and manifest Myself to him." John 14: 21 Nkjv.*

Therefore, it's no surprise that as children, we benefit from our fathers' presence and his good reputation, or else we are tarnished by his bad reputation, but above all, we suffer even more when he is absent.

My father was never good at keeping his word. There were many times he would stop by and tell us that he would come for us on weekends. When the weekend rolled around, we would wait for him dressed up and ready to go. Most of the time, he was a no show. In spite of the many times he let us down, once he said that he was coming for us the following weekend, I would be there waiting again with renewed hope. My mother told me that I was the one who would usually fall asleep with my clothing on, patiently waiting for him to show up. There was nothing that she could have said or done to persuade me that he wasn't coming.

On one of those rare occasions when he did show up for us to spend the weekend with him, he sat Vanessa and me down along with his new female friend. It was then he told me that he was not my real father. I was seven or eight years old at the time. My father was living on Soldier Road in an apartment not too far from where he grew up. Right then and there, my world was shattered in a thousand pieces. I sat before the one and only man that I had come to know and love as my father and hero, only to be told by him that I was not his son.

He told me, "When I met your mother, she was two months pregnant with you. I respected her for being honest in letting me know that she was pregnant. I told her that I would raise you as my own. That's why I gave you my name."

My father talked for a while, but I couldn't hear a word of what he said. I saw his lips moving, and I knew that he was still speaking to me, but I was heavily engrossed in a mental conversation of my own. My world, for all intents and purposes, was now turned upside down.

I did eventually hear him tell me that even though I was not his son, that nothing would change, and he would always treat me as if I were his own. To his credit, he did just that. I was treated no differently than before. The only thing is that he was just an absent, unsupportive, and unreliable father to all of his children. I never told my mother about our chat, and I never questioned her to confirm if what he told me was true. However, some several months later my mother sat me down to have the same conversation. It was then that I told her I knew. She was surprised to hear from me that I already knew about it.

She asked, "How did you found out?"

I said, "My daddy told me." Even at that young age, referring to him as my father felt strange and awkward.

"So how do you feel about it, and do you have any questions or anything to say?"

But I just shrugged my little shoulders and said, "No."

Truth be told, I was not used to having this kind of conversation. As a matter of fact, I was not used to having any kind of conversation with any adult. I was a quiet child and my conversations normally took place in my head. However, this conversation was one I wanted to avoid both mentally and verbally. I felt as if I was being asked to let go of someone that I'd come to adore and love all my young life. Yet, who was I going to replace him with? At that tender and fragile age in my life, I didn't want a replacement. I only wanted him.

Oh, yes, I had questions like, "Who is my father, and what is his name? How is it I have never met him? Do I have other sisters and brothers?"

My mother told me that my real father's name was Gregory Bowe. She started to tell me more about my real father, which wasn't anything much except for how they met, but just like with my father, I tuned her out. I had other conversations going on in my head, like trying to figure out who else I knew that goes by the last name Bowe. Why have I never met this so-called father of mine? I did not meet my biological dad until I was fifteen years of age and heading into Grade 11 of senior high school.

Some Background History on My Father's Genealogy
"People say you're born innocent, but it's not true. You inherit all kinds of things that you can do nothing about. You inherit your identity, your history, like a birthmark that you can't wash off." —Hugo Hamilton, The Sailor in the Wardrobe.

Even though the man I called my father is light skinned and I am dark skinned, growing up I never saw the difference. I never once recognized that the color of his skin was lighter than mine. For example, my two sisters' skin is a lighter complexion—more in line with my father's. Generally, the Deals are a light-skinned group of people who are originally from the island in The Bahamas known as Long Island. Ironically, this is one of the outer islands that a lot of the loyalists settled on during their migration from the U.S. According to the Bahamian official website, there was no large settlement/community on Long Island until the arrival of the loyalists. They were mainly from New England, New Jersey, and later the Carolinas. They fled the American Revolution, with their slaves setting up farms and cotton plantations.

Long Island is approximately 80 miles long, but only 1 to 4 miles across at its widest point. Many artists consider Long Island to be the beauty queen of The Bahamas. The Atlantic side is lined with a dramatic, picturesque rocky shoreline, and leeward are some of the best unspoiled white sand beaches in the world. It is very hilly and punctuated with numerous limestone caves.

The Deals were probably a part of the last set of white loyalists who fled from the U.S. during the Civil War. I believe that they were in such a hurry to get out of the U.S. that they left their slaves behind. I came to such a conclusion because when one looks at our last names—which, by the way, were all given to us by our former slave masters—there are three different skin color groups for the average surnames in The Bahamas. For example, one can find a white Johnson, a light-skinned Johnson, and a dark-skinned Johnson. One may also find a white Bethel, a light-skinned Bethel, and a dark-skinned Bethel. This is the way it is with many of our last names, but when one meets a Deal, who are few in numbers, they are either white or light-skinned. It is extremely rare to meet a dark-skinned Deal. I was constantly reminded of this as a teenager growing up, especially when I was sent out to pay bills for my mother. Whenever I had to give someone my name, I usually got the surprised looks and stares, along with comments like "You're the first dark Deal I ever met." I do have an outside sister who is dark skinned; that is because she took on the complexion of her mother. However, one thing that is evident as it relates to the male Deals—they seem to like their women dark. Case in point: my father had a total of twelve children with eight different women. All of his children's mothers are dark-skinned and there are many couples of whom I ran across as well where the male who is a Deal is light-skin and his wife is dark-skin. It is believed that some of the Deals later migrated to the islands of New Providence and Eleuthera. I guess they were in search of the darker-skinned women. It was probably they who coined the phrase "The darker the flesh, the sweeter the juice." If not, then I guess that they were trying to discover for themselves if the saying was really true. However, it seems as if Long Island men on the hold have a thing for the darker-skinned women. It is probably the island with the highest percentage of interracial marriages in The Bahamas.

It is also widely known among Bahamians that Long Islanders are considered to be the most physically attractive group of people in the Bahamas. The Islanders have a heritage of Lucayan-Arawak-Taino aborigines, who inhabited the islands during the fourteenth and fifteenth centuries before Columbus. I guess this blood was mixed in with that of the white loyalists, and then added in with some blacks who were stolen from Africa. The skin complexion that you would end up with is a smooth, flawless light-skinned specimen of a person. The men are ruggedly good looking and strong, but the women are so beautiful that they are called mango skin. Their pretty skin complexion is said to resemble the mango, which is a tropical fruit that grows in abundance in The Bahamas and throughout the Caribbean.

What Went Wrong? A Look at My Maternal Grandparents

"That men do not learn very much from the lessons of history is the most important of all the lessons that history has to teach." —Aldous Huxley the famous English writer

To better understand the following chapters and the rest of this book, it is important for me to now bring in my mother's parents. There were some decisions that were made before I was even born, yet the results of those decisions had a negative effect on my mother and her siblings. Sadly, I believed that my sisters and I would repeat a lot of my grandparents mistakes, without even knowing about them. Simply because my mother would pass them on to us as our inheritance, based on the life she witness and later lived.

To find out more information about my maternal grandparents, I turned to my Aunt Pearlene, whom we all call Pearl. She is the oldest child out of the six children that my maternal grandparents had together. Aunt Pearl began, "Our father, Samuel Johnson Sr., who is your grandfather, was a descendant from Hatchet Bay Eleuthera.* This was the island where his father was from, and where he was born and raised. "Our mother, Leona Blossom Taylor, came from the island of Andros; from a settlement called Mastic Point. # Mum's mother only had two children. The other child was an older boy named Samuel Martin. After the death of her mother, whom I was named after, mum was sent to Nassau to live with her mother's sister, whom we all simply called Aunty Dell. She lived in the Nassau Street area."

Aunt Pearl continued, "Mum was only fourteen or fifteen when daddy first saw her. He took a liking to mum even though he was much older than her. With her Aunt Dell urging her on to marry, so mum and daddy got married. However, before they had gotten married, daddy had already signed up to go on the Contract to work. "When daddy came back off the Contract, they were reunited and would have an additional four children. At some point, they ended up separating for a while over some differences. Daddy left and went to the island of Bimini, where he found work as a painter and watchman. When he left her, mum was pregnant with their sixth child. She had the baby while he was working in Bimini, and somehow family members got in contact with him telling him to come home.

"At this time, I was living in Andros with one of my younger sisters, Rose. Daddy came back to Nassau, got mum and the children, and took them back to Bimini with him, where they lived for several years, but while in Bimini working, daddy got sick. He had to come to Nassau to seek medical treatment from the hospital. [Back in those days, the only hospital was in the capital of Nassau.] However, mum didn't follow behind him. He sent back for her and the children, but she refused to go. She continued living in Bimini on her own with the other children.

They were now separated for a second time, for daddy was now living in Nassau and mum stayed in Bimini. I was sent to Nassau and then to Bimini to be with mum. This was around 1962 or 1963; I was between the ages of twelve and thirteen then. The aunt I was living with in Andros was plagued with asthma, so she was unable to adequately care for my younger sister Rose and me. She kept Rose with her, but she died some time later after I was in Bimini. We later learned that she had died, and Rose was on her own basically living from pillar to post down there in Andros by herself.
***[2]

[3]##

---

[2] *** / # appendix

[3] ## / (i) appendix

"So now we had to try and scrape money together to get her out of Andros. Being the oldest child, I had to go to Nassau, then on a mail boat to Andros where I found her, and we came in on the mail boat to Nassau, and then we went into Bimini on another mail boat. (i)

"The problem between daddy and mum," said aunt Pearl, "was that daddy was extremely jealous, to the point where he would physically abuse mum. So when he took sick and had to go to Nassau, mum said, 'This is a work of God, so I could get away from him.' Like I've said before, daddy used to beat her a lot, and she was tired of that."

Aunt Pearl then said with sorrow in her voice, "Oh! That was a very rough period for us, because my mother never knew anything about working. She was never the working type. She believed in getting involved with a male and having him to support her. So that's why it was very rough for us, and then she just continued to have kids for these different males. She complained about daddy mistreating her but, when she left him, she got mistreated even worse."

I said to her, "I remember mummy telling us when we were young kids how rough those days were for you all. One time she said you all had eaten fish for dinner. Nobody liked the head of the fish and so it was thrown away in the bushes. The very next day you all couldn't find anything to eat, and so you all had to go and look for that same fish head that was thrown away the day before."

My aunt let out a hearty laugh and said, "That's right. We had to go and look for that fish head, clean it up, cook it, and share it amongst us all.

"Mum eventually came to Nassau and put Daddy in court for child support," said aunt Pearl. "Daddy was one who didn't like around the courts, so what he did, he sat down and talked with mum where he agreed to purchase wholesale groceries and other stuff the children needed. He also agreed to send money along with the stuff, that he would put on the mail boat called 'The Bimini Gal'. If he was late in meeting his commitment, in putting what he had agreed to on 'The Bimini Gal', mum would come to Nassau and show her face, and once she showed her face in Nassau then everything got done."

I asked my aunt, "So what led to her moving from Bimini?"

My aunt hesitated for a moment. When she spoke this time, her pace was slower, her voice was lower, and I could hear the pain in it. She began, "Mum got involved with a man who was a mental patient (Psychiatric problems), but she didn't know it. He is the father of one of my younger sisters. After my sister was born, then his true colors came out. To make matters worse, she was still seeing another older fella on the island as well. When my sister's father found out, he tried to catch her to beat her."

"When I came from Andros, I got caught right in the middle of what was going on. Prior to that, I had been living in Andros from the time I was six weeks old. Apparently, when daddy was on the Contract, mum got involved with another man. This man never had any children, so when I was born, he considered me his child. So this is what daddy came back home to. The man would sometimes take mum and me from our home. We would be locked up in his place, where daddy had to go and get the police just to get us back. I was sent to live in Andros with my aunt Margie Dockers just to keep this man from around mum, because as far as he was concerned, he was coming to see his child."

Aunt Pearl then paused for a second, and said with exhaustion and deep pain in her voice, "Oh, we lived a terrible life, we lived a hard life. Mum had a nervous breakdown. They had to send her on the plane to Nassau to seek psychiatric treatment. Running from him on Bimini traumatized her. I had to stay awake at nights before mum was sent to Nassau. She already had her nervous breakdown, and she needed to sleep at nights. This man used to just sneak up. He would appear from through the bushes. So I had to be up and on guard, looking out for him while mum was trying to sleep. When I would spot him, I would scream to Paula [Paula is the second oldest child], tell mum he's coming. I used to have three or four buckets of rocks and bottles, and I would start to throw them at him to keep him from getting mum, which allowed her to escape him. Mum knew that she was running for her life. I guess that's why she had a nervous breakdown."

Aunt Pearl then said, "Mum was finally able to leave the island for Nassau to seek medical help, where she would spend several weeks in Sandilands Rehabilitation Centre." Sandilands Rehabilitation Centre, is a government-run institution for psychiatric, geriatric, and substance abuse patients.

I was shock to learn that mum was once admitted to Sandilands for treatment. However, I would also be admitted to the very same institution and two other cousins of mine. We were the three members of our family, who would become deeply involved in a life of crime.

They All Left Home Early

"Parenthood is the passing of a baton, followed by a lifelong disagreement as to who dropped it." —Robert Brault author
Aunt Pearl continued by saying, "We were left in Bimini on our own, where we were doing very badly. After mum came out of the hospital, when she got her hands on money, she would send groceries down for us on the mail boat. One time it had gotten so bad, we were in Bimini on our own with no food to eat. On top of that, there was my sister, who was just a baby. We could hardly even feed her, much less ourselves. Being the oldest child and realizing our predicament, I went and talked with the captain of 'The Bimini Gal'. I told him of our situation, and right away he allowed all of us to travel to Nassau free of charge. By this time, it was now ten of us. Four of my younger siblings were born on the island of Bimini."
My aunt Pearl then said with a touch of anger in her voice, "We saw some tough days growing up. That is why us girls went on our own so young. When I look at the children of today, they have it good. They have it good because we been through war. When I heard my girls at one stage talking about 'mummy didn't provide for us that's why we have to work so hard,' I had to say to them, 'you all are lucky you have life. If you all know how hard my sisters and I came up, you all would say you have it good.' How could I go and provide richness for you all, when I didn't have it for myself?"
"Our foundation was taken from under us," continued aunt Pearl. "We had nothing to stand on. I thought about it many times. If our parents didn't split up, we would have had it better.
Oh, and I pleaded with daddy to make up with mum for our sake asking them to remarry. You all forget about what happened and try and make it work. I really wanted them to get back together. I wanted us as a family again, but he just said, 'no'. He wasn't going on that road, and Mum didn't want anything to do with him either, because she said 'he fought too much.'"

Mum eventually ended up working as a janitress at C. H. Reeves School." Aunt Pearl went on to explain how this happened, "She had gotten married again, to Daniel Joseph, who was of Haitian descent. The children weren't going to school. By this time, mum now had thirteen children—ten girls and three boys. Some of my younger brothers and sisters never started school until they were seven and eight years old. So the neighbors contacted social services about the children being home all the time and not going to school. Social services came around and started to investigate. They got all of the children's dates of birth and their birth certificates. Mum wasn't working and she told them that she never worked in her life. She thought that was something good, that she never worked in her life. She used to brag about that: 'I never work in my life. I always had a man to take care of me.'"

"You know, when you are dumb, you are dangerous, my aunt said not bothering to hide her anger this time. "Daniel, who she was married to, wasn't making much. So the social services workers got the children sorted out and in school. They then went around and got mum a job, which was the first time she had ever worked in her life."

My aunt Pearl then concluded by saying, still with anger in her voice. "This is what happens when a woman doesn't want to be independent. She wants to always be a follower, and don't try to be a leader. That is when you get mistreated. This is why I was determined to be a leader. I can't stand it when I see a woman being a follower. I saw that weakness in my mother, and she didn't get nowhere in life for that. I rather hustle and work to buy a chair, rather than waiting for a man to buy that chair for me."

Chapter 3
THE UNWANTED CHILD

"I have come to realize more and more that the greatest disease and the greatest suffering is to be unwanted, unloved, uncared for, to be shunned by everybody, to be just nobody [to no one]". —Mother Teresa

As a boy growing up, I felt as if I was the unwanted child in my family. It felt as if I was an unwanted burden. At the ages of eight and nine, these were my thoughts. I even had a favorite song that captured and depicted my miserable life. For this reason, I vowed to myself as a boy that I would never bring a child into this world to suffer as I did. This is why I named my son Lowell, the French and Haitian meaning of which is beloved.

I often tell my son, that his name serves as my commitment to him that I will always be there for him, and I will always love him. I might be disappointed with some of the decisions that he may make in life, but it doesn't change my love for him. I believe that there can be nothing worse to a child than to battle with feelings and thoughts of not being loved and wanted.

While working at Oasis Restaurant, my mother met Mr. Marvin Harding, a married, white Bahamian from Long Island. During some of the slow periods at my mother's work, Mr. Harding would take us some weekends to sleep in the hotels throughout Nassau. This, to us, was a real treat, especially for Vanessa and me, who had never slept in an air-conditioned room. As a boy, I couldn't believe how big those bathtubs were; in my eyes, they were huge. I clearly remember one time my mother had filled the tub with warm water, and as she was bathing Vanessa, I swam under the water from one end of the tub to the other end. It was the first time in my life that I had bathed in a bathtub.

With my mother holding down a job, and with support from Mr. Harding, who was a Pest Exterminator, she was able to move us out of my grandmother's place and into a one-room rental above a bar [club] on Washington Street.

One of my most dominant memories from living there was one evening my mother was getting ready to go out with her sister Paula and some other female friends. I guess they were going out clubbing that night. I didn't want my mother to leave us in this strange place, even though one of her younger sisters would be watching us. I still didn't want her to go; I still didn't want her to leave us. I pretended I was sick as a way of getting her attention, thinking that maybe she would stay home. My aunt Paula told my mother, "Oh, I think he has indigestion. Just get him a warm ginger ale soda to drink." While I was pleased to have a whole can of soda for myself without having to share with my sister Vanessa, I wanted my mother. I dreaded the idea of her leaving us like our father did. My mother soon moved us from the one-room apartment to another part of Washington Street. Washington Street divides into three parts, and we eventually lived on all three of them. This time my mother rented a one-room stucco place, and when I say one room, I don't mean one bedroom with a bathroom and kitchen. I mean just that— it was a one-room shack, with no running water and no kitchen. It was about ten feet wide and twelve feet long. She rented it from a family named Hanna. They were originally from the island of Acklins. The Hanna family supplied us with electricity from their house. In spite of how small the place was, my mother somehow was able to get a bunk bed, a single bed, and a three-tier stove in there. Amazingly, there was enough space left over to hold a coffee table and a sitting chair.

By this time, I was in the fourth grade at William Phipps Primary School. That was the year I got sick with the chicken pox. The chicken pox was really terrible. It was all over my body from head to toe; worst of all, it was even in my mouth. I had no appetite, because food tasted and felt terrible going down. The only thing I could keep down was the hot chocolate that my mother used to make for me.

   There were five of us living in this one-room shack. The ventilation was poor because we had wooden windows. This meant the windows had to be open for fresh breeze to come in, but at night, we had to close them for security purposes. I slept under the coffee table, to ensure that I didn't get my sisters sick. However, it didn't work because just one week later, both Vanessa and Quannie came down with it as well. Thankfully, it did not affect them as badly as it did me. The chicken pox was the only childhood disease we caught.

Since we had no running water, and I was the only male child in our family, I had to fill all of the empty water containers at the public water pump (built on the side of the street that the government provides in some over the hill areas). This was my first household chore as a child. It was my responsibility to ensure that we always had clean water for bathing, cleaning, and cooking. I never complained or felt ashamed about toting water, because this was what I was born into. Toting water was all I knew; it was simply our way of life. As a matter of fact, more than half of the residents of Washington Street toted water at that time. In the evening there used to be a line of people at the pump, everybody just patiently waiting their turn to fill their water containers. Toting water made me physically stronger as a boy growing up. I also developed from it a love for lifting weights, something I still enjoy doing to this very day.

My Worst Beating
"You think about child abuse and you think of a father viciously attacking a daughter or a son, but in my family it was my mother. My mother, I would say, was a . . . very brutal disciplinarian". —Lynn Johnston the Canadian cartoonist

It was no secret in our family that my mother was physically abusive. She even earned the nicknames "Psycho A" and "Super A" from my younger cousins, who were terrified of her. To this day, she doesn't know about either of those nicknames. Even though my mother stands only four feet eleven inches, what she lacked in size was made up with her belt. My younger cousins feared and revered her. Because of my beatings, nobody wanted to cross Angie's path.

My mother gave me my worst beating while we lived on the middle part of Washington Street. Some of the neighborhood kids and I had been throwing stones at each other. Unfortunately for me, one of the stones I threw at them hit a glass window and broke it. My mother was so angry with me for incurring such an expense on her, that she picked me up from the ground and body slammed me in the dirt outside. She then started stomping me in my chest and stomach area. She did all of this while the neighbors were looking on. Mr. Harding eventually got her to calm down. I remember him telling her, "That is no way to beat a child."

My mother just shrugged it off by saying, "Oh, he deserved it."

In an article entitled, 'Children are not born criminals or killers', written by Camila Batmanghelidj who is the founder of the charity call 'Kids Company'. It is a charity organization that works with young ex-offenders and disadvantaged children, through inner-city schools in London. Ms. Batmanghelidj stated, "The children who stare menacingly from the pages of our newspapers are not born criminals or killers… The act of being violated gives these vulnerable young peoples a street-ready repertoire of violence; they know how to kick because they have been kicked, they know how to stab because they have been stabbed, they know how to torment and humiliate because they have experienced the same."

However, my mother was simply disciplining us the way she and her siblings had been disciplined. This was how my grandmother used to punish them. More importantly, above everything else, my mother was angry. She was angry with my father for walking out on her. My father, who had been a good provider in their relationship, left her with three children to struggle with on her own. He never looked back to assist, except for a brief time after he first left. I remember him bringing groceries for us when we lived with my grandmother, but that quickly came to an end. My aunt, who had a child by my father, told him that my younger uncles use to eat our groceries up when my mother wasn't there. After that, he stopped bringing us groceries.

Now that I am older and a father myself, looking back it was as if my father was just waiting for a reason to quit providing for us. He never reached out to assist us when my mother moved out. I cannot even remember an instance when our father assisted us in purchasing school supplies. So my mother had to cope with us all on her own and in the best way she knew how. Was she frustrated? Oh, yes she was. Did she sometimes take out her frustration out on Vanessa and me? Yes, she did, and I bore the brunt of her frustration. We turn to Patrick F. Fagan Ph.D. and the Heritage Foundation again, for he stated, "Abusive parents do not generally vent their anger equally on all their children. Such parents tend to vent their anger on their more difficult children. This parental hostility and physical and emotional abuse of the child shapes the future delinquent."

One time when we were all teenagers, my cousin Carlos was staying with us for the summer break. Carlos had accidentally broken the face bowl in the bathroom from its wall mount. Knowing how my mother can sometimes react, I told him not to worry about it and that I would tell the old lady that I did it. I told my mother, and it was no problem. She simply called the landlord, who had the matter dealt with and fixed before the end of the day. Some years later Carlos told me how appreciative he was of me for taking the blame. He said, "When that happened, I was horrified as to what 'Super A' was going to do."

This was how intimidating my mother was within our family circle, and I was usually the one who bore the brunt of her fury. Am I angry with my mother, for the abuse that I suffered at her hands? No I'm not, yet how could I be? When she was just doing the best she could with the limited coping skills and resources she had.

The Anger We Pass On To Our Children

"Anger is a very contagious emotion. When you come into contact with an angry person, it's often the case that you will become angry, or at the very least uncomfortable and uneasy." —Peter J. Favaro Ph.D., author of 'Smart Parenting During and After Divorce'

I don't believe in physically abusing children, because all it does is perpetuate violence and feelings within a child of being unloved and unwanted. Growing up, I used to get so many beatings from my mother that I started to believe that I probably was adopted. I couldn't have been my mother's child; this had to be the reason why she used to beat me so much. Even though I was but a boy, I felt as if that natural affection between a mother and her child didn't exist between my mother and me. Looking back now, I'm amazed of my mental thoughts when I was between the ages of 8 and 9 years old. Today this is the age of my son, and I'm mindful in assuring him of my love and support.

Yet it was Patrick F. Fagan Ph.D. who stated, "Normal children enjoy a sense of personal security derived from their natural attachment to their mother. The future criminal is often denied that natural attachment."

I used to think that I was my Aunt Paula's son; who had seven boys and one girl. My reasoning was that my mother was doing her a favor by raising me as a way of helping her out. This had to be the reason why she beat me so much. What really reinforced this belief of mine was that it was often remarked that two of my Aunt Paula's sons, namely Pedro and Jermaine, some say could pass for my brothers.

Therefore, I was a child growing up, trying to understand why my father left and why this mother of mine beats for every little thing. My favorite song as a child was "I'm Nobody's Child". It felt as if this song was written just for me, this was the song that I identified with growing up. The song "I'm Nobody's Child" is about an orphan boy whom no one wants to adopt because he's blind. The opening words to the song truly captured how I felt at the time. I was not my father's child, and I couldn't have been my mother's child, so therefore I was nobody's child.

According to information found on Wikipedia, the song was written by Cy Coben and Mel Foree. Hank Snow first recorded it in 1949. Many different artists would also go on to sing the song. In 1961, The Beatles recorded it, and in 1969, both Karen Young and Hank Williams, Jr. covered it. In 1975, Smokey 007, a popular Bahamian musician in the '70s and the '80s, also recorded it.

Many times as a boy, I contemplated running away. It's a feeling of absolute rejection of the worst kind, to think even for a second that your very own parents do not love or want you. It was the author Robert Goolrick who said in his book entitled, *"The End of the World as We Know It: Scenes from a Life"*, he stated, *"If you don't receive love from the ones who are meant to love you, you will never stop looking for it."*

I guess that this is why Buju Banton's song 'I Wanna Be Love', was my national anthem just before I lost my sight. Simply because I was looking for something that I felt deprived of as a child. This was my inward cry, because all my life I just wanted to be loved. The only thing my mother's beatings did for me was to teach me when someone got you angry, you hit, and you hit them hard.

One time I was by my Aunt Theresa and a little fella was harassing my smaller cousins Darren and Vardo. I asked him to quit it and leave them alone. When he did it again, without even thinking I drew back and slapped him across the face. He ran home crying and came back with his mother, who was arguing with my Aunt Theresa. I was later told that I had slapped the boy so hard one could still see the outline of my fingers on his face. When my mother used to punish me, she was always angry to the point of rage. Often it was while in this out of control anger, that she would pick up anything to hit me with, and this was exactly the way that I would go on to fight with others. My solution to a problem was simple: badly beat up the other person and probably he would think twice the next time.

In my interview with Miss Iris Adderley, a Psychologist and the Consultant for the Disability Affairs Division in the Ministry of Social Development for the Bahamas Government, she adds to this point by saying, "What we now have is a lot of angry women, because the men have left them and in some cases he promised his sweetheart that he would leave his wife for her but he doesn't, so she is angry. The majority of the schoolteachers in our educational system are females, some 85 to 90% of them, and research has shown that female teachers tend to spend more time with their female students than they do with their male students.

So therefore, our young men are coming up angry. You have an angry mother at home, you have teachers who are not giving you any attention, and in the churches the majority of persons there are women, so where do you fit into the picture as a young male?"

Miss Adderley continued, "Our young men are angry, and they have a right to be. The reason why they have a right to be angry is because we have failed them."

It was Patrick F. Fagan Ph.D. who stated, "The children of single teenage mothers are more at risk for later criminal behavior. One reason is that teenage single mothers monitor their children less than older married mothers do.

They are more inclined to have an inconsistent, explosively angry approach to disciplining their children."

It is these angry and frustrated mothers, who often take out their problems of life on their children. So is it any wonder that mothers more than anybody else are the primary abusers of children? This was confirmed in the Third National Incidence Study of Child Abuse and Neglect, which was conducted in1996 by Westat, Inc. and its subcontractor James Bell Associates, under contract by the U.S. Department of Health and Human Services (DHHS). Using data from the Bureau of Justice Statistics (BJS), the study was entitled "Child Victimizers and Their Victims," the DHHS and BJS reported that mothers and not fathers commit the majority of child abuses."

I guess that one can argue the point that mothers more than fathers are the main care providers of children. This is especially true in The Bahamas, where we have a 70 to 75% childbirth rate to unwed mothers.

My Interest In Education Left With My Father
"In boys, I see a lack of competitiveness and a lack of desire to achieve and get ahead in life. These boys think poorly of themselves, hate to put themselves out for any kind of work and have little self-discipline. Often these young men don't have any passion; they drift aimlessly and act lazy. There isn't anything they take pride in doing well." —Dr. Kenneth N. Condrell author of 'The Unhappy Child: what every parent needs to know',

I cannot say that I was an average student growing up; rather, I was a low 'D' student. I started my education at William Phipps Primary, which was located in the Claridge Road area. All of my mother's side of the family attended this school. The school no longer exists today, so this often makes me feel much older than I am, especially when people sometimes ask what primary school I had attended. When I give them the name of the school, they don't usually know of it, and with pride, I tell them that it has since closed down. I know that I started the first grade in the top class but after my father left, my interest and drive for learning left as well. My mother tells me that my teacher inquired about my sudden lack of interest in classwork, and the fact that I had become withdrawn and quiet.

In my interview with Mrs. Juanita Curtis (now deceased), who was a primary school teacher for more than twenty-eight years before she went blind. I had met Mrs. Curtis in The Disabled Persons' Organization, where I would serve as President for more than four years. Mrs. Curtis became like a second mother to me, and in getting to know her, I found out that the same thing happened to her son Torrey when her husband walked out on them.

I asked Mrs. Curtis, "When your husband left the home, how did it affect Torrey?"

She said, "Torrey went from an 'A' student to a 'C' student. It also affected his eating habits as well. I guess if he was born to a single mother, it probably would not have affected him as much. But from the time he was born, it was always his mummy and daddy there for him."

"As a parent and an educator, what did you do to get Torrey past this ordeal and get his grades back up?"

She said, "The basic thing was to show him love, and I let him know that I will always be here for him. Most of the things his father did for him, I was able to do it myself, but it hardly made any difference, because he wanted that male physical presence."

I don't know why I did, but I asked her, "So when a parent walks out on a child, it's like experiencing the death of that parent?"

Mrs. Curtis paused for a second and then said, "Yeah. Ironically, Torrey and I were just talking about this subject a little while ago. He was telling me that a friend of his who lives up the road from us told him that his father died when he was at the age of eleven."

Torrey laughed and said, "My father died when I was eleven too, at least in my world. That was when he walked out on us."

Mrs. Curtis went on to explain, "What he did for Torrey then on, really did not matter. Even though he was paying his school fees, it did not matter. I guess what hurt Torrey the most, was that his father did not attend his graduation from high school. He was informed on the time of the church service. He had a special invitation delivered to his father, and he still did not turn up. Even though he was on the same 21 by 7 piece of rock we called Nassau."

I had a chance to speak with Torrey, who was eighteen years old at the time. I asked him, "How did you feel when your father left?"

"When my father walked out on us it was tough, because I was no longer seeing him as much, and I missed just having him around."

"So how is your relationship with your father today?"

"I will see him when I go down there to him. Other than that, I don't really hear from him nor see him like that. My mother tells me she talks to him sometimes, but I don't call."

"So why don't you call him?" I asked.

"Because he wouldn't call, replied Torrey. If my father used to call and come around more, it would have made it a lot more bearable for me when he walked out on us. It felt as if he wasn't interested in me any longer, you know what I'm saying? Even though it has been more than seven years to date, my mind still runs across it a lot. It builds up anger in me, and the fact that he isn't making any effort to see me nor call me. What I feel about the situation is this: if fathers would be around a lot more, then kids like me would not have to be feeding off so much negative association. If you are always experiencing feelings of neglect, anger, and other stuff, you are going to have to let it out somehow. The biggest influence is peer pressure. I would normally get involved in all kinds of stuff contrary to what you would normally be into, because that part of my life would be filled by him. So therefore, it would have to be filled by someone else. It led to me smoking marijuana, drinking, and other negative things."

Torrey then concluded, "The main thing fathers need to do is to stick around, because them not being there is going to have a bad effect on the child no matter how you look at it. A young fella is always looking up to his father. He wants to grow up to be just like him."

It's no secret that boys idolize and adore their fathers, even scriptures bears witness to this fact as it is found in Proverbs 17: 6, "The glory of children is their father. NKJV"

It was His Airness, Michael Jordan, who put the icing on this topic for us when he stated: "My heroes are and were my parents. I can't see having anyone else as my heroes."

I am an information junky; I like to research the lives and background of individuals who stood out in their respective field. I'm always interested in learning what made them tick, why were they so driven and what or who it was that influence them.

One day while reading up on Michael Jordan's upbringing, I learn that his idol and roll model was his father. So much so, that he even brought a trait of his father on the basketball court and to the world. This was the protruding tongue, which was a trait he picked up from his father. James Jordan sr. who was a repairman by profession, had an unique habit of sticking his tongue out when he was hard at work fixing an appliance on their patio. Michael Jordan would inevitably do the same thing as he's going in for a layup, or attacking the rim for a high flying dunk.

During my teenage years there was a guy from Hawkins Hill we all use to play basketball with, name Harold Longley whom we use to call Jam-up. At that time he was somewhat short and chubby, like everything rolled into one. Anyway, every time Harold was coming in for a layup, His tongue would be protruding out of his mouth. Once I told him, "If you keep doing that one of these time, someone is going to accidently close your mouth shut leaving your tongue hanging on the outside."

Yet we all in our own way were trying to be like Mike, on basketball courts around the world young men were driving to the hoop imitating or imagining that they were Jordan. He was our idol and our hero, yet according to Michael Jordan, his heroes were his parents.

However, when our fathers are gone so are our heroes, and we will inevitably replace them with somebody else. Sadly, for us young black men those replacements are normally drug dealers, gangbangers, movie and rap stars. These are the persons who are real to us, and it is their life styles that we set out to duplicate.

In spite of it all, Torrey was able to leave school with six BJCs and five BGCSEs (these are national exams that students are required to sit in grade 9 and grade 12 before leaving school), which is an excellent accomplishment for anybody, especially a male student. Torrey had the potential to pursue any career path, and he would've done well for himself. He was offered jobs in several banks, because of his excellent school grades but he turned them all down. He always told his mother that he wanted to work with his hands, but he was idle for a while, which led to a few scrapes with the law.

After Mrs. Curtis died, I hadn't seen Torrey for a while. Until one day my wife and I were at a traffic light, where she proceeded to purchase two packs of peanuts from her favorite peanut vendor. Another young man came to the window before she could pull off. He called me by name and said that he was Torrey. I hailed him appropriately in the same way he was glad to see me, and when the light changed, we drove off. My wife said to me, "I could tell you are trying to figure out who that was."
"You're right. I know the name for sure, but I can't place the person."
I then asked my wife, "Describe him for me?"
My wife said, "He's tall with dreadlocks. By all accounts, he's a Rasta."
I asked her, "He was also selling peanuts?"
She answered, "Yes."
But I still couldn't place the person, and it troubled me because I knew the name well. But based on the description my wife gave me, I couldn't make the connection. It wasn't until a few days later that it hit me, and it hit me hard. It was Torrey, Mrs. Curtis's son. I said to my wife a phrase often used in The Bahamas, "Mrs. Curtis would turn over in her grave if she knew what Torrey has now become and is doing for a living." Please don't get me wrong; I know of a few Rastafarians who have done well for themselves in terms of a career, and I have nothing against a peanut vendor. As a matter of fact, my wife and I love peanuts, and we have three favorite vendors throughout the island. Whenever we are in their area, we do our best to patronize their business. But I know the sacrifices Mrs. Curtis made for each one of her children. As a teacher she said, "I had both Torrey and his older brother Ken reading before they were even four years of age."
Both of her sons went to private schools, and they both graduated a year early ahead of their age group. So in spite of Torrey's decline in his education after his father left, she worked with him and he was able to not only graduate, but to do so with distinction. To see him not living up to his full potential, was what really hurt me.

The Fear of Sharks Would Save My Life

"Go in step with your fear, but don't allow it to consume you. It can be a friend that cautions you to pull back when the time is right." —Christine Louise Hohlbaum, author of 'The Power of Slow'

At one point, my mother worked for my Aunt Paula, who had purchased a hot dog stand and had a permit to sell hot dog on Porters Cay Dock. During the summer months, I went out to the dock with my mother to spend the day with her. I can't remember where my sisters were or who was keeping them, or how I used to get to Porters Cay Dock to spend the day with her.

However, this particular day I was out there along with Sean, who is my Aunt Paula's third oldest child. Sean was older than me by three years or more. We somehow ended up at Malcolm Park. This was the old Malcolm Park, before they removed all of the old sunken boats and built the new bridge to Paradise Island [this bridge is now name in honor of the American born Bahamian actor, bestselling author and diplomat, Sir Sidney Poitier]. We went out there and saw a group of boys who were just in their underwear. They would jump in the water, which was about seven or eight feet deep, go down a bit in the water, then surface to the top, and grip a rope that was moored to the dock. You couldn't see the boat that the rope was still tied to because it was sunken under the water. Once they gripped the rope after surfacing, they would simply pull themselves to the concrete dock and come up the stairs. Upon seeing their strategy, I said to myself, "I could do that." Even though I couldn't swim and the water itself was a bit deep, I figured that all I needed to do was jump close enough to the rope like the others. Then once I surfaced from my jump, I could grip the rope and I would be in business. How could I go wrong when everyone else was doing it so successfully?

With the decision made, I stripped down to my underwear and told Sean, "Watch me do this." I stepped a few feet back, and then took off in a run. I was quickly airborne from the dock and came down into the water with a big splash. My plan was a simple one: grip the rope after surfacing and pull myself to the stairs of the dock. The only problem was when I came up to the surface I didn't see the rope. I couldn't find it. Apparently, my run and jump was too long. It was probably good enough to qualify for the CARIFTA Games (CARIFTA Games is an annual athletics competition among Caribbean nations), but in this case, it carried me past the rope. I panicked because I had nothing to grip, and I began thrashing around in desperation trying to find something to hold on to. I went back under the water, but when I broke the surface again I still couldn't find that silly rope, and down I went again.
This time I sank to the bottom with my feet touching the ground. There I had a chance to survey the area around and behind me. There was a lot of debris lying about, and as I turned around, I saw a few sunken vessels clustered together. The vessels were about fifteen to twenty feet behind me, but one boat in particular really caught my attention.
This boat rested on one side, and on its other side, there was a huge hole in its hull. It looked like a scene out of the Steven Spielberg movie Jaws. The only thing missing was the shark. Now the fear of drowning was gone, replaced with the fear of being eaten by a shark. Even though this shark was only in my mind, but for a frightened nine-year-old that shark was real.

Expecting jaws to exit the hole in the boat at any moment, I kicked off to the surface with a ball of energy. I wanted to create as much distance as possible between that boat and myself. I was determined more than ever that a shark was not going to eat me for lunch. When I broke the surface of the water, I could see Sean on the dock giggling. By now, the other boys sensed that I was in trouble, and they started shouting something about the rope to me. I couldn't make out what they were saying because I was thrashing around so much in the water. My eyes were now burning from the saltwater, and I went back under the water again. This time I refused to look behind me. I didn't want to see that hole again or what could be lurking in it. Rather, I just wanted to get farther away from that boat and the images that it was creating in my mind. This process of going up and down under the water took place a few more times. Eventually I soon grew tired, and the realization was starting to sink in that today I would probably die. It was then that my mother came to mind. Here I was about to lose my life just a few hundred feet from where she worked. She entrusted me to my older cousin, and within minutes of leaving her, now I'm here drowning. Just then, a hand reached out toward me and interrupted my thoughts. It was as if the hand appeared from out of nowhere. It was a strange but calming feeling. The hand was right there, and it was within my reach. I quickly reached up and grabbed it with my remaining strength, and an older teenage boy pulled me out of the water. With all of my thrashing around and trying to get far away from that boat with the hole in its side, I somehow drifted close enough to the stairs on the dock, where he was able to extend his hand in the water and pull me to safety.

I came up onto the dock coughing up water and trying to breathe. The young man who had rescued me asked if I was okay. I looked at him but his face was not familiar. He had not been there when I first jumped overboard. I just nodded my head in the affirmative, because I was still unable to speak from the whole ordeal. I glanced toward my cousin Sean with both of my fists clenched. He was still there giggling, but this time he was trying to conceal it. I guess by now he realized that I had almost drowned. Let me just say in my cousin's defense—the truth is, when a person is drowning, to the untrained eye of a child it looks as if the person is just playing around. I never learned who that young man was, or where he came from. But I am indeed thankful for the hand he offered to me; he saved my life that day. To this day, my mother never knew that I almost drowned just a few hundred feet from where she worked.

However, just a few months later, the same thing happened to my sister Vanessa. We were on a popular beach for locals, called Montague Beach. She told me, "DD, I'm drowning."
I laughed and said to her, "Yeah, right."
In truth, it looked as if she was just fooling around, bobbing up and down in the water. Again, it took an older teenage boy to extend his hand and pull her in far enough so she could stand on her own. Water and children are a dangerous mixture. It is my firm belief that parents or a responsible adult should not be sitting on the shore watching their kids. Rather, they should be in the water with them so they'll be there in case of an emergency. Tourist are often amazed and blown away by our beautiful beaches and our crystal clear waters, yet the fact is, the majority of Bahamians cannot swim.

I Used to Run through School Shoes
"The one thing children wear out faster than shoes are parents." —John J. Plomp
It became difficult for my mother to keep shoes on my feet, since I was growing up and very physically active as a boy. I used to play hard in school; games like porking, horsey, and play fights were my favorite lunchtime sports.

Unfortunately, my shoes couldn't keep up with the physical demand that I used to put on them each day, and neither could my school pants. Just about every weekend from grade 5, my mother was stitching up my pants. This happened so much that I got tired of going to her, because that meant a tongue-lashing. So, I started to stitch up my own pants, and many times the color thread I had used was visible for all to see.

A pair of shoes used to last me about seven weeks on average, if even that long. As fast as my mother could purchase a new pair, it wouldn't be long again before I needed another. This meant that many times I had to go to school with my shoes flapping or my toes showing. I was never really into sports while in school, even though the potential was most definitely there for track and field. However, I did have a brief interest in running while I was in primary school, which didn't last long because of a flop I made on the tracks.

I was the third fastest runner in our school, behind two classmates of mine name Devon Outten and Rabirdian Hanna, whom we called Bird Man. In grade 5, I was selected to participate in a government school meet at our sports center. I would be running against different students from various government schools throughout the island. The race was the 400 meters, which is one lap around the track. Before the race, I was contemplating whether to run in my tennis shoes or to run in my socks. I was sure of one thing: I was not going to run barefoot. My tennis shoes were fairly new. I decided not to run in them, not wanting to hear my mother's voice complaining about me bursting my shoes again so, I ran in my socks which was a bad mistake.

At the start of the gun, we took off running. There was a boy from E. P. Roberts Primary school—he just took off. Nobody was going to be able to catch him. Halfway through the race, I kept the second lead. But the chap from E. P. Roberts was way up in front; I was a far second behind him. Then I felt something pulling on my legs. I looked down only to discover that it was my socks, which were slowly sliding down my feet. They were now flopping with every stride I made, but I kept running rather than stopping to pull both of them off. One by one the boys began to take me over, but I was able to finish the race in fifth place, barely beating out two of them from another school. That was my first and last time competing in school sports.

I entered grade 7 at C. I. Gibson in September of 1986. I was in 7 (8), which means that there were seven other classes ahead of mine, and there were just four other classes behind ours. My Grade 7 teacher's name was Mrs. Matthews. I remember her name so clearly because she was strict. The principal at the time was Mrs. Borne, and there was a no-nonsense senior master by the name of Mr. Leonard Johnson. Everybody was afraid of Mr. Johnson. He was not a difficult man: he was firm and strict, but he was fair.

After returning from the Christmas break in January of 1987, our homeroom teacher Mrs. Matthews warmly welcomed us back by saying, "I hope that everyone enjoyed their Christmas break, and I hope that you all got good gifts." We had a class clown named Dion White, who spoke up and said,

"Everybody got gifts except for Drexel."

The whole class erupted in laughter. Mrs. Matthews corrected Dion by telling him, "That wasn't nice".

Everyone was laughing over the fact that I had come back to school in a pair of Mr. Harding's old shoes. Trust me when I say they were old; they were 1960s-style shoes that probably were cool back in his days. Not even black shoe polish could've done anything for them, but they were all I had.

Even before school had break for the Christmas holidays, I was wearing a pair of shoes that needed to be replaced. One might have thought that I would probably come back to school, with a new pair of black shoes. However, I came back with some old hand-me-downs that were probably two generations before my time.

Looking back, all of those memories bring a smile to my face today, because in spite of how tough things were back then, those were really some good days.

My trouble in school didn't really begin until I was in grade 9. I was suspended twice for fighting. The first fight was with a student named Neil. It took place during our class period. Neil was messing with a female student named Wendy. Everybody liked Wendy. I asked him to leave her alone, he in turn got angry, and the next thing I knew we were fighting.

The second fight for which I received a suspension was with Dino, another classmate of mine. Dino was a strange one. Every year from Grades 7 to 9, we used to fight. I have yet to figure that one out, because one would think after getting beat up the first time he would learn his lesson. But every year, he and I ended up fighting. For what, I don't know?

It was while I was in grade 9; I began to size up other male students, particularly those who were in my class. I would think to myself, "Now this one, I know that I could beat, because I'm much bigger. This student here who is my size and height would probably give me a bit of a challenge, but I still could beat him. Now this student over here who is much bigger than I am, he poses my biggest challenge." Thus, it was with such students that I often fought against, and as I moved on to senior school, it was the bigger boys and outsiders that I fought. For me it was the challenge I sought more than anything else. Someone might be bigger than I was, or older, or stronger, but I would often take them on in a heartbeat. To me, the strategy was a simple one: if I took on my toughest challenge first, it would eliminate the rest of my potential opponents, or at least get them to think twice.

Life Slowly Began to Improve for Us
"Children born into single-parent families are much more likely than children of intact families to fall into poverty and welfare dependence themselves in later years. These children, in fact, face a daunting array of problems." —Patrick F. Fagan, Ph.D.
While living on the second part of Washington Street, my mother got a job running a daycare nursery for a Mr. Harrison Toote, now deceased. The good part about her job was that it was on the same street on which we were living, and was just several houses down. My mother and Quannie, who was just a baby, headed out early each morning, and Mr. Harding saw to it that Vanessa and I headed out to school in time. Several months later, we moved from the second part of Washington Street into a two-bedroom wooden house on the third part of Washington Street. It had no running water in the kitchen, but there was running water to all of the bathroom fixtures. One could tell that the bathroom had been recently added on to the existing structure. We were now living on the third part of Washington Street where I met individuals like Cranny, his lil' brother Charlie, Warren, Lil' John, Dolan [not my right hand man in chapter 1] and his older brother Jervin.

I now only had to tote water for the kitchen, for cooking and washing dishes. Here again, because it was a wooden house with wooden windows, in the evenings we had to close all of the windows. With our warm summer temperatures and poor ventilation inside, our back room used to get really hot. We had just one standing fan to share between all three of us. Vanessa and Quannie would get the fan because they were females and there were two of them. They slept on the bottom bunk and I slept on the top. This meant during those sweltering hot summer evenings, with the poor ventilation, I often fell asleep sweating. However, I devised a simple plan to get around this. Since I couldn't feel the fan breeze from my bed, I would hang one of my hands out of the bed directly in front of the fan. My reasoning was that once I could feel the breeze on my hand, it could then soothe me off to sleep. It worked perfectly. Looking back at this simple childhood strategy of mine, I realize that I still use it quite often today, but in a slightly different way. For I have come to appreciate a long time ago that even though I might not have the power to change or control a situation, I can change and control the way I think about it, which often makes the issue more bearable.

My mother then got a job working at a Shell Service Station located on Robinson and Blue Hill Road, owned by Mr. Ron Miller. My mother started out as a pump attendant, which was unheard of for a female back in those days. In fact, it caused an argument between her and Mr. Harding, because he was totally opposed to the idea of her working as a pump attendant. I remember my mother asking him, "So what do you want me to do, do you want me to sell my body?"

Now today, almost thirty years later, one may pull up to any service station and it's a common sight to see female pump attendants. Looking back now, I can better appreciate that it's not where one starts out in life that determines one's destination. Rather, the ability to shape and create a better tomorrow lies in our hands through the power of our choices. My mother worked at the service station on the evening shift for more than five years. She eventually became the night manager at the service station, but this meant working seven days a week from 4:00 p.m. until 11:00 p.m. Therefore, for more than five years she was not a part of our lives, because by the time we came home from school, she was gone. At nights when she came home, we were already in bed and asleep for school the next day. Therefore, we only saw our mother on weekends and during school holidays.

Two of the morning shift managers of the station, Allen and Larry, pulled my mother aside and told her, "You cannot be working seven days a week, with three young children at home in the evenings by themselves."

They decided that Larry would work one day out of the week, on Friday evenings, to give my mother a day off. Soon after that, my mother started working during the day, as a cashier at Ron's Auto Parts, which was also owned by Mr. Miller. Now we really weren't seeing much of our mother; however, Mr. Harding filled in the gap for her. It was then that things really started to improve for us during this time. Growing up during those times, we never lacked for anything. We did not always get what we wanted, but we always had what we needed. The only thing that we lacked was my mother's time, attention, and affection. Vanessa once commented to me, "When we were living through Washington Street [the third part], I thought that Mummy was dealing drugs. One day we basically had no furniture, and the next day the furniture company delivers a truckload of furniture."

Our new furniture was made possible through what is called an ASUE. Just about every Bahamian woman has participated in an ASUE, or still participates in one today. Many Bahamian mothers will tell you that because of the ASUE, they were able to save the down payment for a home, or purchase a car, or take their annual summer shopping trips to Florida. Let's say for example that my mother wanted two thousand dollars to go shopping in Florida for school supplies and other items, she would find a trusted person who's holding an ASUE, with some 20 to 25 persons in the ASUE at one hundred dollars a hand. This means that the ASUE will run for 20 to 25 weeks, requiring each person to contribute one hundred dollars a week until the said number of weeks is completed. So each week, one person out of the 25 will receive $2,500 dollars in cash, and the next week it will be someone else's turn. The key component about the ASUE is that the person who is holding the ASUE itself must be trustworthy. If you can respect and trust her with your money, it's understood that you can also trust her to choose the persons who will be participating in the ASUE (I say "her" because the holders of ASUES are usually females). For this reason, a person participating for the first time would often get later draws ("draw" refers to your week/turn for payment).

As one might imagine, there are some horror stories out there, such as when an ASUE gives an early draw to somebody who later disappears. However, what makes the ASUE so effective is commitment and discipline. Once you have given that first hand of one hundred dollars, you are now committed to seeing it through. The person who is holding the ASUE is one you respect and trust, so you don't want to let them down. This brings up the second part of the ASUE, which is discipline. To do without one hundred dollars each week from your paycheck means there will have to be some cutbacks and sacrifice made for the next 25 weeks. If for whatever reason you are late one week, you can be sure that the holder will call upon you.

[4]

When we were growing up, this was how my mother made all of her major purchases. She did not qualify for a loan from a bank, because either her salary wasn't enough or she lacked job stability. But her participation in various ASUES throughout the year allowed her to purchase, in cash, what she needed for the house and for us.

One of the great benefits of such a collective scheme is that there is no financial debt. It is also a good support network; it rewards those who have proven to be responsible to get early draws. With such a financial support network, is it any wonder that our females are outperforming the males upon leaving school?

You can speak to any home developer and they will tell you that the majority of their clients are women. Even in cases where the clients are a married couple, it is normally the woman who is in the forefront communicating with them. Several years ago, I had to speak with the marketing manager of one of our major furniture stores on the island, who told me that some 85% of their customers are females between the ages of 25 to 45. I guess if one spoke to a car dealership owner, one would get similar numbers. The point of all of this is that it's our females who are outperforming our males in just about every area in life, because they have a better support network than us males.

---

[4] +appendix

Chapter 4
MY QUIET AND ANGRY YEARS

"Without positive male figures or strong mothers, these boys are left to figure out manhood on their own. They have holes in their lives that they sometimes sadly fill with rage and hatred." —Dale Sadler school counselor and author of the book, 'How to Argue with Your Teen and Win'

When I look back over my teenage years, it is sad to realize that I spent the majority of that time angry. I saw a lot of wrong things taking place around me, and I was powerless to speak up about it. As a result, I learned to bottle up things within me, but eventually what was bottled up so tightly came out, all because of these quiet and angry years at home. As a young child growing up in the '80s, it was not as if I was a deeply religious person, yet I knew what adult behaviors were morally and socially acceptable. I remember quite clearly at the age of 12 saying to myself, "Parents really must think us children are stupid in not knowing what they are doing is wrong."

However, I have now come to appreciate better, as I look back today, that one of our main problems is children having children. We have young people who are biologically capable of having a child, but they are not mentally capable of raising one, simply because they are but children themselves. This point is expanded a whole lot more in my interview with the former Member of Parliament for the Fox Hill Constituency, the late George Mackey. He was the only politician in The Bahamas who was referred to as a statesman, because it is said that he treated everybody equally and greeted both friend and foe as beloved.

Mr. Mackey was a historian in his own right, having been born and raised in the old historic Fox Hill community. It is the over the hill community on the island of New Providence that holds the largest cultural heritage festival each year known as Fox Hill Day. I met with him at his office, when he was serving as the Chairman for the Antiquities Monuments & Museums Corporation of The Bahamas. The interview started with Mr. Mackey reading an article that he had written entitled "Save the Family, Save the Nation." He began, "History has vividly shown that some of the world's greatest empires were destroyed not by superior military might from without, but rather by moral decay from within. The greatest contributing factor to most of our social ills, particularly crime, is the breakdown of family life in The Bahamas. This is reflected in the high rate of illegitimacy, particularly between teenagers, which now produces grandmothers in their late 20s. In this latter group in childrearing and nurturing becomes tantamount to the blind leading the blind. Added to this sad state of affairs, the ever increasing number of divorces, which nowadays are easy obtainable and which often leave in their wake many frustrated young children."

What Mr. Mackey is speaking about, is now becoming widely accepted as a fact of life. The simple truth is this, the state of a community or a nation, are directly connected to the state of the homes within. One of my favorite African proverbs really captures this point, when it states: *"The ruin of a nation begins in the homes of its people."*

In my interview with Iris Adderley, she also touches on this point by saying, "The reason why the social ills are the way they are in our society is because the family is nonexistent. One of the things I did when I came back home, after spending 21 years in the US working for the Ministry of Tourism selling our country. I went out and purchased a couple of history books that were written by Bahamians. One of the things that surprised me, and I don't know why it did— I guess it surprised me to see it in writing—was this sweet hearting business, this common law stuff, this thing about a man having two or three different homes that he is taking care of. This existed way back in our history, but what amazed me is that it still exists today, and has now become a culturally accepted thing where you wink your eyes, and turn your head that says its okay."

She continued, "If we are supposed to be a Christian nation based on our constitution, which means that the majority of our citizens our Christians or hold fast to Christian beliefs, why do we have a childbirth rate where 70% of children are born out of wedlock each year? Why do we have the majority of homes in the Bahamas headed by women? Something is wrong with that picture."

We are not alone in this high child birth rate to unwed mothers, a Pew Research Center Report on the rise in children being born to single mothers, provides the following numbers: "In 2008, a record 41% of births in the United States were to unmarried women, up from 28% in 1990. The share of births that are non-marital is highest for black women (72%), followed by Hispanics (53%), whites (29%) and Asians (17%), but the increase over the past two decades has been greatest for whites—the share rose 69%."

Patrick F. Fagan Ph.D. and his team of researchers at The Heritage Foundation, said the following, "The scholarly evidence, in short, suggests that at the heart of the explosion of crime in America is the loss of the capacity of fathers and mothers to be responsible in caring for the children they bring into the world. This loss of love and guidance at the intimate levels of marriage and family has broad social consequences for children and for the wider community."

Speaking about his own upbringing, Mr. Mackey said, "My mother ran a little shop that was right in our yard and my father drove a truck that he had applied for hire out there. But my mother was always in the home. She was able to exercise discipline in the household while my father was out on the truck.

Sometimes if we did something that was wrong, she would punish us with a belt or a switch. When my father came home in the evening, she would tell him what had happened, and in many instances, my father would give us another beating."

Mr. Mackey continued, "In today's society, the Americans call that child abuse and will arrest the parent for corporally punishing their children. But look at the mess. When you take away that level of discipline that causes us to be the way we are now, how could we expect for them to be just like us, when we deprive our children of what made us what we are today? Do you see what I mean?"

The Heritage Foundation actually refers to an independent study on this point, when they wrote, "Over forty years ago, this phenomenon was highlighted in the classic studies of the causes of delinquency by Sheldon and Eleanor Glueck of Harvard University. They described in academic terms what many children hear their mothers so often say: "Wait till your father gets home!" In a well-functioning family, the very presence of the father embodies authority, an authority conveyed through his daily involvement in family life. "

Mr. Mackey went on to explain the structure of the family when he was growing up. "The father was the provider and the mother took care of the home, and took care of the nurturing and the upbringing of the children. But both of them shared in the discipline of the children, and that caused us to be manly where we had to say 'Good morning, ma'am,' 'Yes, ma'am,' 'Good morning, sir,' 'Yes, sir' to people older than ourselves. That was a tradition. That was passed on from their parents and their grand-parents straight on down the line."

He continued, "We have now become so Americanized in our outlook on life, many of the things that the Americans have done, we are doing as well. Whereby, when I went to school, teachers had a right to beat me. If I did anything wrong, I got the cane. The teachers went even further than that because when school was out, they would report the matter to my parents and I was beaten again. My parents beat me for embarrassing the family's name for having done something wrong that cause the teacher to beat me in school. This was how the community was back in my days, for the community did indeed raise the child. Not only did the teachers have the right to beat us, but if any older person in the community saw us misbehaving, cursing, or doing anything wrong, they too could have even beaten us and we dared not go home and tell our parents. For example, I still live in the yard that I was born in. Back in those days, in the front part of our yard, my aunt had two rooms that she rented out to other families. One of the lady's daughters who were renting from my aunt was my schoolteacher, who was known as Gloria Pinder at the time, but she is now Gloria Goodman. One day, Miss Gloria beat me with the tamarind switch and a piece of the stick got stuck in my hand. I thought I was doing a world of good, when I ran home and showed my mother my hand with a piece of the stick in it. I told her that Miss Gloria had beaten me and done this. She called Miss Gloria to her when she reached home, and my mother beat me again right in front of her.

My mother told me, "'If you were not doing anything wrong, then Miss Gloria would not have beaten you.'"

He continued, "Today my brother Charles Mackey (we call him Macadoo) is very active in high school basketball. He is the vice principal of R.M. Bailey, but Charles told me that if he were to beat a child in school (and sometimes he doesn't have to even beat the child, but just deprive them of some privilege) as a means of punishment, the child goes home and reports him to his mother. Most

likely, instead of the mother coming to the school and asking what her child did and why they had to be punished, she brings the child and sometimes some member of the child's gang to the school and she would jump in that school cursing and so forth, asking her child, 'Which one of these teachers mess with you?' The teacher is automatically wrong from the parent's perspective, and mind you, the teacher is only trying to bring up her child properly. This is the difference between parents in my day and parents today."

Mr. Mackey explained, "I am not talking about excessive punishment, where you beat up the child in the school and the child has to be hospitalized. That's not corporal punishment to the extent that is expected in the school; that is brutality. I am not condoning that in those instances. How do you expect a teacher to take a special interest in your child's education, in your child upbringing? If when the teacher tries to discipline the child, you come there and hop down on the teacher. You want to beat the teacher and take the teacher to court. Once you demonstrate that lack of maturity and responsibility, what the teacher now does is put the lessons on the board and run it by the children one time. If you learn, fine, but if you don't, then so be it. They are not going to push any longer, because they have lost interest and they do not have the support of the parents in the education of their children. Not just teaching them from an academic standpoint, but also teach them about life, how to behave, Christian virtues, and all of that."

Miss Iris Adderley adds to this point. "It is my belief that our generation has failed this nation; our parents did not. They taught us the way we should have been taught, but what we did, we got up and got fancy, and in doing so, we destroyed our nation. In my day and time, I couldn't curse an adult. I couldn't call an adult by her first name. When an adult spoke to me, I had to say 'no sir' and 'no ma'am,' and if I didn't act right, they would have spanked my bottom. I couldn't tell my parents, and if they were to find out, I would have gotten another spanking, because my parents would have known that I had to have done something for that to occur."

Miss Adderley continued, "I was at a school the other day, where I had to pick up my niece to drop her home. While waiting for my niece I saw a child gave a note to her parent, and I saw the parent's whole countenance change. She dashed out of her vehicle, leaving the child behind, racing up to the classroom, and I knew she was going to give the teacher a piece of her mind. What she didn't understand was what that attitude was teaching her child.

Each time I see a kid accused of murdering somebody and is in chains walking up to the court to be remanded to prison, it really hurts my heart because that is a reflection of our failure. They did not grow up in the crib saying 'I want to be a criminal,' but we taught them how to be criminals. When they see us as parents running the red light and when we ask them to tell the insurance man that we are not home, what are we teaching them? We are teaching dishonesty," Miss Adderley said.

It was the American author, Robert Fulghum who stated, *"Don't worry that children never listen to you; worry that they are always watching you."*

We Have Turned our Backs on what Worked
"When the U.S. Sneezes, the Bahamas Catches a Cold."
Bahamian saying

The above saying is often used in the financial arena, as a way of denoting how closely the Bahamian economy is connected to the US economy. Therefore, when there is a dip in the US economy, there is a drop in our local economy. Simply because, our economy is built on tourism, and the majority of our tourist comes from the US market, so when they are not traveling it is us who really feel it.

However, we are also joined at the hip in our social ills, and the breakdown of our families is a common bond we share especially in our inner city/ over the hill communities. This point is enlarged on by Patrick F. Fagan Ph.D. and his research team at the Heritage Foundation when they stated, "More recent figures indicate the illegitimate birth rate in many urban neighborhoods is a staggering 80 percent. And today's researchers, like those before them, find that a neighborhood composed mainly of single-parent families invariably is a chaotic, crime-ridden community in which assaults are high and the gang -- " the delinquent sub community"-- assumes control. "

They continued, "It is no coincidence that one of the central rules in the traditional moral codes of all communities at all times, in all places, and in all cultures is the prohibition against giving birth to children outside of marriage. Societies all over the world have recognized that this prohibition is essential to social stability and to raising members of each new generation with the proper respect for their community and their peers. Unfortunately, and with disastrous consequences, this prohibition is ignored today in American society at all levels, but most especially in central-city neighborhoods. Having a child outside of marriage virtually guarantees a teenage woman and her children a life of poverty, low education, low expectations, and low achievement. It gradually puts in place the conditions which foster rejection and, ultimately, crime."

Then they said, "Whenever there is too high a concentration of such broken families in any community, that community will disintegrate. Only so many dysfunctional families can be sustained before the moral and social fabric of the community itself breaks down. "

Mr. George Mackey continued, "The tragedy is the price that we have paid for this modern way of life, is that we have abandoned most of the wholesome things that caused us to be different, that caused us to be better persons toward older people and other people's property. Sad to say, but when you lose that type of tradition, that type of family life, all you can expect is anarchy in society. We have drifted that far away from the basic principles and tenets. God taught us how a family should dwell. The man should be the head of the house, as Christ is the head of the church, his bride. There should be family worship, family prayer. All that type of stuff help to keep the children on the straight and narrow path and to nurture a fear of God and you will have a better society. What do we have today? We have children 12, 13, and 14 having children."

In fact what Mr. Mackey is saying, when our morals decline then our social issues will rise simply because our social problems are as a result of our moral breakdown. Therefore, it can rightly be said that a nation's best defense against social ills is a well-functioning family that serves as an immune system against social deviants. This point has been mention thousands of years ago, when God told the Israelites that it is through the union of marriage do they achieve godly offspring as it is found in Malachi 2: 15. It was the American actor, director, producer and author Stephen Baldwin, who stated, "I think it's really terrifying that a country based on the foundations and ideals of God, is now systematically removing God from everything. Everything!"

We now turn to another study conducted by Patrick Fagan and The Heritage Foundation, it is called, 'Why Religion Matters, The Impact of Religious Practice on Social Stability', which was published January of 1996. They stated, "Religious practice appears to have enormous potential for addressing today's social problems."

They then went on to quote the following individuals, starting with Allen Bergin, professor of psychology at Brigham Young University who stated in 1991, "considerable evidence indicates that religious involvement reduces "such problems as sexual permissiveness, teen pregnancy, suicide, drug abuse, alcoholism, and to some extent deviant and delinquent acts, and increases self-esteem, family cohesiveness and general wellbeing."

"Rockford Institute President Allan Carlson summarizes the pattern: "Social scientists are discovering the continuing power of religion to protect the family from the forces that would tear it down."

Mr. Mackey said, "When I was growing up, you had that religious input along with the academic input that made you a total person. The academics help you to get the skills to survive in this world, the religious prepared and taught you Christian virtue that will enable you to live in peace with your brothers here, and assured you of eternal life in the next world. So we were well rounded. The kids today do not have that, because seven out of every ten children born in the Bahamas are born outside of wedlock. They do not have that family upbringing. A lot of the boys do not know their daddies. A lot of the children are exposed to situations that if they have five brothers and sisters, in some cases each one of them has a different daddy. The type of lifestyle they see their mothers live, children either succumb or become creatures of their environment, or they develop such a repulsive attitude toward that type of lifestyle."

A Love Gift Stolen

"Beware how you take away hope from any human being." — Oliver Wendell Holmes, Jr.

I was in the seventh grade when I got my first job. It was Mr. Harding who got me a job as a packing boy, at Super Value food store on Blue Hill Road. I was paid twenty dollars a week plus tips. The Manager at the time was Mr. Nixon and his two assistants were Mr. Williams and Mr. Johnson. The head cashier was Ms. Sands, who could've competed in the Miss Bahamas beauty contest and probably won hands down. The security guard for the store was Mr. Bain.

While I was working at Super Value, out of the blue my father surprised me one day with a brand new, cherry red BMX bicycle. It was every 11-year-old's dream bike, and everything I could have asked for in a bicycle and more. Yet what made this bike so special to me was the fact that my father bought it for me. Even though he said that he was not my biological dad, to receive such a gift was more than I could've asked for, and for that, I loved him even all the more.

I used my bicycle to get to and from school, and also to and from work at my packing job. My mother had instructed me to stop at the service station each evening, which was about three blocks away, before making my way home. I never understood her reasoning behind such a request, but nevertheless, each evening I went to her work before heading home.

On one of those evenings while waiting for her approval to ride home, I decided to occupy my time with some bicycle stunts. I made a makeshift ramp in the back of the service station. Everything was going well until I got off my bike to make the ramp a little higher when an older boy, perhaps seventeen or eighteen, hopped on my bicycle and started to ride off. I shouted to him, "Hey, that's my bike!"

He looked back at me and said, "Well, it's mine now, shorty."

In desperation, I shouted to him, "My mummy is out front there!"

But he just shouted over his shoulder, "Who cares."

I ran to the front crying and shouting, "Mummy, Mummy, someone just stole my bike!" By the time she came out of the service station, all she saw was the back of the boy riding away on my bike. I have no shame whatsoever; but I cried like a baby that evening. How dare he ride off on my bike, and the very one my father bought for me.

I guess back in those days a bicycle theft was a big deal, because my mother called the police and within minutes, two officers in plain clothing arrived to take my statement. They sat me in the back of their unmarked police car. I was crying and trying to give them my statement of what had happened. But I was crying so much that one of the officers asked, "Shorty, that's only a bike. Why are you crying like this?"

I said to him through my sobs, "That was the bike my daddy bought for me." This officer couldn't understand my hurt and pain. Even the color of my bike was my father's favorite color. He didn't understand; that bike was my most precious possession in this world. The officer would never be able to appreciate that the bike to me was a gift of love, and now some nut head had just ridden away with my love gift. I cried for weeks over the loss of that bike. I even asked God why he had allowed this to happen to me. I blamed myself for not fighting back. I blamed myself for being so careless, and I blamed myself for losing my father's gift. How could I now look my father in his eyes when I had failed to keep what he had given me?

When I was twelve, I started working at the service station with my mother. I was heading into the eighth grade. I was a pump attendant, making eighty dollars a week. For the first time, I was really able to contribute to the home, which made me felt like a man. For me, there's no feeling that beats supporting those you love by contributing to your home. In Sir Sydney Poitier's bestselling book entitled, *"The Measure of A Man"*, he stated, *"Children need a sense of pulling their own weight in contributing to the family in some way. In some sense of the family interdependent. They take pride in knowing that they are contributing. They learn responsibility and discipline through meaningful work. The values develop in any family operates on those principle then extends to the society at large."*

Out of the eighty dollars I made each week, my mother would give me thirty dollars for lunch to last the whole week. However, by Wednesday, I was normally broke because I was awful when it came to managing money. Thankfully, my tips made up for my lack of discipline. Now for the first time in my life, I was able to purchase a pair of the durable but stylish Clarks shoes. These were the most popular shoes back then, and I'm told that they still are today. The Clarks shoes were the first pair of shoes that lasted me for the entire school year.

My Angry Years

"Sometimes you see the behavior on the surface from these boys, but for the most part they are acting out the experiences that many of them have at home." —Pastor Wilbur Outten from Grand Bahama Island

It is widely accepted that the family is the first institution and the main foundation that our communities and the wider society is built upon. Our job as fathers is to prepare our kids today to fulfill properly their role as parents of tomorrow. The values I live and instill in my son today will be the same ones that he will pass on to my grandchildren and great-grandchildren of tomorrow. Isn't it amazing to realize, as fathers, the power we have to influence the future? When one takes a serious look at it, for better or worse, we could determine the quality of life that our grandchildren and great-grandchildren will live. As pointed out to us in Proverbs 13:22, *"A good man leaves an inheritance [of moral stability and goodness] to his children's children. Amplified Bible"*

The major question is this. As fathers, are we living up to this responsibility? Do we value our offspring enough, whom we have not seen as yet, to give them an advantage in life? This is what this book is about. I'm not trying to fix my son; better yet, I'm trying to fix myself, and in the process of doing so, I will make his life better. It was the Swiss Psychotherapist and Psychiatrist, Carl G. Jung who said more than 70 years ago, *"If there is anything that we wish to change in the child, we should first examine it and see whether it is not something that could better be changed in ourselves."*

This means that when it comes to parenting, we will only be able to pass on what we are, and not what we hope to become one day. It is not our best thoughts and ideas that are pass down to our children, rather it is our actions both bad and good, small and great that we pass on to our kids. The truth is who I am today; it will be the man my son will be tomorrow, to which he would also pass on to his children, my grandchildren. This is why scripture says, *"Children are fortunate if they have a father who is honest and does what is right."* Proverbs 20: 7 GNT.

There's an old African proverb that is quite in line with this point, which states, *"If you know his father and grandfather, don't worry about his son."*

I spent my early teens angry and bitter with my mother. This was during the time I worked at the service station with her. As parents, we somehow fail to appreciate that the example must come from us. More than ever, parents, we must lead the way for our children to follow. While we were still living on the third part of Washington Street, my mother got involved with another married man, by the name of Ricky, and this led to a temporary split between her and Mr. Harding. My mother and Ricky then broke up and she resumed her relationship with Mr. Harding.

We then moved in with Mr. Harding where he and his family had lived after his divorce was final. He lived in a three-bedroom, two-bathroom home in a middle-class area called Danottage Estates. This was where I spent the majority of my bicycle riding days, and it was the first time I had my own bedroom.

Mr. Harding was excellent with my two sisters, having raised four children of his own, three of them girls. He picked up my sisters from school in the afternoons and saw to it they got a hot meal. Afterward, he inquired if they had homework and made sure they completed it. If they needed help, he provided it. As a Vietnam veteran who was once a prisoner of war, he was very resourceful and knowledgeable about world affairs. He was a walking, talking encyclopedia. There was almost no issue that he didn't know about.

While living with Mr. Harding, to my dismay, my mother got involved with Ricky again. This time, she even helped him get a job at the service station. I was angry with her. I knew that my mother was wrong for what she was doing. I took it personally, but I never told her and I never acted out toward her. The reason why I took it personally was that everyone at the station knew that we lived with Mr. Harding, and everyone also knew that she was seeing Ricky on the side. Even though nothing was said to me, I knew what people were thinking and it was not good.

One time Mr. Harding came to the station, took a hatchet, and broke out all of the glass of Ricky's car. Now it was hard for people not to talk about that.

The fellas at work said to me, "Boy, your stepfather is crazy." It was a compliment for Mr. Harding, but it pointed out a character flaw within my mother. As a result I felt ashamed, and I was embarrassed about the whole incident. This would be the burden that I would carry through my teenage years. As parents we must appreciate that when we fail to be that good example, then we rob our children out of their dignity, their self-respect and their self-worth. It was Stephen Covey the American educator, businessman, keynote speaker and the author of the wildly successful book, *"The Seven Habits of Highly Effective People"*. Mr. Covey stated,

"When it comes to developing character strength, inner security and unique personal and interpersonal talents and skills in a child, no institution can or ever will compare with, or effectively substitute for, the home's potential for positive influence."

As parents we must understand, that our children are pulling for us to do what's right, we may not always understand or even agree with your principles, but at the end of the day we would respect you for them. However, as we move on into adulthood, we would come to appreciate that your principles did indeed stood the test of time, and now it becomes easy for us to make those principles our very own. Fathers and mothers, this is how we as parents leave behind a legacy for our children.

In Robert James Waller bestselling book entitled, *"The Bridges of Madison County"*, that I had the pleasure of reading which is based on a real life story and has also been made into a movie. The main character Francesca Johnson stated, *"When a woman makes the choice to marry, to have children; in one way her life begins but in another way it stops. You build a life of details. You become a mother, a wife and you stop and stay steady so that your children can move. And when they leave they take your life of details with them."* Those details that we take with us to our own families are our parents' examples both good and bad. What we witness and see as a child, we now live out for our children. Thus this cycle repeats itself, where the values and principles that we observe in childhood we now live out in adulthood.

None-the-less, Mr. Harding and I never really connected, because I never allowed anyone to get that close to me. However, in the preparation of writing this book, I read somewhere that my actions were somewhat defensive. I had been hurt by the man I thought was my father, so therefore I was not going to allow anyone to do it to me again.

I knew that my mother was wrong in what she was doing, but I couldn't tell him what was going on. On top of that, I couldn't approach the subject with my mother, nor could I speak with my sisters. So I just shut down, but I went on raging on the inside. As parents it's foolish to believe that we could live our lives as we please, without it negatively affecting the lives of our children. Dr. Robert Coles, a noted teacher and research psychiatrist, touches on this point when he said, *"Within the child there is a developing moral sense. I happen to think it is God-given, that there is a craving for a moral order."*

I was always somewhat quiet and reserved, but now I became even more so. Sometimes my mother would be talking with me, and she would try to get some sort of confirmation that I heard her. Instead of saying "Okay" to her, I would only say "K." Unknowingly, the "O" was said in my mind, and only the "K" would come out verbally. Once, my mother asked me, "Why do you only say the letter 'K'? Do you mean to say 'okay'? If you mean to say 'okay,' then you need to say the 'O' and the 'K' together."

In my interview with Mr. Vincente Roberts the Counseling Psychologist at Adolescent Health Centre (AHC), where he was the coordinator of psychosocial support. Mr. Roberts is presently a lecturer at the University of the West Indies, in the area of counseling psychology for their Master's degree Program and he is pursuing his doctorate in Clinical Psychology. He stated, "When another adult is bought into the family, the parent cannot assume because they have decided they want this person to be a part of their life, that the child is going to accept the other adult just like that. It requires a process. You still have this reference point of the absent father, or the reference point of the father they had a relationship with. So you are now asking me to have a relationship with two males - one male who is trying to come into my life, when the other one has really not acknowledged me as their child. So there is a lot of emotional dynamics that goes around this whole issue, parents in particular mothers, because we live in a country where 75% of the kids are born outside of wedlock, so this whole concept I think we need to start looking at more specifically."

However, in this case my sisters and I had already accepted Mr. Harding, but now my mother was venturing out with someone else. Yet I was the only one who knew about it, because my sisters were clueless as to what was really going on.

One evening while at work in the station, my mother and Ricky had a disagreement that spilled over after work. Upon leaving the station, he followed her. She pulled over in the parking lot of Fat Boys restaurant which was on Robinson Road. I was in the back seat of her little blue Honda Accord which was her first vehicle, and Ricky was at the driver's door talking with my mother. He said something to her that really got her upset, and my mother pushed the pedal to the metal to exit the parking area. She didn't even stop to see if any vehicles were coming; she just plowed onto the main road directly into traffic. Even though I was sitting in the back seat, I saw the pending danger, for traffic was coming from both sides. I looked at my mother in disbelief but it was as if she didn't care what happened. I screamed at the top of my lungs, "Mummy, NOOOO!"

Just then, I heard the sound of tires screeching on the road as drivers braked to avoid hitting us from both directions. I felt and heard when the front part of our vehicle was hit, and we came to a sudden stop. There was a few seconds of quietness with no movement; then my mother opened her car door and got out. I was pretty shaken up, for I couldn't believe what had just happen.

I opened my eyes then, though I don't remember closing them. I was also now sitting in the middle of the back seat, which was strange to me, because when my mother sped off I was sitting at the right passenger door. Again, I didn't remember moving toward the middle of the seat.

However, it was a truck that hit the left side of our vehicle, and my mother and the driver of the truck were outside talking with each other. After the accident, I didn't come out of the car. I just sat there in the back seat frightened, angry, but relieved that we were okay. I rested my head in my trembling hands, in my attempt to stop them from shaking. I remember saying to myself, "She almost killed us."

I thought about Vanessa and Quannie, who were no doubt at home asleep in their beds. My mind also went to Mr. Harding, who was there waiting on us to come home. Yet we were out here in an accident, one that could've been avoided if my mother would only leave Ricky alone. I wondered to myself if we had died, who would've delivered the bad news to my sisters? Who would've taken care of them? Even worse, because the truck had hit my mother's side of the car, if she had died, who was going to take care of us? We didn't stay at the scene long, because the accident turned out not to be that bad. I guess the truck driver who had run into us had done his best to avoid hitting us. Only the front left fender of my mother's car was visibly damaged, but the car was still drivable. After the exchange of telephone numbers and my mother's agreement to pay the driver for his troubles, we left and headed for home. My mother and I never spoke about the incident. I never told anybody what had happened. I had now become accustomed to keeping things to myself.

Mr. Roberts continued, "One of the things that is happening is that a lot of families are not transparent in many ways, I'm the parent and you're the child. One of the things that happen in that kind of context is, the child sometimes sees this parent being hypocritical and as a result the whole order and structure is broken down. So what happens in that kind of context? It has to do with the family being up front, being transparent, honest and open. It's important for a parent to be open with a child, he or she needs to make sure whenever they're not sure where the line falls, the parent can say, 'you know mummy is trying to work that one out right now, mummy is processing this right now. I know that I told you not to do this, but I'm doing this right now because of so and so'. If it's wrong, then she needs to say, 'listen I should not be doing this'. It's this sense of being up front with the child, so that the child doesn't have to get this confused message of the mother saying not to do this, but mummy is doing it; or the father saying do this but he's not doing it. It's as simple as someone coming to the door, and the parent is telling the child to tell them that they're not home, or it can be someone calling on the phone. Those are all lies."

My Fascination with Fire
"I became captivated with the very same instrument that was once used to try and kill us."

While I was going through my quiet rebellion, there was a young man name Kevin Hanna who had been talked about for years. He had allegedly killed his entire family, and he was later convicted and sentenced to life in prison. It was the first time, to my knowledge, that anything of this nature had ever taken place in The Bahamas, where a young man from a prominent family killed all the members of his family. Ironically, their home was also located in Danottage Estates and I would later meet Kevin in prison. It was said that Kevin was always reserved and quiet. Upon hearing that, my mother sought out professional help for me. She took me to see psychiatrist Dr. David Allen at the Princess Margaret Hospital. Along with my reticence, I also liked playing with fire. I had a serious fascination with flames, to the point where it was almost addictive. Many times, I stayed in my room with the door shut lighting matches and just watching them burn out. There were times my mother came into my room and smelled the scent of smoke. She would inquire what I was doing, and I would just say, "Nothing."

Then she would ask me for the matches, and I would promptly hand them over to her. My mother told me that after my father left us, we lived with my Aunt Paula for a short time, and I set one of the beds on fire. Fortunately, they were able to put the fire out, but I only vaguely remember that incident. Isn't it interesting, that I would later develop a fascination for the very same thing with which my father tried to kill us with? Dr. Allen arranged for me to undergo a test of some sort at Sandilands Rehabilitation Centre. I had to return some two weeks later for the results, but I never knew what their findings were. It wasn't until writing this book that I asked my mother what were the findings of the psychiatric evaluation. She told me that the test revealed nothing was wrong with me mentally. She said that Dr. Allen put my behavior down as really missing my father and probably my home conditions.

Dr. Allen was right about one thing—my home conditions. I was indeed angry with what I saw taking place around me. While I loved my mother, yet I hated what she was doing. Many times at work, I would go to serve a customer, and while asking them how much gas they wanted to purchase, they would somehow sense my anger and say something encouraging to me. These were female who were blessed with a mother's intuition. They would say to me things like, "It isn't that bad," or "You are a handsome young man, you should smile more."

One lady even insisted of me one time before she handed over her funds to pay for her fuel, 'You must smile for me first'. I never knew who they were, but I'll always remember how they made me feel. Their small acts of kindness lifted me up during a time I needed it most. These ladies took the time to say something encouraging, to a kid who was going through some serious inner turmoil. It was the noted American poet Maya Angelou, who stated, *"I've learned that people will forget what you said, people will forget what you did, but people will never forget how you made them feel."*

Several months after I started working at the service station and we began living with Mr. Harding, my mother purchased another bicycle for me to replace the one that was stolen months earlier. It was my best bicycle ever—a gray-and-white trail BMX with white and gray plastic covers that were over the spokes on each wheel. My best bicycle riding days were while we were living in Danottage Estates, which was the perfect place for riding bikes. There was never much traffic; it's a small community and its most striking features are its four or five hills. It was these hills that made bicycle riding a blast.

I went everywhere on that bicycle. I rode to school on it and I rode to work on it. On my days off from work, I would spend hours riding in our neighborhood. That bicycle brought me a sense of freedom, and it was my escape from home.

Eventually the relationship between my mother and Mr. Harding came to an end. I was in the 9th grade then, and it was around the same time I was sitting the Bahamas Junior Certificate (BJCs). We moved in with my stepmother Theresa, who was living on Gibbs Corner just off East Street [which is just two blocks north of Strachan's Corner, the base of the Rebellions street gang]. We stayed there for about two and a half weeks before my mother found a two-bedroom apartment on Mount Royal Avenue.

More than 20 years later my mother would admit, that she really made a mistake when she walked away from Mr. Harding. But I'm sure that my sisters and I could've told her that back in 1989. In truth Mr. Harding was the only father that we knew, and he was the only father that Quannie ever had. In fact, she even called him daddy. My mother said to me once in conversation: "When Mr. Harding and I had separated, Quannie who was just eight years old at the time, looked up at me with pain in her eyes and asked, 'Mummy, who's going to be my daddy now?'

CHAPTER 5
MY ERUPTION IN SCHOOL

"Any emotion, if held down long enough, tends to become more concentrated, sometimes turning into a simmering rage you may feel frightened of or uncertain how to handle." — Author Gay Hendricks, Ph.D.

As Mr. George Mackey revealed in the last chapter, he is the brother of Mr. Charles Mackey who at that time was the vice principle of R. M. Bailey. In my interview with Mr. Mackey he spoke highly of his younger brother Charles by saying, "He is my idol; he is my role model. I admire him. Even though I am almost ten years older than him, I look up to Charles because I like the example that he sets and the work he does with young people."

Ironically before my interview with Mr. George Mackey, I had already interviewed his younger brother Charles; I just never knew that they were related. However, I too was really impressed with his brother, during the time I had attended R. M. Bailey. This was why I went and searched him out, in my interview with Mr. Charles Mackey, he began by saying, "School in itself is a microcosm of society. These kids bring a lot of baggage with them, and as teachers with 30 plus kids in your classroom you have to take the time to get to know them, and not just see them as people you have to teach. And if they want to learn they will learn, and if they don't want too then to bad. But you have to see them as your surrogate children."

Mr. Mackey continued, "I can always tell when this economy is shabby or sluggish. And that is not through reading the newspaper. You can tell from students' purchases of lunch, and the lunch venders claiming they have to take their food back home. It is not that the food is not good or Wendy's is right across the road. It is due to the fact that I am (students) not getting those five dollars on a daily basis anymore.

Drugs are also a part of school life in particular marijuana. Alcohol beverages, prostitution - not so much on campus - but that is a way of survival for some young women and young men. These are societal ills. Schools are a small scale of society.

The girls today are not platting their hair in two ponytails. They are coming to school in a 35/45 dollar hair do. When I see the girls coming to me in the middle of the month, to change a one hundred dollar bill it makes you wonder. One can jump to conclusion, and I don't have to always be right. But there are some drug dealers out there, or a prominent member of society they see these young children matured in a physical sense, and they wage war on them taking advantage of them – pay to play."

Looking back over my life it is now easy for me to see and appreciate, that the anger I held within about my own family failings came out in school. It was the American entrepreneur and investor in high-tech startups, John Sculley who stated, "We expect teachers to handle teenage pregnancy, substance abuse, and the failings of the family. Then we expect them to educate our children."

It was in the 11th grade at R. M. Bailey that I erupted like Mount Helen. I guess this was my way of crying out for professional help. This was during the same time Michael Jordan shocked the basketball world, by beating my team at the time the L. A. Lakers for his first NBA championship title. Yet my volcano of compress anger was about to erupt in school, and it would take more than five years for my molten lava to be brought under control, which was through the loss of my sight. However, shouldn't there be a way of detecting and reaching out to kids like me before there is a massive problem? Why wait until there is a devastating eruption before we intervene? Please tell me why our government experts seem to be better at trying to contain a problem rather than preventing it?

In 1989 at the age of 14, I was transferred from C. I. Gibson to R. M. Bailey Senior High to complete my remaining three years of schooling. Quite a few of us were transferred to R.M. Bailey from other junior schools. Being the new kids on the block, we did what anyone else would do. We walked around the school to familiarize ourselves with the premises, and at the same time, look at the girls. Our exploration brought us to the gym, where all of the school activities are held, basketball games along with assemblies. We were making our way upstairs to the music block, which were to the southern side of the gym when I accidentally walked into another male student. I was walking around with four friends, and the student who had accidentally walked into me was all by himself. I looked up at him and asked, "Are you blind or something?"

He just looked at me with an angry stare, and so I stared back at him with my most angry face. I knew that I had more practice at this; for goodness sake, I was looking angry since the eighth grade, so I was now a pro. I guess he realized that my angry look was more menacing than his, plus he was outnumbered, so he just quietly walked off. We continued on our way with my friends patting me on my back saying, "Boy, you sure put that fella in his place."

Feeling a little smug, I mumbled to myself, "I guess I won't be having any problem out of him."

The next day we were doing our thing again, walking around the school campus, and of course, looking at the girls. In all my life, I'd never seen so many pretty girls in one spot as I did at R. M. Bailey. With new hairstyles for the first week of school, all the girls were looking pretty and smiling. It was the Jamaican reggae artist Shabba Ranks, who sang about a trailer load of girls, but I was looking at an entire school load of beauties in every skin complexion imaginable.

I knew that my time here was going to be fun. It was then that my thoughts were interrupted when I heard someone got slapped. By the sound alone, one could tell that it was a hard one. I figured whoever got slapped had to be close by, so I spun around in search of this person who had just gotten the daylights slapped out of them, only to discover that the person was me. The left side of my face went really numb, and I was somewhat confused as to what was going on. Whoever had just slapped me must have sneaked up on me from my blind side, because I didn't see it coming at all. I turned around looking for the culprit to see who had the nerve to do such a thing especially, when right behind me, was four of my boys. Spinning around on my heels, I discovered that it was the chap I had accidentally walked into yesterday. Now I was really angry and it was visible on my face, because I thought I had already put this fella in his place. I said to him, "What you dealing with bey?" ("Bey" is a local term use for boy.")

In answering me he just repeated my words, "What I'm dealing with?"

He drew back and hit me with another big one. Now this is going to be a slug out between us. But just as I was about to retaliate, I saw where his nerve and inspiration were coming from. The day before we had him outnumbered; it was five of us to him. He was smart in knowing he couldn't win, so he just walked away.

Now today they have us outnumbered—correction; they have me outnumbered. It was about fifteen or twenty of them, and my boys were doing what they did yesterday, standing there watching me get slapped, as if I wasn't even with them. To top it off, the girls I was admiring earlier were now looking at me getting slapped about. It's amazing how things can be so different just a day later. I realized that this was a no-win situation for me. I had already been slapped twice—and I mean two really big ones.

When I had insulted him the previous day, it was more or less a private affair with very few spectators. However, today his assault and insult of me was a public affair. It felt as if everyone was watching me being humiliated. The only thing I could've done to come out with a piece of my dignity was to begin to reason with this fella.

I said to him, "Big man, we don't have to go through this." Again, he just repeated my words. "We don't have to go through this?"

He drew back and hit me with another big one. I then said to myself, "Ah, forget it, if you're going to go down at least do so fighting."

I drew back, and punched him hard to the face. While saying to myself, "That's right, tell me how this feels?" When I punched him, it felt as if I hit a home run straight out of the park. It felt good.

However, that feeling was short lived; in fact, it was the quiet before the storm for I had totally forgotten, that I was outnumbered. For that I would pay greatly, because all of his friends attacked me at once. It was like a shark feeding frenzy; everyone was trying to get a piece of me. The only good thing for me, looking back, was that no weapons were involved. I would later learn that they all were from Price Street in Nassau Village, a subdivision where my aunts Pearl and Paula lived. The individual I had accidently ran into in the gym the day before, was known as Pen he was an 11 grade student. This was the first time I had been ganged, which was less than one week after I had been transferred to a new school.

Teachable Moments
"Especially important in this day and age is conflict resolution. With society becoming increasingly disaffected and volatile, the ability to defuse trouble quickly and efficiently has never been more important." —Kevin Dutton, Ph.D., author of Split-Second Persuasion

As parents one of the biggest jobs we have, is teaching our children how to resolve problems effectively. We live in an era where everyone is quick to act the fool over simple issues. As we used to say when I was on the streets, 'everybody wants to cut a movie'.

Our children are inundated with so many scenes of violence from the media, and from what their peers expects of them. It's not surprising that so many of our children lack the skills on how to reason and defuse a situation properly.

Let's look in on when I was ganged in school, and let's pull out the lessons from that situation. When both of us accidentally walked into each other, it was an honest mistake on both our part. However, what did I do? I ridiculed him. I made him feel small, all because I had the upper hand. Life is a funny thing. You might have the upper hand today, but it doesn't mean that you will have the upper hand again tomorrow. I quickly found this to be true enough.

Firstly: what if I had said to him, "Pardon me, big man, I didn't see you." In this simple little phrase are three essential components to defusing any situation relating to conflicts. The very first two words (pardon me) acknowledge a mistake on my part. There's nothing wrong in admitting when you have erred; it's a sign of maturity. It was the author Jim Fiebig who stated, *"It takes a big man to admit when he's wrong, and an even bigger one to keep his mouth shut when he's right."*

Secondly: by referring to him as "big man," I would have paid him a compliment, without making myself look small. By using the term "big man," what I'm saying is, "I acknowledge that you are worthy of respect." This simple acknowledgement is true with everyone we meet, they are all worthy of our respect. It was the German-born physicist Albert Einstein, a Nobel Prize winner and Time Magazine person of the century who stated, *"I speak to everyone in the same way, whether he is the garbage man or the president of the university."*

The sooner we acknowledge this fact - by treating everyone we meet with respect, then their respect towards us would multiply.

Thirdly: I am acknowledging the reason why I made the mistake of walking into him, simply because I did not see him. What do you think he would have said? What do you think he would have done? He probably would have nodded his head, and said, "Everything was cool." Then he would've continued on his way, and that would have been the end of the matter. When we would have run into each other again in school, we would have both probably nodded our heads toward each other in some sort of acknowledgement, that I see you and hope everything's cool. We probably would have become good friends. But instead, what did I do? I poured gasoline on a spark that was not even a fire, and reaped a whirlwind of events that was out of my control. As scripture says, *"The lips of fools bring them strife, and their mouths invite a beating." Proverbs 18: 6 NIV.*

When I had spearheaded the all-boys youth program called Brothers Against Crime & Killing [BACK], Daynette Gardiner, who is considered to be one of the best School Psychologist within The Bahamas, assisted me on assessing the reading level of our young men to which she discovered through her assessment, that the majority of them were reading way below their grade level. Some of whom were in grade 10 and 11 of senior school, yet they were reading at the primary school level of grade 3 and 4; these were individuals who were soon going to be entering our work force.

In my interview I asked Daynette, "We know that reading comprises of decoding [word recognition/spelling] and comprehension, so how can a parent improve not just their child's decoding skills but mainly their comprehension skills?"

She said, "First of all, you have to talk to your children about things, a lot of our parents don't do that. You have to explain things to children as to why certain things happen. I think that a good way of improving comprehension is to read the newspaper with your child. A lot of times certain sensational things happen and children want to find out why it happened. And sometimes you would hear them talking to each other passing on erroneous information and the rest of it.

You can use those times as teaching times for children. Or teachable moments to explain what happened, why it happened and what the consequences are. Not only things that make it to the newspaper but in everyday life. Parents need to see that every situation that their kids find themselves in is a teaching situation, and they need to take the time to explore cost and effect. So talking to your children, explaining things to children as to why things happen in the world. Getting them to see cost and relationships between events is the best way to increase comprehension skills. But the main thing is talking to your children."

Daynette then said in earnest, "you cannot improve your child's comprehension skills without talking to them, without spending valuable time with them."

Based on Daynette's information I can now appreciate God's instructions to Joshua, found in the fourth chapter of the book bearing his name. In verse 2 & 3 God tells Joshua: *"Take for yourselves twelve men from the people, one man from every tribe, ^{and} command them, saying, 'Take for yourselves twelve stones from here, out of the midst of the Jordan, from the place where the priests' feet stood firm. You shall carry them over with you and leave them in the lodging place where you lodge tonight.'"*

Joshua then helps us to understand God's reason behind this strange instruction, when he later explains in verse 6 and 7, *"That this may be a sign among you when your children ask in time to come, saying, 'What do these stones mean to you?' Then you shall answer them that the waters of the Jordan were cut off before the ark of the covenant of the LORD; when it crossed over the Jordan, the waters of the Jordan were cut off. And these stones shall be for a memorial to the children of Israel forever." NKJV.*

Therefore, those stones that were used to make a memorial pillar, were in fact conversation starters. Those stones reminded the older Israelites about the awesome power of God, while at the same time they were also use to inform their children about the same.

Likewise, the Jewish holidays such as the Passover all serve the same purpose; they were teachable moments to pass down their history, their heritage all through story telling. This is how a people preserve their history, and safe guard their future. Simply because the lessons learn the hard way by our forefathers, are not forgotten by those alive today.

The truth is these story telling or teachable moments, provides us with a vast reference base of real life antidotes for possible future problems. They not only entertain and give us a resource of proven solutions, but they also help shape and mold our character. Therefore, when we don't take our time to communicate with our kids, then we rob them of critical life lessons that we and our forefathers learn the hard way - lessons that they would needlessly have to learn through trial and error themselves.

Daynette then gave an example by saying, "You are driving along the street in your vehicle with your child, and a guy on a motorbike just whip through traffic on one wheel. That is a good opportunity for parents to ask, 'what do you think could happen to this person because of the way they are driving?' Just by presenting questions like that gets your child to start thinking and reasoning within themselves. You don't necessarily have to tell them everything just engage them so that they can start thinking for themselves."

I like how Patrick Rothfuss puts it in his book entitled, *"The Wise man's Fears"*, *"It's the questions we can't answer that teach us the most. They teach us how to think. If you give a man an answer, all he gains is a little fact. But give him a question and he'll look for his own answers."*

One day in our house to house ministry, my wife and I ran into an individual that I grew up hearing about on the streets. The individual's name was Mallory Bullard, who was a soldier from the old school. It was said that he was once the fist, for a popular drug dealer back in the day.

However, Mallory said something to me quite interesting when he stated: "It is our job as parents, to instill principles and values in our children. So that when they depart from you, those principles and values won't depart from them."

It's rather simple then, as parents, we are able to instill those values and principles that we live by in our children through story telling. This is how we are able to determine what our child should think. It's what we give them to think about, that would determine what they will be as an adult - as scriptures says, *"For as he thinks in his heart, so is he." Proverbs 23: 7 NIV.*

Mr. Mackey adds to Daynette's point by saying, "As we talk to younger teachers we tell them sometimes, the mood of the class might be an opportunity to scratch your lesson plan for today, and use it as a teaching moment because that might be where they are. They came from the yard with an issue and they are not settled, so make that a lesson and you can serve as a great resource person for all of them."

In my interview with Superintendent Hulan Hanna, who I believe was the best Press Liaison Officer to date for the Royal Bahamas Police Force. Supt. Hanna is not only a great communicator, but the public knew that he was real, honest and fair as they come. It's not a surprise for me to learn, that he has risen to the rank of an Assistant Commissioner of Police (ACP).

ACP Hanna talks about the challenges from a person with limited reasoning skills, "So a person who takes a gun holds it to somebody's head, and intimidates them for money or take their property from them. The person who gets into an argument and his only resort is to take a gun or some offensive weapon and eliminate the other person. I understand that many of these persons do not have reasoning skills. They do not have the basic conflict management skills, to resolve basic issues between themselves and others. So they resort to what they know best, which is violence. I'm talking about the animalistic instinct."

In these story telling moments we equip our children, with crucial solution tools for life. To deprive them of these necessary teachable moments is like denying a carpenter the tools of his trade. It was the psychologist Abraham Maslow who stated, *"If the only tool you have is a hammer, you tend to treat every problem as a nail"*

My Second Car Accident
"It takes 8,460 bolts to assemble an automobile, and one nut to scatter it all over the road." —As seen on a bumper sticker.

When I was in the tenth grade, my aunt Rose tried to hook up my mother with one of her coworkers, who was a chef. The relationship never really got off the ground, especially after I almost lost my life in his car. He told my mother that he was having some plumbing problems with his clogged up bathtub. My mother suggested that he take me to have a look at it. I was the Mister Fix-It of the minor things around our home. On our way there, I could tell that the man had been drinking, because he was driving recklessly by overtaking every vehicle that he could, and then the scent of alcohol was heavy in his car. At first, it was not a problem for me because I was enjoying the ride. He was burning the rubbers of his tires with every turn, as his tires squealed their protest; people looked at us and got out of the way. This was a road show, and I was front and center loving it all the way.

When we got to his place and I stepped into his bathroom, it was a different story altogether. The little respect I had for him was now gone. The bathroom was a mess. He told my mother that he was having a problem only with his bathtub. Yet his toilet looked and smelled as if he hadn't flushed it in weeks. The bathtub was filled with dirty water, and floating around in the water were lumps of feces. I looked up toward the ceiling in disbelief, and wondered how could someone be so nasty?

I stayed in the bathroom for a minute or two, just passing the time. I then exited his bathroom, where I told him, "I think you need to call a plumbing company, this is beyond me." Even if I could have fixed his problem, I was not going to touch it.

So he proceeded to take me back home. On our way, he did the same stunts, speeding and driving recklessly. But I was no longer amused or impressed; rather, I just wanted to get home and out of this vehicle. As we drove over Market Street hill, he opened the engine up and we flew to the top. As we came over the hill, he didn't bother to ease up off the gas. I noticed that there were cars parked on both sides of the road, and right away, I sensed that we were going to crash.

Everything started to move in slow motion. A vehicle was coming up the hill in the opposite direction, facing us but in its own lane. With vehicles parked on both sides of the road, this meant that there was just a narrow passage area for both vehicles to pass through. However, he had yet to reduce his speed, and now I knew which car he was going to hit. I was frozen stiff with fear in the front passenger seat, as I helplessly watched him slam into the back of a parked car. I was not wearing a seat belt, so upon impact my head crashed into the windshield. I was then slammed back into my seat, but with such force that everything went black.

I was in a semiconscious state; even though I was unable to see anything, I was still conscious. I remember saying to myself, "This car is going to explode; so you need to get out now, Drexel."

I guess this was because of my years of watching movies, where a high-speed chase usually ended with a crash and one of the vehicles exploding on impact. Without being able to see anything, I made my move. I had no clue as to where to go for safety. I only knew that I had to get out. I opened the door of the mangled vehicle and staggered out onto the road, where I walked to the rear of the car and made a right turn onto the sidewalk.

I heard voices speaking all around me, but I saw no one, nor was I able to understand what they were saying. When I was finally able to see again, I was in the parking lot of one of our local food stores. A guy in softball clothing stood in front of me and asked, "Are you okay?"

Without saying anything to him, I blinked twice first, just to make sure that my sight was indeed back. I then nodded my head to indicate, "Yes, I was fine." That was when I felt something trickling down my face. I brought my hand up to my forehead to investigate. The guy in softball clothing caught my hand and said to me, "No, there is a lot of glass splinters embedded in your forehead."

When my forehead made contact with the windshield, it broke upon impact, which resulted in the splinters in my forehead. Neither of us wore a seatbelt, because back in those days we did not have any seatbelt safety laws, so seatbelts were not widely used. When I got around to looking at the vehicle, it was completely smashed up in the front. But his vehicle just stood there by itself, and I tried to figure out where was the parked car he hit. But when I looked down the hill, there were other persons in softball clothing standing around another accident. Apparently, when he hit the rear end of the parked car, the impact was so forceful that the vehicle rolled down the hill and hit another parked vehicle.

Writing Graffiti in school
"In the black culture, certain kids are given nicknames that they roll with forever; the nicknames outweigh their real names. I'm one of those scenarios." Snoop Dogg/ Snoop Lion
It was in the eleventh grade at R.M. Bailey that I picked up the naughty habit of writing graffiti. When no one was around or looking my way, I was writing the name Raw Deal on the school walls and classroom blackboards.

In the ninth grade at C.I. Gibson High School, a classmate of mine had recently seen the movie Raw Deal starring Arnold Schwarzenegger. He told me that I had given another student a raw deal, and ever since then the nickname "Raw Deal" stuck. For some reason or another, my nicknames were always associated with my last name. While at William Phipps, I was called Deal the Cards, and then later Deal the Dope. It was due in part to the emerging drug trade in the '80s, where drugs were being trafficked through The Bahamas en route to the U.S.

However, it wasn't until the eleventh grade at R.M. Bailey Senior High that I really took on the nickname of Raw Deal. With some artistic creativity, I would draw a face around the name, with the mouth in a mean, angry snarl. Every clear surface that I could find, I was leaving my angry, artistic touch behind. It got to a point where everybody was trying to figure out who this Raw Deal chap was. Since I was the only person in R.M. Bailey whose last name was Deal, it did not take the school officials long to figure out who I was, especially after receiving a tip from a female student that the most wanted graffiti artist's name ends with Deal.

One of our senior masters, Mr. Butler, soon approached me, and I denied knowing what he was talking about, of course. Mr. Butler also tested my handwriting by asking me to write the word return on a slip of paper. I had a unique way of writing the letter R. I know that he wasn't expecting me to hang myself by writing the letter R the same way as I do in my artistic handiwork. I wrote the word for him on the paper he provided, intentionally leaving out the second R in return. I was trying to get him to doubt himself, because if I couldn't spell the word return correctly, then it was highly unlikely I was the person he was looking for. I was able to slip away on the impromptu handwriting test because there's no way he could've connected both handwriting and say they were the same.

However, if he really wanted to bust me, all he had to do was ask to see my schoolbooks. The front and back covers are the first place graffiti artists start to draw. We practice and perfect our handiwork in our books before displaying them for the world to see. In a book entitled The Graffiti Subculture: Youth, Masculinity and Identity in London and New York, author Nancy Macdonald found in her research that the construction of identity operates to a large extent behind the practice of graffiti writing. In particular, she claims, it becomes "a way of building masculinity."

Eventually, Mr. Charles Mackey, who was a senior master at the time, busted me on my graffiti writing. Some two weeks later, Mr. Mackey came to me and his approach was completely different from Mr. Butler's - who had been trying to prove that it was me, to have me suspended from school. However, Mr. Mackey came to me and said, "We know that it's you, so we're not going to argue over that. There are some who want you to be put out, but I'm prepared to work with you if you are prepared to work with me."

At that time, I had moved from just writing on the outside walls. I was now putting my graphic touch on the blackboards in the classrooms. Mr. Mackey said, "This is what we are going to do. I'm going to provide you with some paint, and you will go to every blackboard that has your name and repaint it over. When you are finished with the blackboards, I'm going to provide you with wall paint where you will do the same."

I did not put up an argument with Mr. Mackey, because it's difficult to argue with someone when you know that they have gone out on a limb for you. At the same time, I didn't confess that it was me, but it was a reasonable request, and so I agreed to paint over my work. He provided me with a disposable lab coat to put over my uniform, because the male students of R. M. Bailey wore white pants, and off I went to work. Most of the classes were in session while I repainted some of the blackboards. This meant that while the teacher was writing on one side of the blackboard, I was repainting on the other side. By the time I had finished painting over all of my graffiti at the end of the day, I was even more popular and well known than before.

I will always respect Mr. Mackey for the way he dealt with me. His approach was not hostile, rather his approach was one, "Look here, I'm working with you, so I need you to work with me." He showed me first that he had my back, and it was easy for me to do the same for him.

Mr. Mackey was well known in the entire school as a no-nonsense but fair person. There are some school administrators that aren't intimidating at all, but with Mr. Mackey, it was totally different. When we saw him, even if we were not doing anything wrong and our uniform was intact, we still tend to avoid him by going in a different direction. His presence alone demanded that kind of respect. In speaking with Mr. Mackey, He talked about how most administrators are quick to punish students. He said, "The cane is just not going to cut it. I shared with some of my colleagues that these brothers live in neighborhoods where they are getting whapped with a piece of stick all night, stabbed with knives, and pegged with screwdrivers that have been sharpened down, and they are leaking blood. When you come to a fella without even interviewing him, without sitting him down to find out why you did what you did, your only interest is caning him, because you are burned out and frustrated yourself. You say to him, 'Bend over, you are getting six.' And the boy grits his teeth, skin up his face, takes those six cuts, and he is gone. But have you really been effective? Caning him is no big deal, because he's probably ducking bullets at night. He has a lot more things on his mind than that. On the other hand, we can further send our delinquent students into damnation by telling them they are no body and all we want to do is punish, punish, punish.

Here at R.M. Bailey, we have been trying a lot of different things. But at the end of the day, nothing that we do is better than the voice itself. Nothing is better than talking to the child, listening, developing trust, developing a friendship. Feel free to come to me anytime if something is bothering you, because I was your age once before."

Chapter 6
KICKED OUT OF SCHOOL

"I'm not going to fight because I mean too much to our team, and I can't afford to be suspended for a game or do something stupid to get me kicked out of a playoff game." NBA super star LeBron James

When I look back over my troubled teenage years, I have come to appreciate that many of the problems I got into were for others. I was generally a quiet teenager growing up. This meant that for the most part, I kept out of people's way. There was a friend I used to hang out with named Owen Williams. He was the mouthpiece and I was the muscle. This was not to say that Owen couldn't back up his talk with action, but somehow he would always get himself entangled in arguments, and I would be the one who would resolved the issue physically. I could see that the name I made by acting out in school as a fighter followed me to my neighborhood. In 1991, while I was still in grade 11, one day some fellas from Hawkins Hill (which was just up the street from where we lived on Mount Royal Avenue) came seeking my assistance. They needed a fighter, and I was more than happy to lend a helping hand. They used to attend a church youth group on Wednesdays at Evangelistic Temple Church on Collins Avenue, and were having some problems with some fellas from the Yellow Elder area (it is a community opposite the service station where my mother and I once worked). I never used to attend this youth group, but for some strange reason they sent for me to help them out. I should also point out that some of those who sent for me were much bigger than I was. Anyway, I went up there and slapped this fella name Sean. When I did so, he pulled out a knife. The fellas who had brought me in to handle this situation started to run away as Sean came toward us. I stood my ground, pulled out two screwdrivers from the waistband of my pants, and charged at him. When he saw the two screwdrivers in my hand, he turned around and ran away. I couldn't believe that this was the fella who was giving the Hawkins Hill fellas problems. For goodness' sake, that was just too easy.

The next week I went back around there with them, just to show my face and ensure that everything was under control. However, the Yellow Elder fellas went and brought their top fighters to handle their situation. As we were leaving the church and heading for Hawkins Hill, a car sped toward us. When we looked back at the quickly approaching car, there was a person hanging out of each passenger window with a cutlass in hand. There were three of us—I can't speak for what they saw but what I saw were lights gleaming off each one of those cutlasses. I knew right away that we were in trouble. We took off running. Even though things were getting serious with them bringing more fella's, for us this was fun. The street that we were on was a dead end enclosure off Collins Avenue called 4th Terrace. It was connected by a foot passageway to another dead end street, which led out to Hawkins Hill. We just had to make it to the passageway, and we would be home free. We all were running our hearts out to reach this goal. The car passed us—I guess to block our escape route home—but they went past the passageway and started to reverse back. My two friends made it through just in time, but I didn't because they were ahead of me. I made a left and ran behind a building, where I believed another shortcut to Hawkins Hill was located. If not, I could always hop over the fence, but when I made it to the back of the building, in my frantic state I couldn't find the short cut. I attempted to climb the fence, but it just sagged under my weight. I wasn't going to be able to climb it, I was out of ideas as to what to do, and I was not a MacGyver.

I heard the car doors opening and shutting, then the sound of footsteps running my way. What was fun just a few short seconds ago had now drastically turned very serious. I turned around to face my pursuers. I still had my screwdrivers in the waistband of my pants. But I didn't bother to pull them out, because there were five of them with knives and cutlasses. I figured there's no reason to provoke them; maybe I could reason my way out of this one.

As they slowly started to surround me in a semicircle to ensure that I couldn't escape past them, I knew that tonight was not going to be a night for reasoning, and I wondered how in the world I got myself in this mess again. Fortunately for me, these were not fighters, because they came at me talking. Sean, who was the one I had slapped last week, asked me, "Why you slapped me, bey?"

I thought to myself, 'This fella has to be kidding; that's the dumbest question I ever heard in my life. You have me surrounded, outnumbered, and this is what you gon' ask?' I wanted to say to him, "Because it felt good doing so".
However, I just went along with him by saying something even dumber. "I didn't slap you, bey."
"Yes, you slapped me!" he shouted.
I was tempted to asked, "And so what?"
But I guess it must have shown on my face, because one of them came at me with a cutlass and swung it at my chest as if he were swinging a baseball bat. I jumped back trying to avoid the blade, but it just slightly caught me which could've been worse had I not reacted.
I guess this action motivated them, because another one came at me, this time with a hatchet. He let loose a scream as he swung for my head, and I instinctively put up my left hand to block the blow. The blade of the hatchet caught me squarely in the palm of my hand. Upon impact, I heard the sickening crunching sound of steel cutting through cartilage and connecting with bone. But to my surprise, that was it. The fight was over, if it could even be called that. I then walked through them and went on my merry way, without anyone saying or doing anything else.
I received four or five sutures in my hand. The doctor told me that I was fortunate, because any deeper and I could've lost the use of my left middle finger. It took about six months for my hand to heal, and for me to begin using my hand again. But it would take more than a year to heal properly inwardly, and years later for the numbness to leave that finger.
As soon as I was able to manage to use my left hand, which was some six months later, I went back at them for my revenge. I caught Sean's brother, Welly where I smashed a glass bottle into the side of his face. Sean then came at me with a knife, but again I pulled out my trademark two screwdrivers and kept him at bay. When I took out my revenge on them, I told no one of my plans and went there on my own. I had already been put out of school, and had already been arrested and charged with a criminal case before the courts. As a result I had to sign in at the Central Police Station on East Street once a week, which was the condition for my being released on bail.

One morning on my way to work (by this time I was working at the Hill York Air Condition company), I stopped at Central Police Station to sign in. There was a female police officer who came to the counter to assist me in this process outlined by the court. She looked at her watch to write down the time, and then she asked my name, which I politely told her. She opened the sign-in book and read a piece of paper that was folded inside, after which she asked me my name again. I thought nothing about it, so I repeated my name to her once more. She then opened the short gate on the side of the counter and said, "Please step behind the counter."

Somewhat puzzled, I said to her, "Excuse me?"
"I need you to step behind the counter," the officer ordered.
I looked at her closely but was unable to read anything on her face, so then I reasoned with myself, "This must be my lucky day. For goodness sake, I have a police officer cutting up with me."
I politely stepped behind the counter toward her. I couldn't believe my good fortune. I came here to do a simple signing in; now it looked as if I would be signing out with a female police officer. However, she brought my little fantasy to an end when she said, "You're locked up."
This is the Bahamian version of "I'm placing you under arrest." In the Bahamas, we have a unique way of shortening everything.
The officer then said to me, "You are locked up for causing harm."
I asked her in surprise, "Causing harm?"
This is the Bahamian version of assault or battery.
"We have a complaint here against you of causing harm to one Mr. Wellington."
The second she said "Wellington," I stopped listening to her. In my mind, I said for goodness sake, she meant Welly. I was stunned, and my jaw might have even dropped open, because I couldn't believe what I had heard. Those little snorts went to the police and actually made a. report against me. When they ganged me several months ago, I didn't go to the police crying. I took my beating like a man; I didn't get the police involved.

The officer took my phone number and called my mother, because I was still a juvenile an adult needed to be present when they question me. An hour later, I was brought out front to the interview room where my mother was there with tears running down her cheeks. I was charged with causing harm, and was shortly released and continued on to work. I was convicted a year later and sentenced to one month in prison for that offense.

Suspended for a Third Time
"We need to change the life stories of the young people who too often end up dead or seriously injured on our streets or are sucked into a life of violence and crime." Theresa May Home Secretary in the British Government
I know that I somewhat jumped ahead, but it was necessary in order to facilitate what's coming next. In the 11th grade of school, what was bottled up in me for so many years just erupted. I was angry, bitter, and out of control. It was not as if I went looking for fights, but at the same time, I wasn't backing down from any. My third suspension of the 11th grade came about while we were in the middle of our end of school year exams. A classmate of mine named Claude was making noise during the exams, so I politely asked him to quiet down. He quieted down somewhat, but a short time later he picked right back up where he left off. This time other classmates asked him to be quiet as well. I told him, "Man, Claude, you're killing us. Keep the noise down, brother." However, he somehow got offended with my words, so he said, "You can't tell me to be quiet. Who in the hell do you take me for? I'm not afraid of you. Whatever you for, I'm ready."
I was shocked by his remarks, because Claude and I never had a problem before. So to hear him carry on in such a way led me to conclude that he was trying me, because my left hand was bandaged up. The bandages were from the fight I lost with those fellas from Yellow Elder a few days ago. I took on his challenge by saying to him, "Okay, we will pick this up during break time."

He kept running on during the whole exam, but I didn't answer him again because I had already said what I had to say. The only thing left to be said between us would now be said in action at break time. Even though my left hand was still in bandages, I wasn't going to back down from this little joker. This is not to say that he was smaller—quite the opposite, because Claude is taller and about my size in body, but the nerve of this fella. Oh, the minute he saw my hand in bandages, he took it for a sign of weakness, an opportunity for him to challenge me. Besides, even if I wanted to back out, I couldn't, because the whole class had heard me when I told him that we'd pick this up during break time. Now I was bound by my words. If I win, lose, or draw, at least my reputation would still be intact.

As soon as the bell rang to signal break time, I calmly put my school supplies in my bag and cleared out my desk. I knew that I was going to be suspended again, and probably kicked out of school but I just didn't care any longer. There were classmates just milling about acting uninterested, but I knew that they were waiting to see what I was going to do. I walked outside and broke off a solid piece of tree limb, and went after Claude with it. When he saw me coming at him with the branch in my hand, he took off running toward the office area. I was right behind him, though, and as I was bringing the limb down on his back, I caught sight of Mrs. Parker, who was one of our school's Senior Mistresses. She stood there in shock watching this scene unfold right before her eyes. When our eyes locked on each other, it was as though the whole world froze for a second or two. This was a real photo op moment; it's as if somebody had turned a spotlight on me from out of nowhere, and I didn't know what to do. In this case, there was nothing I could have done; the tree limb was already in motion. My hand came down with the tree limb. When it made contact with Claude's back it broke in two upon impact with a cracking sound. I guess for Mrs. Parker that made it even worse—the fact that the branch broke when it hit him.

Claude continued running, but I stopped, with the other part of the branch still in my hand. Mrs. Parker knew exactly who I was, so it made no sense to try to run away. She stood still for a second, shocked at what she had just witnessed. She looked at Claude, who was running away, and then she looked at me intently. This was like one of those Fresh Prince moments, when Will Smith was caught red-handed doing something wrong. He would normally be fidgeting around, scratching the back of his head. Well, I couldn't do any of that, because my left hand was in bandages and I was still holding the remainder of the limb in the other. So I just stood there looking at her, and she was there looking at me. I was busted; there was no doubt about it. Mrs. Parker then quickly snatched me by my arm, and said, "Okay, Drexel. Let's go get your school bag." My bag was sitting right on top of my desk already packed; I knew that I would be returning to get it. I just didn't think that it would be so soon. As we exited my classroom, Claude reappeared from nowhere with a glass bottle in his hand. He shouted at me, "You joking, bey, you joking, bey."

But Mrs. Parker stood her ground between us, while Claude tried to throw his bottle at me. Each time he tried, Mrs. Parker got in the way and told him to put down the bottle. I broke away from her and gave Claude a clear shot. I couldn't have it said that Mrs. Parker stopped me from getting smashed over my head with a bottle. Besides, this fight was between Claude and me, so it made no sense to cause her to get hurt. By this time there were a lot of students gathering around to have a look, this meant that the fight was on now and I was on center stage. Seeing his opening, Claude took his best shot. This was what I wanted him to do. I knew that it was difficult to hit a person with a rock or bottle, especially when that person is facing you. He threw his bottle at me aiming for my face, and I ducked, the bottle flew over my head and smashed onto the wall behind me. I rushed at him again, this time connecting a blow to the left side of his face. I was about to land another one on him, but I was held back by Mrs. Parker. I had totally forgotten that she was there. She hooked both of us up by our collars, and was prepared to carry us to the office like that. I mumbled to myself, "This lady has nerves of steel. Instead of getting out of our way and letting us battle it out, she kept intervening." Mrs. Parker stood about five feet nine inches tall and had a solid build. She was not fat; she was just a solid Bahamian woman, firm in body and in the way she dealt with you.

With such a large crowd of onlookers, I just couldn't get past the image in my head of a woman carrying both of us to the office hooked up by the collar. On top of that, she was wearing high-heeled shoes. I had my reputation to consider; I couldn't afford to let Mrs. Parker ruin that. So I wiggled out of my shirt, leaving her holding it in one hand and Claude in the other. Now she could carry my shirt and Claude to the office. As for me, I'll get there on my own and in my own time.

I ran around one of the school blocks bareback, where I ran into another student by the name of Owen Moss. This Owen and another student name Cyprian Smith (Sip) were good buddies. He stopped me and asked, "What happened, Deal?" I briefly explained what had just taken place, and how I left my school shirt in Mrs. Parker's hand. Owen then took off his school uniform shirt, and gave me the white T-shirt he was wearing underneath. I put it on and then made my way to the office, where Claude and I were suspended for two weeks.

My Expulsion Out Of School

"Not a lot of people would think that I spent most of my early years totally rebelling against anything I could, getting suspended from school, going on demonstrations. I was a pretty difficult teenager." —Dan Stevens, English actor

Somehow they allowed me back in school to start the 12th grade, even though the rule said that any student who was suspended three times in a given year would automatically be expelled. At first, they said that Mrs. Parker had expelled me during the last term. Mrs. Parker was no longer there, for she had been transferred to another school over the summer break. When they went and checked my record, they discovered that it was only a two-week suspension. So I was let back in for the 12th grade, but not before being warned on our assembly by Mr. Butler. Unfortunately for me, my time in grade 12th didn't last long at all, because just two weeks into the start of the school year, Owen Williams and I were expelled.

The date was Friday, September 16, 1991. We were both expelled for fighting with students from the neighboring school of C. H. Reeves. Owen says, "I had everything wrapped up and you came in there and blew it."

I got the word that a school administrator had pulled Owen out of his classroom. As soon as I heard about it, I knew that I would be next on their list, so I skipped my class. If they want me, they'll have to find me. However, it didn't take long for Mr. Butler to find me, and I have to give him credit for how he went about it. The brother was sharp in the way he approached me, for he never told me that I was wanted at the office. Rather, he simply asked me,

"Drexel, what's this I'm hearing about you and a hammer?"

I stopped short in my tracks and asked incredulously, "Me and a hammer?"

"That's right, because Owen is in the office telling us and the police that it was you who hit a student from C. H. Reeves across the head with a hammer."

I thought to myself, 'How in the world Owen could be telling the story that I had the hammer, when in fact it was he who had the hammer?' I then said to Mr. Butler, "I didn't had any hammer. It was Owen who had the hammer."

In my haste to defend myself against an obvious lie, I had unknowingly implicated both of us as being involved in the school brawl the day before. Not missing a beat, Mr. Butler then said to me, "Well, you better come into the office and clear your name." Then he just walked away about his business, as if he was never even looking for me. He said it as if he was doing me a favor by letting me in on what was being discussed in the office.

Sip and Owen Moss, who were standing there with me, had heard the conversation between Mr. Butler and me. They were outraged at what Mr. Butler had just said about Owen Williams. They said to me, "If Owen is telling them that you had the hammer then you need to go and straighten that up for them."

So off I went marching to the office to clear up my name. I stepped inside Mr. Steven Surette's office, who was the Acting Principal. There were three students from C. H. Reeves School, along with one of their administrators, a police officer, Mr. Surette, Mr. Butler, and of course, Owen. As soon as I stepped inside, Mr. Butler asked me, "So, Drexel, who had the hammer?"

Without hesitating and believing that I was clearing up my name, I pointed at Owen and said, "Owen had the hammer." Owen just hung his head down and shook it. Mr. Surette then said to us, "Okay, that's it. Both of you are out of here."

It was not until Owen and I were exiting the school premises that Owen asked me angrily, "What you came in there for? Secondly, why in the world would you go and tell them that I had the hammer?"

I replied, "Mr. Butler said you were in the office telling them that I had the hammer."

"Deal, use your head. Do you think I am going to lie and tell them that you had the hammer when I know it was me who had the hammer? Mr. Butler lied to you. He used you to speak against me, and now both of us are out of school. Before you came in the office, I had everything going my way. They were only going to suspend us for two weeks, but you came in there and blew everything up," said Owen.

ACP. Hulan Hanna continues by talking about the challenges we face, as a community from the high school dropouts.

"When I say high school dropout, I mean two things. I am actually talking about people who stop going to school before graduation day. I am also talking about a group of people who remain in the education system, who simply stop learning. So they, too, have dropped out of school, because they are not actively participating in the learning process."

It was as if ACP Hanna was actually referring to me, because I had stopped participating in school a long time ago. Sadly, school for me was like a playground. I went there not to learn; rather, it was just to have fun. Breaking the rules were the high lights of my day, and acting the fool was just the exciting topic for the day among the female student. So after I was put out of school I wept, because for me R. M. Bailey was like a stage that I was performing on. This was where I was being recognized, respected, and revered, and outside of that, I was a nobody.

Here again The Heritage Foundation and Patrick F. Fagan were right on the money with their study, for they wrote, "Professor David P. Farrington's Cambridge University study finds a high correlation between school adjustment problems and later delinquency: "Youths who dislike school and teachers, who do not get involved in school activities, and who are not committed to educational pursuits are more likely than others to engage in delinquent behavior."

The administrators at that time might have gotten rid of us that day, but all they did was send us somewhere else, which was on the streets. There, Owen and I would once again find our playground, our performing stage, in the street gang the Rebellion Raiders, where we would go on to do more sinister things that brought us the recognition, respect, and the attention we so desperately craved. To top it off, I learned a crucial lesson on that September day that would serve me well in a life of crime. If the police told me that an accomplice of mine said I did something, I would tell the officer who was questioning me, "Then you're wasting your time questioning me. You need to speak to the person who provided you with that false information, because they know way more than I could ever tell you."

However, Mr. Charles Mackey has a different view about expelling students from school. He stated, "Dressler Sherman [the School Principal at R. M. Bailey during the time of our interview] and I are very close and we share a lot of thoughts. I think we have done a tremendous job in regards to not being quick to expel our students. Over the past five or six years, we have done well in that area. We tend to talk more and hold more parents' conferences, so if we suspect someone of smoking or being involved in drugs, the Guidance Department comes in because that is the agency on our campus to deal with that. Guidance then contacts the parent, whereby they make certain that what they suspect is true or isn't true. The student is sent to a government agency to have a test done, and if it comes back positive, they will undergo counseling through this particular agency. This is better for us and more meaningful than saying if we catch you smoking, you are out of here."

Mr. Mackey went on to give an example. "I caught one of my basketball players from last year's team, him and another student in the back of the Plumbing Block, smoking. I mean, you are talking about smoking a joint [marijuana] big lunchtime [a time when everyone is moving about, which wouldn't be a good time to do anything illegal]. They just came out of their classroom. I guess they thought a quick pull while everyone is walking around no one would suspect anything. They did not anticipate anyone to be in the back of the building. But we are very vigilant like that. That is one of our policies among the administration, to be vigilant. We do break time and lunchtime yard duty. You just have to be out there. We have more than 1,100 students who are all over the place. Someone has to be watching them.

So the two students went through the program. My player came back to the team. Both him and the other young man, they came to me one day and thanked me. They said, 'Thanks, coach.'

I guess from the program they were able to discover how much further they could have gone through damnation and destroyed their live."

In my interview with Superintendent Allerdyce Strachan, of the Royal Bahamas Police Force, who was once the officer in charge of Community Policing and was the first female officer to rise to the rank of Superintendent on the Police Force where she served for 35 years. The interview was conducted at the Headquarters of the Royal Bahamas Police Force, East Street Hill at the Day Care Centre, (which was named in her honor) for children of police officers.

Supt. Strachan shared something similar with me by saying, "There were times I went into the schools and the administration was ready to expel the student, and I said to them, no, give them a chance. I would then work with the kids, and they would turn their lives around. But a lot of us just give up on these kids too quickly."

To bring home Supt. Strachan's point, I would like to introduce Troit Lynes, a former death row inmate of Her Majesty's Prison and one who has tremendously changed his life for the better. He is now married with a family. Troit has his own home, and has been recognized and awarded numerous times by his place of work as an outstanding worker, and is now one of their managers. Troit was also once a part of the Rebellions, and in 2001, we founded the youth program Brothers Against Crime & Killing [B.A.C.K.]. It was our way of reaching out and giving back to our community, as a way of trying to prevent what happened to us from occurring to another young male.

Troit once said to me, "When I got put out of school in 1992, I later learned that it was so much of us from different schools that were put out. That the Ministry of Education was faced with a serious problem: what they were going to do with all of these young men? As a way of preventing us from ending up on the streets, they established the SURE Program in 1992 to allow us to carry on our education."

He continued, "During my trips to prison, I met more than 90% of those young men who were the first to enroll in the SURE Program with me. All of us were eventually charged with very serious crimes, and some of us would go on to be charged and convicted for murder."

The most notable person from Troit's 1992 group is gang leader and drug lord Steven "Die" Stubbs, who would go on to be charged with several murders, including that of a police officer while trying to shoot two Rebellions. Mr. Mackey continued on this point. "Putting children out of school is not the answer, for it just creates another problem. Some of these same students who were put out of school, you will see them coming around in the morning and the afternoon because they still have a linkage to R.M. Bailey. That relationship has not been severed through the official process, which would have been graduation. So you put them out of school, then they create more problems for us by being out there in the mornings and afternoons, because some of them come back with negative wibes."

When I first was ganged in the 10th grade, there were three individuals by the name of Sean, Jamain Longley and Monk who were all kicked out of R. M. Bailey the year before they had ganged me. Yet after Owen and I were kicked out of school, we also frequented the school grounds looking for problems. During which time we would sometimes get into fights with current students. I was arrested one afternoon in May of 1992 from the R. M. Bailey campus. This time, we had done nothing. I guess the administrators got tired of us just coming on the campus causing problems. So Ambry Armbrister (now deceased) and I were arrested and charged with trespassing on the school grounds. This arrest led to my being sent to Sandilands Rehabilitation Centre, our local mental institution, for a three-week mental evaluation. It was after this particular arrest that the magistrate for the juvenile court, Mrs. Cheryl Albury at the time, wanted to know what was going on with me, and what was going on at our home. The arrest for trespassing at R. M. Bailey made the fourth weekend in a row, that I was not only arrested but also charged with a criminal offense before the juvenile court. Therefore, Mrs. Albury ordered a three-week evaluation at Sandilands, which actually turned into a three-month stay. I would later learn from my mother that Mrs. Albury inquired of her as to how involved my father was in my life. She also wanted to find out if he was financially supporting us? It was then that Magistrate Albury instructed my mother, to make an application before family court for child support assistance from our father. Prior to that, my mother had never sought assistance from our father. I don't even remember my mother seeking government assistance from Social Service for us. After following the advice of the magistrate, our father was summoned to appear before the court. Once he was before the magistrate of the family court, he did what the majority of deadbeat dads do: he requested a blood test for Vanessa and Quannie from the court. According to my mother, "His concern was that after all these years, why is my mother just seeking financial support for them?"He didn't bother requesting a test on me, because they both knew that I was not his child. But here's what ticked me off upon hearing this. After preventing my biological father from being involved in my life by telling my mother that he would raise me as his own, he gave me his name, he signed my birth certificate as my father. So now that he's no longer involved with my mother, his commitment to raise me as his own is off the table. Now, please tell me, who in the world was supposed to be responsible for me? Which one of those jokers I had as a father was obligated to provide for me?

Oh, any male can impregnate a female, but it takes a real man to look after what he has reproduced. How does a man look in the mirror and not feel badly about not supporting his child? How could a father not fight to be involved in his child's life? How could a man just disregard the life that came out of his loins as if it was nothing?

In spite of those two jokers I had for fathers, my mother never turned her back on us. She may not have been perfect, but she was our rock. I am comforted in the knowledge that she did her best in raising all of us. Did she make some mistakes? Yes, she did. But who hasn't made mistakes, especially when it comes to raising children? As the old English proverb goes, *"He who has never made a mistake, never made anything."* However, I believe that one of the biggest mistakes my mother made was choosing to be involved with those two jokers. As the American astronomer Margaret Turnbull puts it, *"No man is responsible for his father. That was entirely his mother's affair."*

Margaret Turnbull is right on the money with her statement, yet one key piece of information is somehow over looked. The fact is a woman's ability or the lack there of, in choosing a mate is directly related to her relationship with her father. Having grown up without a father, my mother simply lacked the ability to make an inform decision on the men she chose to be with.

We Don't Remember the Expensive Stuff

"Your children need your presence more than your presents. Jesse Jackson"

It is only fitting to close this chapter, on how we as a people are becoming very materialistic. To make matters worse it is affecting our children's ability to value and appreciate anything. In so doing we are developing a generation of young people, who feel as if they are entitled to the best of everything without working for nothing. This in itself will lead to another problem, because when our children lose their drive to achieve worthwhile goals, then they will pursue worthless goals with more vigor and zeal.

Mr. Mackey touches on this point by asking, "Why in the home these children are given so much expensive things? Parents would come and tell me 'But Mr. Mackey this boy wouldn't come to school if I don't by him a pair of Edwin Jeans.'
I would ask the parent, how much is for the Edwin?
They would say, '$68 to $90.'
Yet I am wearing a pair of $29 slacks that I bought while on vacation in Florida or New York."

In his bestselling book *"The Measure Of A Man"*, Sir Sidney Poitier talks about how his mother used to buy flour sacks and make pants and shirts for his school clothes.
"Endless fun was made of me because I wore the emblem of the flour company on my bottom. But knowing that my mom and dad did the best that they could gave me the strength to suck it up and move on."
Mr. Mackey talks about how this materialistic culture has even made it to the church. "I understand that God promises life and life abundantly, and we should aim for the top. If I want a Lincoln continental tomorrow I would get that Lincoln if I pray and believe in God and work towards it by making an effort. But, why do I need a Lincoln Continental?"
He continued, "My value system is just different. I believe in saving for rainy days. In the next 12 years if God spears my life, they could tell me I can go home, even though they move the retirement age up to 65. But who says I want to work after the age of 60? Our value system, a lot of it the children are persuaded by the parents. Come on man, two hundred dollars for a pair of tennis? The most I ever spent on a pair of tennis in a long time is one hundred dollars. It's the parents who are perpetuating this nonsense. These kids are wearing more Land belts today in R. M. Bailey, than I believe is in the store at the Mall who sells them. But I don't want a land belt. I have money and I am not cheap. But like I told you earlier, my value system is different and it was influenced by my mother. She taught us how to be satisfied with what we have, and to put up something for a rainy day, which has been useful for me in assisting others too."

Mr. Mackey then goes on to illustrate, "One of my former students came to me the other day. He was in a financial bind. He had committed himself to holding an asue, and some people dropped out. The other person had paid in advance some ten thousand dollars, because that was the total of the asue draw. I loan him some money so he would not get into problems with these people. He said, 'By the end of a particular month, I would pay you back.' But that money I loan him the other day did not cause me not to eat today."
Mr. Mackey continued by sharing more about his childhood, "I came from a poor family. My mother was a lunch vendor, and the funds were just not there. I had to spend a lot of my adolescent years working, from the age of 9 to the age of 14 I was a gas pump attendant. It was so difficult to focus on the book, when you had survival to deal with. I had tips along with my salary and that help my mother keep the household going, because there was certain period when school was close and no money was coming in."
Mr. Mackey then goes on to say, "I never had no permanent father in my life. My mother was very enterprising. I was introduced to all kinds of uncles. This here is Uncle Tom, Uncle Joe and Uncle Mike. My father died before I was born, so my mother had to survive. When she ran into different men who wanted friendship with her, I guess there would be remuneration for times she spent with them. However, those men impacted my life, in that they would tell me some positive things if they saw me misbehaving and put me back on the right course," concluded Mr. Mackey.

At the end of the summer months of grade 9, which was 1989, my mother quit working evenings at the service station. She had been absent from our evening life for so long, it was as if we were getting to know her all over again. However, for me it was too late, because I was already getting into minor mischief at school.
After I was put out of school, my mother said to me once, "I provided you all with everything you could possibly need, just look around you." She gestured her hands at the stuff in our living room. "You have a computer you can use, video games, telephone, videotapes of the best movies. Everything is at your fingertips, so what else do you want?"
I heard myself saying in my mind, "You provided us with everything except yourself. I want you." Of course, I did not tell her that. I probably would have been knocked upside my head.

What my mother said was indeed true. Growing up as children, we may not have had the best of everything, but we always got what we needed plus more. During the Christmas season, we had new toys, new clothing, and the food was always off the chain. There was never anything lacking except my mother's presence, and in spite of all those great Christmases we had growing up, I don't remember much about the toys I received on Christmas Day. As a matter of fact, most times before the end of December 25th, my toys would be destroyed.

Looking back over my life, here's what I remember the most: Sunday dinners as a family. My mother was always a great cook, and she would sometimes set up the dining table as if we were at a buffet. At the end of the meal, none of us children wanted to clean up the dishes, but those were some good times. Then there was the Sunday drives after our meal, where we would sometimes drive out west to get ice cream or to pick coco plums. During those Sunday drives into the affluent areas out east and out west on our island, my mother put the desire to strive for better in our hearts.

Then there was the time in grade 8 when she taught me how to drive her little blue four-door Honda Accord. Or when she and I would sit down to watch an action movie together. My best childhood memories are those in my mother's presence and not her presents.

In a column written by Christopher Toh, he stated, *"Time is a luxury that we don't have because we're too busy trying to make sure our children have the luxuries we never had."*

Chapter 7
FROM IDLE TO CRIMINAL

"All things truly wicked start from innocence." —*Ernest Hemingway*

After being kicked out of school at the age of 16, reality quickly slapped me in the face. The verdict was in—I had eleven years of schooling but nothing to show for it. With no idea of what to do and no clue of where to go, I was hopelessly lost and adrift out in the sea of life.

I believe that my main reason for getting into crime was my idleness and the desire to get lucky, which can be a really dangerous and volatile mixture. It was Napoleon Bonaparte the first emperor of France, and a military genius who stated, *"We are made weak both by idleness and distrust of ourselves. Unfortunate, indeed, is he who suffers from both. If he is a mere individual he becomes nothing; if he is a king he is lost."*

Therefore, not only was I idle, but I also had no confidence in myself, and nothing worthwhile to work towards. I would soon learn that this in itself can be a very dangerous state to be in. It's rather simple, when a young man doesn't have anything he's working towards, some three to six months or even twelve months away then his presence becomes his worst enemy.

Each day becomes a lot more difficult to get through, because any and everything that sounds like fun you want to do. Goals not only provide us with something to aim towards, but they also empower us to take control of each day. We don't jump forward three or six months into the future rather the future comes into our lives one day at a time. This is why scriptures remind us, *"Where there is no vision the people go unrestrained, but happy are they that are keeping the law." Proverbs 29: 18 NWT.*

So how did I get involved in a life of crime? All criminals get their start somewhere, but normally from another person in most cases. However, I got my start from no one but from somewhere, which was right in my neighborhood. The first set of crimes I got into other than petty juvenile fights were shop break-ins.

People who normally committed such crimes were referred to as Crackers. These were individuals who, for the most part, were strung out on drugs, and used shop break-ins as a way to support their habit. Therefore, shop break-ins were considered the low and petty crimes, largely because they were normally committed by drug addicts who roam the streets at nights. Yet shop break-ins would become my area of specialty, my skilled trade, so to speak. This would also be my crime of first choice, right up to the day I lost my sight.

The very first shop break-in that I committed occurred about three months after I had been thrown out of school. Up to this point, I had never been arrested by the police and charged with a crime before the courts. To put it rather mildly, I was squeaky clean in the eyes of the law. However, this would soon drastically change and I would go on to become a career criminal. My journey into a life of crime was completely innocent. It was an unexpected turn in my life. The only thing I wanted to do was to help my mother, but as the seventeenth century English scholar Dr. Samuel Johnson once stated, *"The road to hell is paved with good intentions."*

I remember my mother complaining about how high our utility bills were, especially the electricity bill. I was not working at the time, so I took extreme care to cut off all the lights that were not in use as a way of doing my part to ensure that we kept the bills at a minimum. Yet this was barely enough even to begin to reduce our electricity bill, so this really began to bother me as a male since I was unable to contribute and assist my mother.

I always liked working and was never a lazy person. Of all the jobs I ever had, only once was I fired. So from the age of eleven I worked and just being able to reduce the load off my mother's shoulders was a good feeling. But to contribute to the upkeep of the home was an even more gratifying feeling. Even though those contributions were nothing much to talk about, they made me feel good about myself, and made me feel like a man.

I knew how hard my mother struggled with us, and she did so all by herself. This is why my goal has always been to assist my mother, from the time I was just a boy. In spite of the hand she was dealt, my mother did a great job providing for the three of us. She never once turned her back on us; she never gave up on us, so not being able to contribute to the upkeep of the house made me felt rather awful. During this same time, Vanessa shared with me that she had found $110 in a brown paper bag on the side of the road in our neighborhood. Right away, an idea took shape in my mind. I figured if she could find more than a hundred dollars, then I could too.

Lady Luck Sucks
"The way for a young man to rise is to improve himself in every way he can, never suspecting that anybody wishes to hinder him." —Abraham Lincoln, the 16th President of the United States

I remember quite clearly taking a lot of Sunday walks after the family dinner in hopes of getting lucky. I patrolled our community like a foot soldier, checking every brown paper bag I came across. However, I was never as fortunate as Vanessa, and after several weeks on foot patrol stopping to search every bag, I came up empty-handed, with absolutely nothing to show for my efforts. Looking back now, I can better appreciate that it's really sad for any young person to live their life with the hope of getting lucky one day. Rather, life should be purpose-driven in the pursuit of our goals instead of waiting for our luck to fall.

It was Thomas Jefferson, the third President of the United States who stated, *"I'm a great believer in luck, and I find the harder I work, the more I have of it."* Thus, luck is nothing more than opportunities that we create for ourselves through hard work, discipline, and persistence. This more than anything else is what determines the quality of our lives. It's a pitiful existence for anyone to go through life, depending on chance, hoping for lady luck - who by the way sucks. It's a travesty to believe that our life would improve one day, when lady luck smiles on us. To do so is to remove our will power, and place it out of reach on a shelf somewhere. As a result we don't take charge and control of our lives; rather we give it up and squander each day of our lives by rolling the dice in the hope of getting something we already have.

I like how Lucille Ball puts it, the American comedian, model, television actress, and star of the hit TV series I Love Lucy. She stated, *"Luck? I don't know anything about luck. I've never banked on it, and I'm afraid of people who do. Luck to me is something else: hard work and realizing what opportunity is and what isn't."*
So there I was at the age of 16, walking my neighborhood in the hopes of getting lucky. Yet I believe that my time would've been better spent if I had applied that same energy toward looking for a job, or going back to school to learn a trade because wanting something without working toward it is nothing more than wishful thinking.

After each of my Sunday walks, I always ended up at the same location. This was at the back of Mount Royal Shopping plaza, which was adjacent to where we lived on Mount Royal Avenue. I used to sit on the stairs at the back of this building and spend the remainder of my Sunday afternoon there thinking. When dark came, I would get up and walk the few steps to our home. The reality of life had started to sink in, and it was one that I wasn't prepared for. I could still hear those questions I used to ask myself. "What are you going to do with your life now Drexel? You have no education or any particular skill, so what are you going to do?" All I had was an idea as to what I wanted to do, which was to simply help my mother. Yet I was clueless as to how I was going to do that. So in looking for Lady Luck, mixed in with idleness I stumbled right into a life of crime. There's an old Turkish proverb which states, *"The devil tempts all other men, but idle men tempt the devil."* Oh, yes indeed, I would be tempted like never before. However, a bizarre thing happened. During these mental conversations with myself, I was keenly aware of sitting on the bottom stairs, at the back of the shopping plaza but as the weeks went by, I somehow unconsciously worked my way up to the top of the stairs. I started out at the bottom, then on to the middle, and then I sat at the top. One evening I just happened to look behind me, and a light bulb came on in my head. I stood up from where I sat and took stock of everything. From the makeup of the steel grill door keeping me at bay, I saw two doors that led out to the stairway. After a quick assessment of the locks, I realized that I could easily cut through the steel bolt with a hacksaw blade. During my summer break from school, I worked on the construction site of C. R. Walker Secondary School as a plumber's helper. So I knew what a hacksaw was capable of cutting through, and this steel bar would be a piece of cake. I concluded that the only thing needed to open the other locks, would be a simple kitchen butter knife. Being the only male child in our family, many times I was called on to open a door that was accidentally locked. I quickly walked home and got a hacksaw blade, a butter knife, and a screwdriver just for good measure. Once I got back within fifteen minutes, I had already cut through the steel bolt, picked both locks, and was inside. My heart was racing a mile a minute; I couldn't believe how easy this was.

The building I had entered was once used as a gym. All of the weight lifting equipment was still in place, along with a complete DJ audio system that worked perfectly. I couldn't carry anything home except for a few of the weights, which would not look out of the ordinary to my mother. I had always been into lifting weights. I might never have had a complete set, but there were always the odd pieces of dumbbells and barbells around our home. The weights I had selected didn't look their best; they were a bit rusty in certain spots. It worked out perfectly for me, because my mother didn't even give them a second glance. I took apart the DJ system piece by piece and gave them to Michael, a friend of mine who was a brown belt in karate. Michael lived on the top of Hawkins Hill, which is the highest peak in Nassau. Even though he and I were close, he never knew where they came from. As a matter of fact, I told nobody. By this time, I was really good at keeping things to myself, so keeping quiet about this wasn't difficult at all.

For the next several weeks, I was in and out of the building. I now had my own personal gym, and I made good use of the various exercise equipment that was there. This building also became my sanctuary away from home, my private spot to think and exercise. Until one day, I tried to enter the premises only to find everything tightly locked down. I guess the owners of the building, discovered that the premises had been broken into during one of their random checks. They took the necessary steps to secure the building by fixing the steel bolt to the back gate. However, once I had discovered what they had done, I broke into the building again. But I didn't feel as safe as before; rather, I was simply exercising my newfound skill of break-ins.

I then moved on from the Mount Royal Plaza, because there were other businesses that had now caught my attention, and I wanted to try my hand at them. Besides, the plaza itself was too close for comfort anyway, being right next door to where we lived.

Mastering My Newfound Skill
"Ah, mastery... what a profoundly satisfying feeling when one finally gets on top of a new set of skills... and then sees the light under the new door those skills can open." —Gail Sheehy, journalist, lecturer and author

Here's what I find to be really interesting when I was depending on lady luck. When I couldn't find this elusive cash on our streets, somehow I became willing and ready to do whatever it took to create my own luck. I figured sense lady luck wouldn't come to me, then I'll simply go to her. Just one year prior to all of this, I had despised anyone who would commit such a crime.

Case in point: during the summer months of grade 10, I learned that a neighborhood boy with whom we all played basketball with was arrested and charged with shop break-in. I had never said anything to him about it, but to the individual who had told me the story I asked, "How dumb could he be to do such a thing?"

Yet I went on to do the very same thing, but I made a career out of it simply because when those things we want without working for them are slow in coming, then we begin to look for them in undesirable places and faces. To put it plainly, when your character is weak in one area, it will also be weak in another. Therefore, life becomes a downward spiral from bad to worse. As my mother use to say to me growing up, whenever she caught me in a lie: *"A liar is a thief, and a thief is a murderer."*

I resumed my foot patrol again, but this time I was on a mission. I not only knew what I wanted, but I also possessed the skills to get it. I now took a second look at businesses that I passed each day. This time it was with a different set of eyes. It was exciting, to say the least, to know I could get into businesses using a little household trick. To top it off, we lived in a well-known commercial area, so the potential was huge. I could pick, choose, and refuse among many targets. I began to look at shop breaking as a means to an end. With so many stores to choose from, I was getting a lot of practice. One of the great advantages in my favor was that there were more businesses than residential homes in our area. So at night the area was virtually a ghost town, and a lot of stores were for the most part isolated—where the closest home was probably a block away. It was these stores that I would break into from around 8:30 at night and by 10:00 I was heading home.

I figured that once inside a building, I would no doubt get lucky in finding cash on its premises, and thus I would be able to assist my mother. In my survey of different buildings, I quickly realized that I was not the only one with this ingenious idea. As a matter of fact, from the look of things I was really late. Someone, or several some ones, had already beaten me to the deal, for many of the buildings I saw the unmistakable signs of past break-ins.

Undeterred, I decided to focus on the most difficult buildings, the ones I'd really have to work to get into. I settled on targeting businesses that were located upstairs. The next store that I broke into was on the second floor of a two-story shopping plaza. I used an old TV antenna as a ladder to get to the bathroom window. The antenna itself was not that sturdy, but being five feet six inches and only weighing 150 pounds, it was strong enough to support my weight. It was around 1:00 or 2:00 in the early morning hours. I had to be extremely quiet because there was a house just behind me. I slithered through the bathroom window within minutes. Upon entering the premises, it was easy for me to conclude that the electronics store downstairs was using this space for their storage. There were a lot of electronic toys, radio and cassette players, and other small electrical devices.

My focus was on the latter two; I took as much as I possibly could. As I got to the window, I realized I had a small problem. First of all, the window was too small for my loot. Secondly, how was I going to get them down to the ground? I had come up on a flimsy antenna for a ladder that could barely hold my weight. I quickly devised a plan by tying electrical drop cords around the boxes that I had found on the inside. Then I gently lowered them to the ground, one box at a time. I was able to move everything successfully and hide each box in the bushes behind the Mount Royal Shopping plaza. Eventually, over a three-day period, I was able to sneak everything inside where I hid them under our beds to the very back, close to the wall.

My sisters and mother didn't have a clue as to what I had done and what was hidden inside our home. I eventually gave the majority of the stuff to Carlos, a cousin of mine who used to sleep by us from time to time. As the weeks and months passed on, my list of accomplishments really began to grow, but I never ran across this elusive cash as I'd hoped. So I would often take just small electronics that I could hide out of sight from my mother. But in the mean time I was getting good, and my confidence was really growing. I had finally found something in life that I was good at; the only thing was I had no one to share in my excitement or to tell me, "Well done."

The various tools I collected from different places along the way made the task of shop breaking even easier. There was not a business in my area that I couldn't get into. However, I was still unable to carry anything home, because a lot of my targets were mainly business offices. Then I didn't had a connection, who could get these office electronics and supplies sold for me, so I basically left them behind. Whatever little stuff I carried with me I mainly gave away. I can clearly remember my mother finding a brand-new telephone that I had brought home from one of my night adventures. I told her that I had purchased it from a friend of mine for little or nothing. But she wasn't buying that line, so she threw a fit and threw me out of the house that night. I took advantage of the opportunity, and simply broke into another store. When I was finished, I hopped our fence and slept on the back porch.

The next day my mother told me, "Don't you never, ever bring anything stolen in my house again. I don't care who you bought it from; if it doesn't have a receipt from a store, don't think about bringing it here." Even though I was angry with her, I respected her position and the stand she took that night.

Caught Red-Handed

"A thief is a king till he's caught." —Persian Proverb

I believed that there's absolutely nothing worse than being caught red-handed. It's like someone taking a photo of you on your worst day. But what makes it so bad is that the photo was taken while you were naked.

By this time, my mother was dating another married man, whom I'll simply refer to as Pat. I guess that my mother had complained to him about the stolen phone I had brought home, because a few days later he pulled me aside and said, "I have a brother who wants to buy a fax machine. Do you know where I could get one at a good price?"

I couldn't believe it. This was like music to my ears. My assistance was finally being sought. I straightened my back and even stood taller in our little conversation, for I was now conducting business. I told him, "Let me check with my people. Just give me a day or two and I'd get back to you."

He didn't know where I was getting my stuff from, but how does a sixteen-year-old come across a fax machine unless it's hot? I was now motivated and pumped up. I had someone on my side who could probably get some of this stuff sold for me. I would've been more than happy to give it to him for free, because I was always coming across fax machines; I just never had any use for them. Before our conversation was even finished, I already knew which office to target for this fax. I can remember my first arrest clearly, as if it were yesterday. I came home around 11:00 p.m. on a Friday night, after attending a church revival with some neighbors who had invited me out. My mother, knowing in advance that I went to a church service, and aware that I would be coming in a bit late, was already in bed. If not for that, she would've probably been up waiting for me. When I came home, I changed my clothing, watched some TV, and by midnight, I was gone.

I had already scouted out my latest target, and again it was a two-story building. I don't know what it is about me, but I always got a kick out of doing the more difficult things. I used an aluminum ladder this time; I was stepping up my game, so to speak. The ladder itself I had stashed behind the building in question some two nights earlier, having stolen it for this purpose. However, this building had a residential home just two doors down, and the residents inside were still up watching TV. I figured if they had their TV blasting so loudly, they wouldn't be able to hear me and they'd have their eyes glued to the screen.

I was glad to have Pat's support, so much so that I did away with all caution—the very thing that had kept me from being arrested by the police so far. I was reckless, to put it mildly, taking no steps to be quiet. It was the most noise I ever made trying to get into a building. But as the Nigerian novelist, poet, and professor Chinua Achebe puts it, *"A boy sent by his father to steal does not go stealthily, but breaks the door with his feet."*

I put the ladder against the wall and made my way up to the bathroom window, but it was taking longer than usual for me to get in. I also learned the hard way that aluminum ladders can be very noisy, and in the still quiet of the night the sound seems louder. Some twenty-five minutes later, I was still there trying to get in. Shortly thereafter, I heard two car doors closing in the distance.

I paused for a brief moment, and hearing nothing else, I went back to my work at getting inside. Just seconds later, a guy in a black trench coat and a matching cowboy hat ran toward me with a big chrome revolver in his hand. The thing that really caught my attention was the chrome gun he was holding. In spite of the fact that it was dark, the gun looked as if it generated its own light.

Right away, I knew that I was busted; nobody had to tell me that he was a police officer. He stopped several feet from the ladder and took up a shooter's position, legs apart; arm extended, and pointed his revolver at me. I remember thinking to myself, this looks just like in the movies. The only difference was that no one here was acting. This was as real as it gets. He then shouted at me, "Don't move!"

I just stood there on the ladder looking down at him, while he was there looking up at me. I guess he figured that he needed me on the ground to arrest and handcuff me, because after a few seconds he said, "Come down from there, and really slow. No sudden moves."

I said to him in a somewhat annoyed tone, "Ah, heck, I'm coming down now."

I did as I was told, taking my time to make it to the ground. I was angry with myself for not taking heed of the two doors shutting in the distance. By this time, Trench Coat's partner was at his side, where he also took up a shooter's position. I was handcuffed and patted down. After removing my few tools of the trade, they handcuff me and bundled me in the backseat of their unmarked car. These were not regular police officers in uniform; rather, these were officers from the Criminal Investigation Department (CID), which could be compared to the FBI among our local law enforcement officers. These were the bad boys of our police force, and I was quite familiar with their reputation, having heard countless of stories from people who were arrested by them. However, I also knew that before the night was over, I would have stories of my own to tell, provided I lived through the night.

They took me for a long ride on the taxpayers' dollar, which was the longest ride of my life. As we drove, it slowly became clear to me that they were not taking me to a police station. Rather, we were heading south. Everything started out nice and polite; this was the calm before the storm. They asked me my name, my age, and where I lived. I could tell that they didn't believe me when I told them that I was sixteen years of age. To be sure, Mr. Trench Coat asked me, "What is your date of birth?

I rolled it off my tongue without hesitating. "July 3rd, 1975."

"What other stores have you broken into?" Mr. Trench Coat asked me.

I lied and said, "This was my first one."

He looked back at me as if to say, "Come on kid, do you expect me to believe that?"

Believing that I had made a mistake, I said, "I mean, that was going to be my first attempt."

Mr. Trench Coat said to me in a cool and calm voice, "Drexel, don't you know that it isn't wise to lie to us? But don't worry my friend, before the night is over you're going to tell me all of your darkest secrets."

He looked directly in my eyes as he spoke in his cool and calm voice. I knew then that I was in trouble. Sensing my fear, he smiled and said, "You could begin to unburden yourself by telling me the truth."

They took me out to South Beach, where there were not many residential homes around the beach area. It was there that they started to work me over. Mr. Trench Coat started the melee by punching me in the mouth, because my hands were still handcuffed and my feet somewhat unbalanced, his blow knocked me to the ground. My fall was cushion by the sand on the beach, and I tasted my own blood in my mouth. Then they were all over me, punching me in my chest and stomach, and I started screaming, "I don't know nothing! That was my first break- in!"

They shouted questions at me like, "What other stores you then break into? Who else does go with you? What was the last store you broke into?"

The blows themselves did not hurt much, and I sensed that these officers were really trying to scare me more than anything else. These were grown men with much practice, so their blows should indeed be more powerful and painful. I decided to play their game with them by acting the scared part. Growing up, Vanessa and I had become quite good at this. When our mother would hit us once for doing something wrong, we would fall to the ground crying, putting on a real show. However, as soon as she left the room, it was as if nothing had ever happened. One day she caught us giggling after one of her beatings. She dashed back into the room, this time with the broomstick, and she went ballistic on us. Now when she left the room this time, we were both crying our lungs out.

So I reasoned to myself, Oh, I could ride this out. To give them the impression that their blows were working, I turned to my acting skills that we used to perform for our mother. I started to tremble, so that I could at least look scared. Then I allowed some tears to fall down my cheeks. Added in with that was another scream I let loose from the pit of my stomach for maximum effect. We all saw when someone cut on their outside light to see what was going on outside.

The officers shouted at me, "Shut up. Shut the hell up!" They grabbed me by both arms, lifted me to my feet, and walked me away from the houses further down the beach. To ensure that the few residents wouldn't hear my screams as they worked me over for information. This didn't really concern me; rather, it just enforced my belief that they were trying to scare information out of me. However, as they guided me farther down the beach, Mr. Trench Coat said something to me that shattered my resolve to resist and hold out.

He pulled out his weapon and said through clenched teeth, "Listen here, boy. Nobody knows where you are, nobody knows that you were arrested, nobody knows that we have you. We could kill you out here tonight, and nobody would know a damn thing. So you better talk, and you better tell us the truth."

My resolve sank like stone in water upon hearing those words, because he was indeed right. No one from my family knew where I was, much less that I was in police custody. So just like that, the mental game was over, and Mr. Trench Coat and his sidekick had won. I started singing like a canary. I now felt every blow. I agreed to things that I didn't even do, just to get them to stop and take me off this beach. Encouraged by what they heard, the officers rained down more blows. They wanted more information out of me, and they pumped away at me with their fists. They swooped in for the kill, like Mike Tyson when he's about to knock his opponent out. Mr. Trench Coat then said to me, "We're going to strip you naked out here, and then feed you to the sharks. Now tell us everything."

I wondered to myself, 'How in the world he knew that I was afraid of sharks?' It was as if I was drowning all over again, but this time I was drowning in a sea of blows.

He then asked, "Who else do be breaking into stores with you?"

"Only me one!" I screamed out in agony. But he didn't believe me, and kept asking me the same question over and again between his blows. This was the truth; I was always alone during my midnight adventures. He landed another blow on me, bringing me back to his question. He wanted an answer from me, and not the one I gave him. I thought about it quickly. He didn't want the truth, so a lie would have to do. I called out my neighbor's name—Donald. Don and I never did anything together, but early one morning he saw me breaking into a store. He stopped and we chatted for a minute or two, and he went on his way. It wasn't until the next day that he told me that he did the very same thing. So just to get them to stop, I called his name.

Encouraged by the information that they got out of me, they went even further by broadening their questions. Mr. Trench Coat then asked, "Which one of you has the gun?"

Now that one really caught me off guard. I thought to myself, 'A gun!' I wanted to ask him, "Officer, you caught me about to break into someone's store, so what I gon' be doing with a gun?" I was sixteen years old at the time, and I didn't even know anyone who had a gun. But again, I called Don's name, because he had told me once that he had a flare gun. On that night, they got everything out of me and a whole lot more than they had bargained for.

The Moment Of Truth
"For nothing is secret that will not be revealed, nor anything hidden that will not be known and come to light." Luke 8: 17
Satisfied with themselves and the fruits of their labor, they took me back to their vehicle some 45 minutes later. But before they put me inside to leave, they made sure that I cleaned up. I particularly noticed that Mr. Trench Coat was taking great care in making sure that no trace of the beach was on my clothing. They brushed me off really well, to ensure that no sand was in my hair. Then they took me home to search our premises, which was the thing I dreaded the most. I could've endured their blows for several more hours on the beach, but I wasn't ready to face my mother. This was the moment of truth for me; now everything would be brought out in the open. For my mother always told me, *"What's done in the dark always comes out in the light."*
We were outside our front door, but before knocking on our door, Mr. Trench Coat inspected me one more time. The only thing that was out of the ordinary was that the left side of my mouth was slightly swollen and I was in handcuffs. This was my first official arrest, even though I had been arrested months earlier for damaging a vehicle with some friends at a church youth group meeting. I was never placed in a holding cell, because the vehicle's owner didn't want to press charges against us. They just wanted their car glass to be replaced, and so my mother, along with three other parents had to pay eighty dollars.

On the night of my first arrest, the lessons I learned prove to be very valuable in my life of crime. Chief among them was this: when being beat by the police to reveal information, it's obvious that they don't know all they say they know. So I never focused on what they said to me, because I knew if I could block out their threats and intimidations, I would also be able to block out the pain. When you take an honest look at it, interrogation is nothing more than a psychological game, more so than any physical pain and discomfort. Therefore, my focus was on controlling my mind, and in so doing, I controlled what came out of my mouth.

The sound of police officers knocking on anyone's door 2:00 a.m. is never a pleasant thing, and I dreaded hearing the sound of my mother's voice answering the door. After a few minutes of banging on our door, my mother came to the window and asked who it was. Mr. Trench Coat identified himself as a police officer, and asked, "Do you know one Drexel Deal?" My mother said, "Yes."

Before Mr. Trench Coat could go any further she asked, and I could hear her voice starting to break with fear, "What do you want with Drexel?"

"We don't want him. We have him outside with us."

"What do you mean you have him outside with you? Drexel is inside sleeping."

As cool as a cucumber Trench Coat replied, "Ma'am, we have Drexel outside here with us. I guess he can best explain to you what we caught him attempting to do."

My mother then swung the door open, and I could see that her hands were shaking. It was both her and Pat at the door, but my mother did all of the talking. I was embarrassed and kept my head toward the ground. I didn't dare look her in the eyes. My mother asked, "Drexel, what were you doing to be arrested?"

I mumbled something under my breath. She quickly said, "Drexel, I can't hear you, and look up at me when you speak." As I brought my eyes to hers, it was clear to see that she was shaking all over. She asked me, "Drexel, what did you do?"

I took in a deep breath, and let it back out by quickly saying, "They caught me trying to break into a store."

I gestured toward the officers with my chin. My mother broke down and started weeping. "Why, Drexel, why?" she cried.

Looking back at it all, I put my mother through an emotional roller coaster ride of shame and disappointments. I was that boy talked about in Proverbs 29:15, which states, *"A boy let on the loose will be causing his mother shame."* NWT.

They searched the room I shared with my sisters and found a few small items that I had kept stashed away. They also took me to the Old Lightbourne Trading Building on Montgomery Street where Paradise Fisheries is now located. I was using this building as my own personal warehouse, to house some of the stuff I had stolen.

At CID, another round of questioning took place, but this time it wasn't any physical intimidation. They had what they wanted out of me. On the beach, I had confessed to some fifteen shop break-ins. However, during the interview process it was cut down to eleven, because they realized the other four I had confessed to was just to get them to stop beating me. Don was also arrested that night as well, and he was charged with one count of shop break-in. Yet some of the CID officers found it difficult to believe that I was only 16, especially realizing that these crimes were mainly committed on my own in the early morning hours. To top it off, I was using another building as a warehouse to stash some of my goods.

I was charged with eleven counts/cases of shop break-ins and receiving stolen property, which added up to some 22 charges. I appeared before Magistrate Ian Bethel. The total value of everything that I had stolen from the eleven stores was more than twenty thousand dollars. Therefore, they set my bail at twenty thousand dollars, and my Aunt Pearl had to put up her property as collateral for my release.

Chapter 8
A CLOSE CALL

"Sweet is the remembrance of troubles when you are in safety." —Euripides

I never told anyone about Pat's request to locate a fax machine for him, because it was not his fault. I just was caught in the act of doing something that I had been doing for months. This is not to say that Pat himself wasn't shady, because he indeed was. Case in point: he got me a job doing plumbing during the summer months of grade 11, when I was heading into grade twelve for my last year of school.
The company he worked with had the contract to do all of the plumbing work for the Bahamas Financial Service Center building, which was under construction. I was paid sixty dollars [$60.00] a week as a helper. At first, I didn't have a problem with the pay, until we went to work at The Bahamas Faith Ministries which was also under construction and is one of the largest churches in The Bahamas today. I was outside in the hot sun, digging trenches with a pickax for the first time in my life. To me, this is the most difficult part about plumbing work—the digging of trenches, especially in the heart of summer. But after a few days of having backaches and both palms of my hands blistered with sores, I quit and walked off the job. I reasoned to myself that at the age of 13 I was making $80 a week at the service station; now three years later I'm making less, and the work is five times more difficult. So I just walked off the site and walked all the way home which was some eight miles away.

When my mother came home I told her of my decision, and of course, she gave me a tongue-lashing. However, over the weekend Pat told me, "I spoke to the boss and he's going to increase your pay. But they will need you to now work at C. R. Walker, to have it ready in time to start the school year."While working at C. R. Walker, I learned from one of the workers name Jones, that the helpers' pay was one hundred and twenty dollars]$120.00] a week, oppose to the sixty dollars]$60.00] a week that Pat was giving me. This meant that he was stealing my money each week, and then probably adding $40 of his own money to give to my mother as if everything was coming from him alone. So in fact, he was using my labor to pay his sweetheart bill, even though the sweetheart in this case was my mother. But my issue is this: if you're dumb enough to take on the responsibility of another household, because you want to play around as if you're Mack Daddy, then pay for your pleasures out of your own pocket, rather than having me foot half of your bills for your cheap thrills. So when he saw me over the weekend, in passing he made the remark, "Boy, I heard the boss doubled your pay." During the same summer months, my cousin Carlos came to stay over. Pat got him a job at The Bahamas Financial Center, where of course Pat did the very same thing, he paid Carlos only sixty dollars [$60.00] a week. I had told Carlos of Pat's dirty trick, but Carlos didn't have a problem with that. He was just heading into grade 10, and he was working to purchase his school uniform and supplies. Besides, this was his first real job, and the most money he had ever made so he was cool with that.

Some three weeks after my first arrest for shop break-ins, I went back to the same store where Trench Coat caught me. But this time I was able to get inside within two minutes, using a simple kitchen butter knife. It has always been my nature not to quit and not to allow anything or anyone to stop me. However, the only problem was I was applying my determination to the wrong pursuits.

Ironically, just four years later, Mr. Trench Coat and two other officers would come to my job to arrest and question me for murder.

One would think that after I was caught red-handed attempting to break into a store, and not to mention the beating on the beach that I would stop and give it up. Instead, I got deeper into shop break-ins; actually, I got deeper into the world of crime and violence. As a matter of fact, I was just getting started in what would become my profession. With each successful shop break-in, my confidence grew to a point that I was unstoppable. There was not a building in our commercial strip that I couldn't get into if I wanted. The only question was how badly I wanted to get inside, which was due in part if the building was an easy or a difficult one to enter. My two favorite places for entering a building were either through the door using a screwdriver or a simple kitchen butter knife. Then there was the roof, which is normally the most vulnerable part of a building. Here's what I can say about shop break-ins: no building is burglar-proof. The only thing we could do is to make it difficult, because criminals are opportunistic in nature. They strike at what seems to be the easiest target at the time. However, the best defense against shop break-ins is an alarm, which works best with burglar bars, steel grill doors, and a well-lighted area. Not to mention a guard dog if you could afford one. An alarm doesn't prevent a house or a shop break-in rather it chases the intruder away like a guard dog. No one in their right mind wants to take the time to search a building when an alarm has gone off. Criminals work best under darkness and in silence, but when an alarm has been triggered, it removes those favorable working conditions. Thus, he has no other choice but to flee. As John 3:20 states, *"For everyone practicing evil hates the light and does not come to the light, lest his deeds should be exposed."* NKJV.

An alarm system today is quite effective and affordable, so I don't know why some people have not protected their homes and places of business with such an affordable system. Often it's not until their home has been broken into, or their business ransacked, do they purchase such a system. They say, 'prevention is better than cure'; then protecting our loved ones and our financial interests should be proactive rather than reactive.

One time I had broken into one of our major wholesale food distributors on the island. I looked at their building and whispered to myself, "Now this one will be a good challenge." Early that morning, around 2:00 a.m., I sneaked out of the house and climbed to the very top of the warehouse roof. There was no need for me to bring a ladder this time. They had one already provided on their building, in the form of the rainwater drainage pipes that ran down the side of their building. I gripped the pipe that ran to the ground from the roof, with my foot on either side of the pipe. I simply walked right up to the roof, as if I were Spider-Man.

Once on top of the roof, I walked to the eastern end where I knew the office was located. I had been to this office on two different occasions—the first time to pick up a job application form and the second time to return it once I had filled it out. So I knew the office was at the eastern end of the building and upstairs. I was quickly able to make a hole in the roof and get inside, where I lowered myself onto a support bracket that was holding the ceiling tiles. The support bracket was unable to hold my weight and it gave way. Realizing the impending fall, I braced myself for impact, and a good-sized portion of the ceiling tiles and I fell to the ground. I landed on my feet in the office area, right where I wanted to be.

Upon landing inside the building, I heard a beeping sound start to go off. I knew right away that it was an alarm. This was my very first time coming into contact with one. This meant that the motion sensor had been triggered, which resulted in the beeping sound. I figured if I could just keep still and not move, maybe the beeping sound would stop and the alarm wouldn't go off. Some thirty seconds or more passed and nothing happened. I couldn't believe my luck—I just beat this alarm system without doing anything. I don't know how many seconds the alarm delay was set for, but just when I was about to move, that alarm screamed to life with that sickening sound. On top of that, the lights in the warehouse came on at the same time. This gave me the impression that someone else was also in the building, maybe a security guard who was probably downstairs.

To this day, I don't know how I got out of there, but in a flash, I was through the hole and on the roof. All I knew was that in no time, I was home.

Back For More
"He that seeks trouble never misses." —French Proverb
Having made it back home without incident, shortly after nine that Saturday morning, I came back to the warehouse to see if anyone had come to check on the building. I was in a short, white Chicago Bulls basketball pants, a t-shirt, and Nike tennis shoes. It looked as if I were just an ordinary teenager; you wouldn't have even looked at me twice. Seeing no vehicles in sight and noting that the door was still locked, I used the rainwater drainage pipe again to make it up to the roof. This was a weekend and the store was closed.
The warehouse was situated at the back of other stores, so I was able to do my climbing without anyone noticing me. I made it back to the hole in the roof, where I proceeded to look inside. I was glad to see that everything was the same as I had left it. I lowered myself down to the ground, and just like before the beeping from the alarm started all over again.

This time when the alarm went off, instead of running I tried to find the source of the noise in an attempt to disable it. However, after two minutes with no success, the alarm just stopped by itself. Relieved, I started to search the building. I knew that I couldn't carry much with me, so I gathered together the stuff I would be carrying. This time, I was in there for about half an hour to forty-five minutes when I heard a familiar sound, and I stopped what I was doing to listen carefully. The noise that I heard was something vibrating. I stood there puzzled for a moment, racking my brains because I knew that sound. I was sure that I'd heard that sound before, but where did I hear it? The answer almost knocked the wind out of me, and I quickly crouched down low to the ground as if someone was shooting at me. My heart was racing a mile a second. I knew where the sound was coming from. This was not good news at all, for the sound I heard was the glass vibrating by the stairway. This was why the sound was so familiar, because the two times I visited this office—to pick up and drop off the job application form—I heard the same vibrating sound each time while walking up and down the stairs. When I had visited this office, I never really paid much attention to the glass vibrating. However, the lessons learn from my first arrest, taught me to pay attention to every little sound. My senses were now more alert, and in a quiet, empty building you are more keenly aware of everything. I knew what this meant: that someone or somebodies were coming up the stairs. Still crouching down, I made my way over to take a peek in the stairway. Sure enough, to my horror, there were two persons walking up the stairs. Two white adult males were coming directly toward me. The one that was leading the way, I guessed, was one of the owners of the building. He was a plain and regular-looking office person. However, the person who really caught my attention was the one bringing up the rear. He was thick and muscularly built and wearing camouflage fatigues from head to toe. There was no doubt in my mind that Mr. Muscle wasn't here for pretty, or to marvel at how clever I was in getting inside. He was hoping to catch someone in here. There was this no-nonsense look on his face. I could tell that he meant business, and by the look of him, I knew that he could handle himself. The way he was walking up those stairs—it was as if he were a big cat stalking his prey, about to pounce any second.

As a little sixteen-year-old black male, no one had to tell me that I was in some serious trouble if caught. There was no doubt in my mind that Mr. Muscle was carrying a handgun. They were the owners of a multi-million dollar company, a part of the financial elite, and on top of that they were white Bahamians. Oh yes, I thought to myself, he's strapped. I knew if they saw me, I would be as good as dead. With their influence and financial clout, this would be a justified killing. Without a second to spare, I quickly ducked into the nearest office to hide. I had been in this office before, but I had taken nothing. It looked like a plain conference room. The only thing inside that could have hidden my body entirely was a table. The table ran from the back wall almost to the door of the room. Just as I ducked under it, I heard the glass door open up in the outer office. Several seconds later, I saw the camouflage pants standing to the entrance of the room. Right then, I believed that my heart stopped beating. I thought to myself, "You are busted. He saw when you ducked into this room." Before I could register another thought, he took one step inside the room. However, the other one out front called to him—I guess to look at something else. He stopped, quickly turned around, and then exited the room.

I could hear them talking as they made a brief search of the building. I guess they determined that whoever had broken in was now long gone. I was unable to see what they were doing further back. However, I could still hear them talking, and this gave me an idea of where they were in the building. Then everything went quiet for a while. A short time afterward, I heard when office boy got on the phone and made a call. Just by listening to his end of the conversation, I could tell that he was talking to the alarm company. He told them that it was in fact a break-in. They were discussing the two different times that the alarm had been triggered. He then made several other calls—I guess one of them was to the police to report the break-in because two police officers showed up some forty-five minutes later, and then a roofing company came to repair the hole that was above our heads.

One of the police officers took a statement from him, while the other one dusted for fingerprints. Some fifteen minutes later, one of the officers came to the door of the room that I was hiding in. I thought to myself, "Now you're busted."

The officer took a step in the room, but Office Boy said to him, "Nothing was disturbed in there."

Just like that, he backed out and went to look in another room. A short time later, a white lady with a young toddler arrived on site. She looked around briefly as well; I then heard her commenting about the damage to the ceiling tiles lying on the ground. I guessed that she was office boy's wife, and with her was their daughter. She offered to go and purchase lunch for everybody, including the roofing guys working on the hole. By this time, the two police officers had left. As she was getting ready to leave to purchase lunch, she stopped in front of the door to the room that I was still hiding in. The young toddler with her turned around and looked me straight in the eyes. Right then I stopped breathing. I was able to avoid being seen by muscle man, plus that nosey police officer. But now it was over; I was going to be busted by a two or three-year-old little girl. I held her gaze and she held mine. For what felt like an eternity, we just kept staring at each other.

I dared not blink or even move a muscle. If she just pointed at me, I'd be dead. She doesn't even have to talk, just point in my direction. Her mother would no doubt bend down to her level to see what she was pointing at. If this happened, I knew that it would be over for me.

But she just looked at me, and I looked at her. At the same time, I prayed to God, "Please get me out of this one. I promise on my grandmother's grave, I will never break into another store again. Please God, do not let her point at me, and do not let her speak."

This was the longest minute of my life. She was unable to break her stare from me and I was unable to do the same. Her mother then took her by the hand, and they left to purchase lunch. I sat back under the table, finally able to breathe again. I knew right away that after they left, I had to make my move. That was too close for comfort.

After they left, the front area got very quiet, and I figured that now was my best chance to get out of here. I slowly came from under the table, where I had been for almost three hours or more. I peeked out the door and saw Muscle Man looking around in one of the back offices. His hands were behind his back, and his back was toward me, which was good. I was unable to see office boy and didn't care; I figured that if I couldn't see him, then he couldn't see me either. My prayers were answered. I closed my eyes for a second and said, "Thank you, God." The door leading to the stairs wasn't far from the room I was hiding in. I took one more look at muscle man, just to make sure that his back was still toward me. Then I quickly and quietly stepped out of the room and made my way toward the door. I was almost home free. Just after taking three long steps towards the door, I ran into office boy. "This can't be real," I said under my breath.

I didn't actually walk into office boy, but it was darn close enough. He sat at the receptionist desk, where he was on the phone talking. I was about three feet away from the desk where he sat. I stood there frozen stiff with fear, but he had yet to register my presence. His right elbow rested on the desk, and his head lay in the palm of his right hand. The palm of his hand covered the right side of his head, which was the very side on which I was standing. The phone receiver was in his left hand, and he held it to his left ear. This was why I couldn't hear him earlier, because he was on the phone having a conversation in a low voice. Looking back now, there's no doubt in my mind that he was talking to a female, and it was someone that he was intimate with. His sweetheart no doubt saved my life. I knew that he couldn't have been talking to his wife, because she had just left.

He sat there looking down at the desk, and his posture was that of a defeated man. All the while, I just stood there dumbstruck, not knowing what to do. I couldn't believe it; I was three feet away from this guy, and he didn't even sense my presence.

Finally, I came out of my shock. I looked back at muscle man, whose back was still toward me. I looked down at office boy. He was still preoccupied with his phone conversation. Even more quietly than before, I quickly made a beeline toward the glass door. Someone inside would have to buzz you in to enter the office after climbing the stairs. However, for people exiting the office, one would simply pull down the lever and be on their way. I pulled on the lever and opened the door slowly. It opened without making a sound. I looked back at office boy, who was still deeply engaged in his phone conversation. I couldn't believe my good fortune. I might have walked away with nothing, but I still had my freedom and my life. Once outside the office, I quietly pulled the door shut behind me and then started down the stairs, careful not to allow the glass to vibrate on my way down. Once I was outside, I saw the roofing company's truck. There was no one inside the truck; they were all on the roof repairing the hole. I couldn't see the people on the roof, but I could hear their voices. Once I passed their truck, I knew that I was home free. Even though I had prayed to God to get me out of that jam, yet I continued getting deeper into a life of crime. As the Scottish Proverb states, *"Danger gone, God forgotten."*

Joining the Rebellion Raiders
The profile of a typical gang member according to the FBI "Is a male school dropout or truant, who is unemployed or has no employable skills. The gang member is usually in trouble with the police and does not receive adequate family attention. The gang provides identity and status and, in return, the member develops a fierce loyalty to the gang and nation."
I joined the Rebellions in early May 1992. Even though they had been around for some time, I had never heard about them. Not until I began to hang with Michael and his younger brothers on Hawkins Hill did I start to hear about the Rebellions. Michael had graduated from D. W. Davis (referred to only as D) School, which was the stronghold of the Rebellions. He also had a younger brother named Shawn, who was still attending 'D' in his last year of school. Shawn was best friends with Kelly, who was a Rebellion from East Street. Then Kelly's younger brother Franz, one of the key shooters for the Rebellions, made up the inner circle.

Every Sunday Michael and I used to go to Canaan Lane to play basketball. There were guys like Cedric "Space" Sweeting, Reggie Parks, Deno, Yellow, Horse, Pie, Peacock, and Annie, who was the biggest of them all. There I got to meet Geno, a.k.a. Silver Fox, who was a Rebellion. He was the cousin of Peacock and the brother of Pie. Geno was not a ballplayer; rather, he was a motorbike rider. This was what he enjoyed doing. Prior to joining the gang, I was mainly into graffiti. I had my name plastered all about, especially on the back of the Palmdale Shopping Plaza.

The Canadian Imperial Bank of Canada (CIBC) rented the northern portion of the plaza, where Fidelity Bank Bahamas Limited is now located. I had the back of that building written right up with my nickname from school. Geno ended up hanging with us a few times, and heard about the one or two fights that I had been in and my love for graffiti. He said to me one day, "If you are carrying on this bad on your own, you might as well start hanging with us. I agreed and he took me around Strachan's Corner the next day. As we were walking, he told me, "Now they are going to throw some blows on you, just to see how well you could handle yourself under pressure."

We entered Strachan's Corner from East Street, which was the Rebellions' stronghold. Even though it was a dead end corner, there were many ways to enter it on foot. The first person he saw was Gray Eyes, one of the gang's chief lieutenants whose street name was as a result of the unique color of his eyes. Geno said to him, "I brought one over for initiation."

Gray Eyes quickly looked me over. He turned around and walked off, and then he threw one of his hands in the air and said, "Let those lil' fellas deal with that."

In their research paper "Alcohol and Violence in the Lives Of Gang Members," Geoffrey P. Hunt, PhD and Karen Joe Laidler, PhD wrote, "For many gangs, new members are expected to go through an initiation, often referred to as 'jumping in.' This induction process, or rite of passage, is important, because it is designed to symbolically test the newcomer's toughness and his ability to defend himself and withstand physical violence."

We continued walking, and Geno found six fellas sitting on a disabled truck. I later learned they were the Truck Boys, Scrooge's (the leader of the Rebellions) little crew. This truck was in front of his yard. Once Geno told them why I was there, they all came down off the truck and looked me over — I guess just to make sure that they didn't have any prior problems with me.

Geno was standing on my right side. He said to me, "Now I'm going to start it." He took two steps out in front of me, spun around quickly, and delivered a punch to my left jaw. My head jerked back from his blow. I remember thinking to myself, at least that wasn't bad. However, before I could register another thought, the five Truck Boys were on me like white on rice. They threw blows and slaps on me. For the next minute or so, I stood there and took it all in like a good soldier.

This was the price I was more than willing to pay to become a member of the Rebellions. After it was all over, they welcome me in with handshakes. Then they started asking me where I lived, and what school I had attended. Just like that I was now in the gang, these were my new best friends, individuals whom I would go all out for, and who would do the same for me.

A few days after my initiation, Archie socialized me into the gang, letting me know of the gang's history like who the top guys were in the gang, areas to avoid now, basic gang rules, etc. But Archie told me, "If the big fellas had initiated you, it would've been a really severe beating."

How the Rebellions Initiation Came to be Instituted
"Group initiations are similar to examples of 'battleproofing' in military training, in which the new recruits experience a situation of stress that allows them to develop confidence in their ability to face danger." anthropologist Suzette Heald, author of *"The Ritual Use Of Violence: Circumcision among the Gisu of Uganda"*

In my interview with Franco Bethel a.k.a. 'Co' (who was also a part of the Rebellions' inner circle, and would become one of the top shooters in the gang. Franco would also go on to become one of the biggest drug dealers who emerged out of the Rebellions and eventually would go on to control his own area called the Big Yard.)

Franco shared with me how the Rebellions established an initiation process, for new members wanting to join the gang. He said, "We were all sitting down one day just talking, like we would normally do through the corner. I can't remember how the conversation came up, but we ended up discussing who all were committed to the gang".

Franco then said, "Somehow, Teddy took over the conversation by declaring in a loud voice, 'Who, me? I'm ready to die for Rebellions. I'm ready to kill for Rebellions. I'm ready to do whatever for the gang.'"

"Scrooge was right there sitting down just listening to everything. So Scrooge asked Teddy in a soft and calm voice, to the point where we almost didn't hear him, 'So you ready to take a shot for Rebellions?' Teddy jumped up and said, 'Who, me? I could take couple shots for the gang easily.'"

"There was a slight pause, then a shot went off. We all quickly jumped to our feet, except for Scrooge who was still sitting down. It was only when I stood up that I saw him put a lil' .25 back in his pocket. You know, we always kept something on hand that we could reach quickly just in case fellas came around joking."

Franco continued on with a smile, "So before I could even register what had just happened, I heard Teddy screaming 'Murder'. Teddy was hopping around and holding his thigh with one hand, where he had been shot. He was screaming and crying like a baby saying, 'Call my mummy, I want my mummy, I gon' tell my mummy you all trying to kill me for true.'"

With the smile now gone Franco said, "Even though that was a big joke for us right then, it really showed us that he wasn't ready, because after that incident Teddy never came back to the gang. At the same time for us who were there, it made us sit up and take notice that this is real, and you could lose your life."

Franco concluded by saying, "After that, Scrooge instituted the initiation process for new members, as a way of weeding out those who were not ready. This was primarily done to toughen fellas up, for when they ended up in the hands of the police. We were having experiences where gang members who were being locked up couldn't handle pressure. The next thing you know, they were pulling right up in the front of your door with the police."

Chapter 9
LANDING IN THE HAWKS' NEST

"It is said that no one truly knows a nation until one has been inside its jails. A nation should not be judged by how it treats its highest citizens, but its lowest ones." —Nelson Mandela

Just one week after joining the Rebellions, I was arrested for the fourth weekend in a row. This prompted magistrate Cheryl Albury to remand me to Sandilands Rehabilitation Center. After I was released from Sandilands, I was then sent to prison because my aunt had taken my bail back. My mother couldn't sign a twenty thousand dollar bail, because she had no land papers to meet the bail requirements. Therefore, I had to tough it out in prison until all of my cases were completed. This was August of 1992, the very same year I was supposed to have graduated from school. Looking back, I was indeed graduating; I was about to step up to another level in my education of crime. I was sent to prison for shop break-ins and other petty juvenile crimes of mischief.

One of the first things a new inmate is greeted with at Her Majesty's Prison is the high stench of rotten food, that smells as if it has gone bad years ago. I was guided through the eastern side of 'B' block to what is called a bulkhead. As I walked with the prison officer, everything was just so surreal. It felt as if I had been transported back in time to the eighteenth century during the time of slavery. Everything moved in slow motion as I passed each cell on my way to the bulkhead. Even though it was dark on the inside of the cells, I could still see the body outline of men. But what I could see most clearly were their eyes. I guess they could tell that I was new; they stared me up and down, some even coming closer to their cell door to get a better look.

There were bits and pieces of garbage in the corridor. The place was really filthy. Not to mention the scent—even though it was a different scent in the air this time, it still smelled awful. The thing that always stands out about maximum security is the scent. It is always there.

According to information posted on Amnesty International website, the following was found: "Amnesty International visited the state's sole prison, Her Majesty Prison [HMP] Fox Hill, in August 2002 with prison reform expert Professor Rod Morgan. They stated, "Many prisoners continue to be detained in conditions amounting to cruel, inhuman or degrading treatment. Unacceptably overcrowded accommodation was evidenced in all prison units, seriously affecting the living conditions for inmates and the working conditions for staff. Cells were dark and fetid, and many prisoners slept on cardboard. Many prisoners are still subject to the degrading practice of slopping out while the prison still has inadequate plumbing and drainage system."

I was put in the downstairs eastern bulkhead. It was about ten feet wide and about thirty-five to forty feet long. There were thirty or more individuals in this unit, and some twenty of them, I later learned, were from the same area, which is Bain Town (Gun Hawks territory, a rival gang of the Rebellions). Unknowingly, I had just landed in the Hawks' nest. As soon as the officer locked the cell door and turned his back, somebody called for a person named Nana, who came and took one look at me from head to toe. Then he said, "He's a Rebellion," and just walked away.

I guess that he was the in-house expert on identifying Rebellions or anyone who was at odds with the Gun Hawks. I knew that I was in trouble. I thought to myself, 'How did he know I was a Rebellion? To make matters worse, he was so sure of it, and he was indeed right.' I had just joined the gang a week before I was arrested, but I'd just spent the last three months in Sandilands. To top it off, the week I was with the Rebellions I was never involved in a fight with them and had never even gone out with them, so he couldn't have known me. Bolstered with this bit of knowledge, I found my voice and said to his back, "I'm not a Rebellion."

This time the dorm went quiet, and everybody looked at me. I thought to myself, 'what in the hell you got yourself into?' These were not fellas my age and size. This was the major leagues of criminality; these were the real gangsters. These guys were built like the Hulk. Just about everybody was bulked up as if they were on steroids. Then the interrogation began. I was transferred from one person to another. They all wanted to know which area I lived in, what school I had attended? What I was charged for and where on the streets I hang out?

As one group interrogated me, I could tell that every word I said was closely monitored and sniffed out for lies. At the end of the day, it was where I used to hang out that saved me and prevented me from being picked apart by the Hawks. My Hawkins Hill hangout was just four blocks from where we lived on Mount Royal Avenue. This was not known as a Rebellion territory, nor was R. M. Bailey known as a Rebellion school. To my surprise, Jason, the Bosun (the person in charge of the dorm), knew Michael, and he also knew that Michael was not a Rebellion, but just someone who was into karate.

Jason stood up and said, "You all aint touching him. There will be no ganging in here tonight." He was one of Bitto's older brothers, and Bitto was the Gun Hawks' leader.

They also had another brother in there named Isaac, who also stood up and said, "Nothing is happening so leave this lil' fella alone."

Prior to my arrival, I had been told that some weeks ago Shaney was in there. Shaney was a Rebellion, but I had never met him before. Shaney had taken a gun from a Gun Hawk, which had started the war between them and the Rebellions. They had led him to believe that everything was cool, and everything was forgiven because they all were in prison. However, after the prison was locked down for the night, they threw a blanket over Shaney's head and ganged him. The beating was so bad that Shaney ended up with a fractured skull.

The same thing almost happened with Galen (a.k.a. Ninja, leader of the Public Terrorist, which was another arm of the Rebellions). The Gun Hawks had convinced him and the officers to let him in the bulkhead. However, Galen said to me, "They jumped the gun by not waiting until lockdown. As soon as the officers left, they threw a blanket over my head and started beating me up. The officers were not far, so they were able to quickly return and get me out of there."

This was the environment that I was in. Even though nothing happened, I felt that I was monitored each day. I knew that they were just hoping for me to slip up and make a mistake. For each day there was an additional question that someone had forgotten to ask me. One day, fellas were writing their street names on the prison wall with paint. I never knew where they got the paint from; nonetheless, I was delighted to participate. Graffiti was my thing. I totally forgot where I was for a second. I was about to draw my signature angry face, but when I had only gotten to write the R and the A for "Raw Deal," I heard the dorm got quiet. Without even looking around to find out why, I could tell that a lot of eyes were on me. I was being scrutinized all over again.

I realized then that the letters R and A are also the first two letters in "Raiders." I guess that they thought that I was about to write the word "Raiders" on the wall. I dared not look behind me; I just continued by writing the letter W and then "Deal." I didn't draw the face, because that would've been too much for them to handle. Somebody would've tried their best to connect it with the Rebellions. When I had finished, before even turning around, I could hear the talking resume. Only then did I breathe a sigh of relief. I was held in the Hawks' nest only for that weekend before I was transferred to the Detention Center. There, I would take my first shower since entering prison. The bulkhead I had been in had no running water. Everybody urinated in one-gallon water bottles, and if you wanted to do number two, there were buckets for that. Looking back over those four days in the Hawks' nest, I don't know how I made it through. It was the Russian novelist, short story writer and former prisoner, Fyodor Dostoevsky, who stated, *"the degree of civilization in a society can be judged by entering its prisons."*

My First Shooting
"The environment you permit determines the product you produce." —Dr. Myles Munroe, Bahamian bestselling author
The first time I ever fired a gun, it was not fired in the air nor at empty cans and bottles, rather, it was when I actually shot someone. It wasn't until sitting down to write this book did I realize, that the first and the last persons I shot were both security guards.

So what brought me to my first shooting? How is it that a teenager who had never fired a gun before, can so easily pull the trigger on a security guard in a busy public place? How does a boy of seventeen get to this point in his life, and what is the mindset of such an individual? What motivated me to such utter violence and disregard for life, and how can we prevent others from following a similar path?

While in prison, I noticed something rather peculiar among the inmates: as to which ones were respected and revered. They were all charged with offenses like firearm and drug possession, armed robberies, attempted murders, and murder itself. These were the bad boys of prison, and the local celebrities we all looked up to. It was them who did most of the storytelling. Their colorful stories became our live entertainment. It goes without saying that I was one of their most captive audience. This was the real thing; there was no acting here. Oh, the fellas would add something new to their stories each time, which made it even more enjoyable. These guys were masterful in their reenactment; they took you with them to each crime scene. This was as real as it gets. It was in this environment/university of crime that I became more like them with each story told.

I believe that the reason why prisons are such effective training grounds for criminals, is because they house a body of like-minded individuals who all share the same interest and passion. Therefore, their story telling moments often serve as peer education group sessions of learning. In fact one is faced with only two choices in prison, to either exit that life style, or get better which means getting deeper into a life of crime. While in prison, I never made a conscious decision to shoot anyone as a way of resolving a problem. Yet if you had told me back then, that just four months after my release from prison, I would return with charges of possession of two firearms, armed robbery, and attempted murder, I probably would've suggested to you that something was wrong with your head. But that is exactly what happened.

I was released from prison in January of 1993. There was a new magistrate in the juvenile court named Rodger Gomez. I first met him while coming down from prison to appear for one of my cases. During which time he said to me, "Drexel, your name is the most frequently heard name before the juvenile panel."

By this time, I had almost twenty cases before the courts, and they all were trying to see what they could do with me. The juvenile panel was willing to work with me and to give me a second chance.

They offered me a plea bargain through my court appointed lawyer, Mrs. Joan Ferguson. If I pleaded guilty to everything, I would be placed on six months' probation, which would not give me a criminal record. Realizing all the evidence that was against me, I quickly agreed to their offer. I was released on six months' probation, and for a while, everything was going well, I was even working at our church. I reported in frequently to my caseworker. What led to my first shooting then? It all started one Saturday afternoon in the Mall at Marathon. My cousin Carlos and I were both looking for a Mother's Day gift for our respective mothers. The Mall at Marathon, back in my teenage days, was the most popular hangout spot for us young people. As a matter of fact, it was the spot. If you were not at the mall, then you were nowhere. While at the mall, I ran into a crowd of fellas from Ida Street (the Ida Street Sharks Gang). I had some problems with them back in the 11th grade of school. So on that Saturday in the mall, a guy who goes by the street name of Red Ants came over and punched me three times to my head. I looked at him and then looked at his friends. There were about seventeen of them just leaning against the wall watching. I knew that I couldn't win, so I just walked off and took those three blows. They won that round; I could live with that. I have survived worse, so what were three blows? On top of that, Carlos was with me, and this kind of stuff was not up his alley. It made no sense endangering his life over something he knew nothing about. I just went on my way, acting as if nothing had happened. But it goes without saying that I was determined to strike back. At that time, I was hanging with the Boys in the Hood, which was another arm of the Rebellions. Their hangout was just several blocks down the road from where we lived. The leader of this group was Anthony Cash a.k.a. "Cash," who was also a former student of R. M. Bailey. I had mentioned to someone what had happened in the mall. One of the members, Puckey (now deceased), came to me with the idea of purchasing a handgun. Right away, I was down with that idea. We agreed to put up seventy-five dollars each the following Friday. My weekly salary from the church was one hundred and fifty dollars. I never knew if Puckey was working, but he had his money ready as he said he would. I gave him my seventy-five dollars as agreed, and he went off and came back an hour later. Puckey was able to purchase a little .22 revolver from a well-known robber named Cedric a.k.a. "Sadie," both him and Shaney were charged with a string of armed robberies together. I would also later meet

Sadie in prison, for crimes I committed using this very same weapon.

The following Saturday I was in the mall again, along with four fellas from the hood. I was strapped and it sure did felt good, oh yes, I could take on anyone now. In a newspaper article headlined, 'Galloway Boys are back on the street', which was published in the Toronto Sun of Canada. The article was written by the reporter Chris Doucette, May 28th 2013. He quotes Dr. Anthony Hutchinson a former gang member, who has turn his life around and is now an assistant professor at Tyndale University, and a court certified gang expert. Dr. Hutchinson stated, "Behind the gun there is a false sense of power, a false sense of identity."

I was hoping to run into my Ida Street friends, and one person in particular—Mr. Red Ants himself. It was time to return the favor, but fortunately for them, they were nowhere in sight. Instead, we ran into seven or eight fellas from Lizzy, another branch of the Rebellions. Apples was the senior man in the crew so once we linked up, it didn't take us long to run into someone we were warring with.

We ran into five or six Fox Hill fellas, Lizzy's archrivals. These guys were well known for toting knives. Just a year prior they had stabbed Mackey Dog from Lizzy to death, so we faced off with them in The Sports Center store and they held their ground. It was clear to all that they were going to stand and fight, even though they were outnumbered. I was lurking in the background, waiting to see what was going to happen, because it was really too crowded to do anything stupid. After a brief standoff with both sides holding their grounds, Apples picked up a stool and threw it at them. It landed helplessly on the floor, but the Fox Hill fellas came at us all of them baring knives.

Everybody from our end took off running, including me. I looked around and saw two of them gaining on me, so I intentionally slowed up a bit, allowing them to close the gap. One of them slowed down as I did, while the other one kept charging at me with his knife. We were more isolated now, as we headed for one of the many exit doors. Without warning, I quickly spun around on him with the revolver in my hand. He stopped immediately with a stunned looked on his face. The barrel of the gun was already pointing toward his chest. Before he could even register that I had lured him into a trap, I pulled the trigger of the gun. To my surprise nothing happened. So I pulled the trigger again, and just like before, nothing happened.

I thought to myself, "Why is this stupid gun not firing?" I spun back around and ran outside, leaving him standing there stunned and mystified. Once I was on the outside, I spun the chamber of the gun twice and slapped it to make sure that nothing was stuck. When I ran outside the mall, I saw Apples fighting with someone in one of the stores. So I charged back in the mall to get him. When I entered the store, both of them were still at it. They didn't even notice when I entered, that's how much they were entangled with each other. I took up a shooter's position, with my legs slightly apart just as I had seen officer Trench Coat done. I extended both of my arms outward, with the gun in my right hand. I then firmly said, "Let him go." Both of them stopped fighting and looked around when they heard me spoke. The individual let go of Apples, who ran out of the door. I didn't know him, nor did I know whether or not he was with the Fox Hill fellas. The individual with whom Apples was fighting was not wearing a security uniform so I didn't know whether he was a security officer. Without thinking about it, I just pulled the trigger, but this time the gun did fire. It was like an explosion, as the sound vibrated off the store's wall. This was my first time ever firing a gun. I saw when a dark circular spot appeared on his chest as confirmation that I had shot him. There was no sign of blood. He didn't stagger or even flinch. Apples was gone and out of the mall by now. I then quickly exited the store and ran out of the mall. I took off after Apples and the rest. I was a runner, so I caught up to them quickly.
Having grown up in Danottage Estates, I was quite familiar with the Marathon area, and thus I led the way through Marathon, into Palmetto Village, through White's Addition, and then soon into Danottage Estates. I ran Apples and everyone hard, for a few of them started to complain about their sides hurting and wanted to slow down. I felt the same pain, but I couldn't stop. We had to keep moving. More importantly, I had to keep moving; not only had I just shot someone, but I still had the weapon on me. Once we made it to the northern end of Danottage Estates at Bernard Road, then the others took over leading the way. We were now on their school turf. We ended up in what they called the wilderness, which was directly behind L. W. Young School that they all had attended. Once safely in the wilderness, I was able to breathe a sigh of relief.

We spent some two hours or more up there, which is a rocky incline with overgrown bushes. Upon exiting the wilderness, we came out on Bernard Road, which was more or less the Fox Hill fellas' territory. We stayed hidden behind a liquor store/bar, and to our surprise, there was a truck of fellas from Lizzy who were heading home after being on East Street. Apples flagged down the truck and we all hopped on the back. The others were dropped off in Elizabeth Estates, leaving just Archie and me on the back of the truck.

Looking back at it all, I went to the mall with the sole purpose of shooting someone that day. It just happened that an innocent person was caught up in the middle of our gang war.

Bait the Hook to Suit the Fish

"Speakers who talk about what life has taught them never fail to keep the attention of their listeners." —Dale Carnegie

The above quotation by Carnegie really captures my next point, which is: Sometimes the best way to reach gang members is through someone who has lived and overcome that life. The church I attended at the time—Calvary Bible Church—was working with me. The Assistant Pastor of the church, Fredrick Arnett, really did his best in trying to reach out to me. However, I was unable to connect with him, and thus he was unable to pull me out of a life of crime.

Please don't get me wrong. He tried his best, but it was just not enough to reach me. I remember Pastor Arnett sharing with me once, a little about his early years growing up. I sat up straight to hear what he had to say. This was the first time in all of our counseling sessions that he had my undivided attention.

He told me of his flamboyant playboy years and that he had been a ladies' man before giving his life to Christ. Listening to his story, I just had to smile inwardly, because I would never have guessed that Pastor Arnett was sweet on the ladies. Even though I had enjoyed his story, for me it wasn't enough. Deep down within I honestly wanted help, but there was no one that I could have identified with. There was no one who understood my pain and frustration. I was angry and didn't know why. People were talking to me, but they were not connecting with me. There was just no connection to what I had been through and still lived with.

I walked out of counseling that day shaking my head, mumbling to myself, "He doesn't know what I'm going through. My struggles are far different from his. He just doesn't know."

Now to be fair to Pastor Arnett, I never talk much in those sessions. I kept my problems to myself, something I am still good at doing today. However, today I can better appreciate that we witness best when we share with others the mess the Lord has brought us out of. I needed a successful guide, someone who had been through what I had been through and made it out. I needed an ally who was familiar with my pain and the uneven terrain of what was my life. This is why today I cannot effectively counsel a drug addict or an alcoholic, because I've never been there so it's difficult to identify with them. If I can't feel a person's pain, then it becomes difficult for me to lead them to healing and recovery.

In an article entitled, "There's No Glamor In Gang Life', written by Mark Cantrell and published February 20th 2013 in the British Housing Excellence Magazine. Mr. Cantrell writes, "The world of gangs is, of course, anything but glamorous. The ones who know this best are those who have managed to escape, so it makes sense to harness their testimonies and their experience to try and influence young people away from gang life."

Here's what I've come to appreciate, when it comes to reaching out to people: you have to bait the hook to suit the fish. For young men who are somewhat deviant and going astray, you have to speak about what interest them, and not about what's in their best interest. If they were really concern about what is in their best interest, then they wouldn't be considered deviant or going astray.

Therefore, one has to speak the language of those we want to reach, and this is where we who once walked that road can best talk about it to those who are leaning that way. Case in point, Troit and I spent about a year reaching out to young men, who were in the Simpson School for Boys [the government's facility for wayward adolescent boys]. During our first visit there, we had the opportunity to share our life story and what we been through. One of the school's warden said to us afterwards, "I've been here for more than 20 years, and I've seen a lot of people who came here and spoke to the boys. But I've never seen what I've witness today, you guys really had their attention."

Then he went on to explain, "Our biggest challenge when we have guest speakers, is maintaining order and getting them to pay attention. Who ain't putting their heads on the table falling asleep, are either talking or doing something else to distract the others. But with you two there was none of that, everybody was wrapped up in what you were saying even me."

In the article entitled, 'Former Modesto gang member devotes his life to reaching at-risk youths', which was published in the Modesto Bee and written by Garth Stapley. Mr. Stapley interviewed Ignacio Pizano, a former gang member who was sentence to life in prison for murder at the age of 15. "Teens recruited by gangs, Pizano said, are best reached by those who survived them." Pizano continues, "(Former gangbangers) are who the kids want to hear from, not someone who read it in a book. When you're dealing with young peoples' lives, they want to relate to somebody who's been through it." Ignacio Pizano's book is, 'Soldier Field', which captures his life spent on the streets of Modesto, California.

This is not to say that persons like Pizano, Troit and I, are the only ones capable of reaching such individuals. Our life stories simply serve as a hook, to get their attention long enough where we can now say something meaningful to them. It's the same principle in selling anything, you must first capture your prospects attention with what interest them, then meaningful dialog can take place.

This is the same principle use when fishing, the bait that is used to catch crawfish/ lobsters, Nassau groupers and sharks are all different. Simply because the food they eat is different from each other, what may interest one set of fish, may not interest the other set. Even the benefits of the gospel must be interesting. This is why Jesus said *"come follow me and I will make you fishes of men." Matthew 4:19.*

Thus getting young people to do the right thing must also be interesting if they are to buy into it.

Even though Troit and I may have an edge, it doesn't mean that others without similar experience cannot be effective. The truth is we all know of someone who took the wrong path in life, and as a result suffered greatly for doing so. Well, that's what they want to hear about, that there is your hook. Once you have their attention, for they are now listening to you. Now you can pull them in by speaking something positive into their lives.

Our lives' experiences and that of others inform us, that enable us to make better decisions and we can pass those lessons on to others. As Daynette Gardener stated in chapter 5, "Getting them to see cost and relationships between events is the best way to increase comprehension skills."

During the time that Troit and I were reaching out to the young men at the Simpson Penn School for boys, I had invited Fred Wallace to speak to the young men. He was an elder at the church I use to attend, which was Mount Tabor Full Gospel Baptist Church. At one point he used to pick me up for Sunday services. I found Elder Wallace to be a down to earth person, and on top of that he was a Defense Force Officer [our local military].

Elder Wallace came in his camouflage fatigues, for he had just come off duty. Right away he had their attention, before he had even uttered a single word. This was not a former bad boy, some street thug who believed that he was a soldier rather this was the real thing, a soldier who had handled all of the high powered weapons out there.

People often ask me, 'Why are young men so fascinated with guns? But what else do you want them to be fascinated with? When they are bombarded with it in the movies, in games, in songs and then you give it to them in the form of a toy. Don't you think that one day, they would want to hold and experience the real thing for themselves? Don't you think that one day they would want to know how it feels just to shoot someone? Don't you think that one day they would now want to know, how it feels to take a life?

One cannot create a culture of guns and violence, in the minds and hearts of our young people and expect them not to act on it. Our young people today are simply regurgitating, the violence that they have been entertained with for all their lives.

In 1993 the American Psychological Association estimated, 'the average child will have seen 8,000 murders and 100,000 acts of violence on television before finishing elementary school.'

It was the 14th century English author, lawyer, statesman and social philosopher, Sir Thomas More, who is better known in the Roman Catholic community as Saint Thomas More. He said almost 500 years ago in his book *"Utopia"* which was published in 1516, *"For if you suffer your people to be ill-educated, and their manners to be corrupted from their infancy, and then punish them for those crimes to which their first education disposed them, what else is to be concluded from this, but that you first make thieves and then punish them."*

However, Elder Wallace was true to form and he didn't disappoint, for he took us all on a boat ride. He told us about his deployments on the high seas, and how they took down drug runners by shooting out their engines. Knowing he had them wrapped around his little pinky finger, he then began to slowly pull them in by speaking into their lives. As it relates to the poor decisions they made in the past, their choice of friends and how they can make something of their lives in spite of their present circumstances.

Elder Wallace was not a former bad boy, but he used his work experiences to inform and pass on valuable life lessons to the young men. By the time he was finish with his stories about drug seizures and boat chases on the high seas, I could have tasted a hint of salt water in my mouth, because that's how wrapped up I was in his stories.

Even if Pastor Arnett had been able to connect with me, I don't think that I was going to change immediately. I was already in a free fall, plummeting head first into a life of crime. The only thing that was going to stop me from my descent was hitting rock bottom. At the same time, if I had been able to identify with him, it would've provided me with a lifeline of hope - a line that I could have used when I was ready, to pull myself up and out of a life of crime once I hit bottom. My reasoning would've been that if he could do it, then I could do it as well, provided I was willing to take advantage of it, because not everyone who needs help wants to be helped.

It was Pastor Arnett who had gotten me a job as a handyman, doing little odd jobs around the church.

I Went From a Zero to a Hero Overnight

"One of the greatest diseases is to be nobody to anybody." — Mother Teresa

After the shooting in the Mall, I didn't sleep home that night; instead, I was officially introduced to Scrooge, who allowed me to sleep at his place. I'm going to let Supt. Allerdyce Strachan introduce Scrooge. In my interview with her, she said the following about him:

"The reason why I remembered Scrooge so well was because he had his name spray painted on the wall opposite the Church of God. His name was all over—Scrooge, Scrooge, Scrooge—and I was wondering who this Scrooge was. When I finally got to meet him, he was a very calm person with a beautiful smile."

Scrooge was slimly build, and stood about 6ft. 1 o 2in. When I had first joined the gang, Archie had given me the rundown on how Scrooge got his name. He said, "There was a gambling game going on under the tree, and Scrooge, who was not called Scrooge as yet, came there and broke the game. I mean, he won everything. Those of us who had lost our money asked him for something back. But he just kept telling us, "no". We followed him straight to his home asking just for a dollar. But he refused to even give us a dime, and so somebody called him Scrooge and the rest was history."

In 1993, Scrooge and I would share a cell together in prison for more than three months. I had the opportunity to ask him about that day, and in response he said, "I got tired of hearing the fellas complaining about losing all of their money in this dice game. So I went there, and even though the game was barely new to me, I was able to win everything. After the game, some of the fellas were behind me asking for some of their money back, for they had lost their entire pay for that week."

He continued, "To be honest with you, I intentionally didn't give them anything, because normally the person who broke the game would give some of the players a lil' something back. But my thing is this: if you are that stupid to gamble away money you worked for—I'm not talking about money that was given to you. But if you gon' gamble away your hard earned money, then you don't need it."

After being introduced to Scrooge as the individual who just shot the security guard in the mall, he wanted to hear from me, what had happened? So I gave him a step-by-step account as to what had taken place in the mall. He listened attentively as I spoke, interrupting only once to ask me to clear a particular part.

After he was finished with my debriefing, he then asked me, "So what are you going to do, because you know that you can't go home?"

"I don't know," I said.

He suggested to me, "Well, ya know, you could sleep by me until the heat die down."

Later that evening when I had phoned home, Vanessa asked me with deep concern in her voice, "What you done? Because the police was just here looking for you. It happened that one of the guys who were arrested at the mall was from the Hood, and he did a lot of singing in custody.

On that same day, some other Rebellions had attended a fair (a gathering and sale of goods with entertainment) where they beat up some rival gang members and ran them out of the fair. Then there was a group of Rebellions from a different area who destroyed the glasses on a jitney (a privately owned bus used for public transportation service). Upon hearing the latter two reports, Scrooge said to the ten or fifteen of us who were sitting around there, "The Rebellions got an 'A' plus today. We have a shooting in the mall, we beat up and ran the Gun Dogs [they were also a part of the Gun Hawks] out of their own fair, plus break up a jitney - now if that does not deserve an 'A' plus, I don't know what does."

It was the first time that I had actually been graded and commended publicly for anything like this, and it felt darn good. Just like that, I went from being a zero to being a hero in the gang. A good friend of mine named Alfred Williams, who also has a troubled past of his own, but he has really gotten his act together in a big way. Alfred said something rather interesting on this matter, regarding the approval that the gang gives to its members. Alfred stated, "All we need is for someone to put their hands around us and tell us that we did good. It could either be for barking open a coconut [removing the husk from the coconut], or for barking open somebody's head."

It was as if I was the new kid on the block that everyone wanted to see and meet, even though I had joined the gang months prior—but since then, I had been to Sandilands and prison. So it was as if I was new and they were all getting to see my potential for the first time.

News of the shooting had spread like wildfire within the Rebellions. The act itself was one that other Rebellions were proudly owning up to. Yes, it was us, the Rebellions, who did the shooting in the mall. This was unheard of on our little island with only two indoor shopping malls, this just didn't happen.

I had people coming up to me each day, giving me the progress of the security guard who was still in the hospital. I was unable to listen to the news, but apparently, they listened and filled me in.

What I was unable to get from home, and from those who tried to reach out to me from the church, I got from the Rebellions. In the gang I found approval, a sense of belonging and on top of that support. In an article titled *"What Gangs Give Kids That You Don't,"* written by Eugene C. Roehlkepartain, he quotes Dennis Rodriguez, a former gang member who became a police officer. Discussing why kids join gangs, Officer Rodriguez stated, *"Young people don't join gangs to be murderers or criminals. They join because they need to belong to something bigger than themselves. They're vulnerable, just like everyone else; they hurt and cry."*

Chapter 10
FROM A YOUNGSTER TO A MONSTER

"Sometimes human places create inhuman monsters." — Stephen King Bestselling Author
After the shooting in the mall, without even making a conscious decision about it, I knew I had to commit armed robberies. It's just one of those things you know you must do when you're on the run, because you're going to need cash, and so anything goes when it comes to getting it. It's no big secret that when criminals are on the run, they tend to be more aggressive and dangerous. If I'm being hunted down for attempted murder, then armed robberies and other crimes are small stuff. I cannot entirely blame this mindset that I had picked up on my trip to prison. Rather, it is a social truth. You see it in the movies all the time when fugitives are being pursued by the authorities they would commit additional crimes that are often worse. I was now on the run and knew I needed money. I couldn't go back home. I couldn't go back to work. So I put the gun I had in my possession to work instead. My first armed robbery was a chicken shack [local term for fast food restaurant]. I stepped in and ordered a chicken snack. There were two other people ahead of me in line. Once they got their orders and left the premises, I pulled out my gun on the young woman working behind the counter and asked her for all of the money. She ran to the back. I leapt over the counter and pursued her. I thought that she was actually running away from me, but when I got to the back, I found her at the cash register. This was what she was running to; it was situated behind a wall. She handed me the money that was in the drawer, and I went on my way. I couldn't believe how easy that was. I repeated this several more times with several different stores, but each time the take was nothing much to talk about so a fellow Rebellion who went by the street name Bing, suggested that I hit Snack Food on Robinson Road on a Saturday. Bing used to work there stocking their shelves, so I followed him up on his suggestion.

Just one week after shooting the security guard in the mall, I stood in Snack Food on Robinson Road getting ready to rob them. Just as Bing had said to me, Saturday was their busiest day. However the place was too crowded, and this posed a challenge for me. I didn't want to rob a crowded convenience store, so I spent twenty-five minutes or more lurking through the aisles. I was waiting for things to quiet down, while at the same time trying to look like a paying customer. As soon as there were just a few customers left, I made my move on the two cashiers. I pulled out the .44 revolver that had belonged to Scrooge. Since I began staying with him, he had trusted me enough to give me a key to the house where he kept his guns. When he was not around, I just went and helped myself to what I needed. It's amazing how the gang leaders and generals think once you have proven that you are ready and capable of shooting anyone, they will give you access to guns, because they know once you are strapped you will always make the gang look good.
Holding the .44 on one of the ladies, I asked her to put the money in the bag. There was a female customer at the counter who looked at me and then sighed. She rested both of her hands over her bag, pulling it to her body as if to say, "Oh, no you ain't." It was a silent act of defiance. This lady was telling me through her body language, "I don't care who you rob and what you take, but you're not going to have what's in my bag." I dismissed the body language that I was getting from her and focused my attention on the two cashiers, because it was the store's money that I actually came for.
I saw a slight movement to my right, and I pulled out the .22 revolver on a male worker who looked as if he was trying to sneak up on me. I told him, "Don't you even move." Here I was, seventeen years of age, and nobody had ever instructed me on how to commit an armed robbery. Yet I knew just what to do. Those storytelling times in prison made it even easier. On top of that, I've seen it so many times on television that I could mimic exactly what to say and do. So I stood in the midst of four females and one male, with two handguns drawn on them. It was like something from those Billy the Kid western movies. It was just so surreal. This was not me, but in fact it was.

Once the lady finished emptying the cash registers, I snatched the bag and ran out of the store. Where I dashed to the back street, that was behind the building. Where my getaway driver, Bullet, was waiting for me on a motorbike. I hopped on the back of the bike, and we took off into traffic. I knew by the amount of money that came out of those cash drawers that this time I was indeed straight. As a matter of fact, right then I was thinking about purchasing some gray Nike tennis shoes, which was going to go good with my brand-new Nike sweatpants.

As we were zipping through traffic, the breeze felt good as it blew across my face, for we were free as a bird. I just had to smile to myself; that was just too easy. Then I got the shock of my life when I heard the sound of a police car, which was right behind us in hot pursuit. Bullet opened the throttle up for more speed, but the police cruiser was still with us and they were gaining quickly.

During our attempt to cross over a four-way intersection, a car pulled out in front, almost hitting us. Bullet turned the handlebar of the bike hard to one side, and we just barely missed hitting the car in question. However, in doing so, the bike slid to the ground, and before it stopped, both of us were off and running. Looking back now, I could see how fortunate I was then, because I didn't even get a scrape when the bike slid from under us. Eventually, I was caught with the bag of money and the two guns, and Bullet got away.

I later learned that as soon as I had exited the store, two of the workers ran outside and flagged down a passing patrol car. Talk about bad timing; it just couldn't get any worse than that. They told the officers that they had just been robbed and provided the officers with my physical description and the color clothing I wore. They then pointed the officers in the direction where I had fled.

The officers quickly followed up on the information. When they turned onto the back street, they saw us in the distance on the motorbike. They gave chase behind us, and it wasn't until they were almost on our backsides did they cut on the police car siren and that was an out of this world experience. One minute I thought that I was home free, and I couldn't wait to get to the clothing store. The next thing I knew, the police was right on our tails, bringing me out of my daydream of new Nike tennis shoes and Tommy shirts. I knew that we had hit a big score. At least a couple grand was in this bag. Looking back now, that wasn't much money to be daydreaming about, but for a seventeen-year-old kid, it was a hell of a lot to dream about back then. This was a criminal's worst nightmare, but this was my living nightmare—one that I would never forget. The motorbike and I were taken to the Grove Police Station. The bike had belonged to Whitey, but he didn't have a clue as to what we were up to. Once we got to the police station, I was put into one of the holding cells with handcuffs still on my wrists, which were now tight and biting into my hands. There were three other fellas who were already in the cell. I knew two of them from living on the third part of Washington Street. We all probably hadn't seen each other for more than six years. One of them was Lil John, who was surprised to see me after all these years. The police treated me as if I was a serial murderer, by putting me in the cell handcuffed.

Lil John asked me with deep concern in his voice, "DD, what in the world did you do?"

I said to him, "They caught me with two guns."

I could see from the look on his face that he was totally shocked and blown away. But at the same time, I also saw a look of respect. Here was somebody I grew up on Washington Street shooting marbles with, and playing cowboys and crooks. Now some six years later we met again, but on the inside of a holding cell of a police station.

Lil John then asked me in amazement, "DD, you had two guns on you?"

I answered him, "yeah."

Even though I was handcuffed, I stood tall beaming with pride. I never knew what he was arrested for. I never had a chance to ask, because ten minutes later I was taken out of that cell and quickly transported to C.I.D. Head Office in Oakes Field.

When I had last been at C.I.D I was sixteen years old, and had surprised them as to the amount of stores that I had broken into on my own. Now little more than a year later, I would surprise them again. When I got upstairs in C.I.D., I noticed that the bench was full with young fellas and as I took a good look, I saw Apples, Dog Man, and one or two others from Lizzy. Just then, two fellas from Fox Hill stood up. They had also been in the mall on Saturday past. They too had been arrested and were sitting on the bench. The Fox Hill fellas started saying, "That's him there, that's him there who shot the security guard in the mall."

The police officers who had brought me into C. I. D. began to put the items on the desk that I had in my possession when I was arrested. One of the Fox Hill fellas, named Parky, then said, "That's the same gun he used to shoot the security in the mall." He was referring to the .22 revolver that the officer had just placed on the desk. So with my arrest, the police were able to solve two different cases that happened a week apart. Apples would tell me later when we were in a police station holding cell together, "If you hadn't gotten locked up today, I had the C.I.D. convinced that Parky was the one who shot the security guard in the mall."

While at C. I. D., different police officers kept coming in calling my name. When I identified myself by raising my hand, they just looked me over without saying anything. I didn't know why they were doing this, until one of the arrested individuals sitting on the bench with me said, "Soldier, that gun they caught you with must be really special, because you have the whole of C. I. D. wanting to see your face."

Unbeknownst to me, one of the guns in my possession was one of the most powerful handguns in the world. This was Scrooge's .44 Smith & Wesson revolver. Someone I knew told me later that there was a news report on ZNS about my arrest. Of course, my name was not mentioned because I was still a minor, even though I was arrested for committing an adult crime. However, the news report was about a juvenile who was arrested with a .44 revolver. Apparently, the news clip also had footage of the gun that was confiscated, and the reporter wrapped up by asking, "If this caliber weapon was found in the hands of a juvenile, could you imagine what's out there on our streets?"

The .44 Smith & Wesson revolver was made popular by the 1971 movie Dirty Harry, starring Clint Eastwood as Inspector Harry Callahan. Here's a famous Dirty Harry line from the movie itself. Inspector Callahan said, "Being as this is a .44 Magnum, the most powerful handgun in the world, and would blow your head clean off, you've got to ask yourself one question: Do I feel lucky? Well, do ya, punk?"

Yet, for me what stands out the most about my arrest in 1993 was not the caliber size of the weapon I was caught with, but rather the year it was released to the public. This particular .44 was released by Smith & Wesson in 1992. Scrooge actually had a gun magazine with the exact same gun on the front cover. So within a few short months of its release in the U.S., it was already on the streets in The Bahamas and in the hands of individuals who were on the wrong side of the law.

According to the Commissioner's Policing Plan for 2012, of the Royal Bahamas Police Force: Commissioner Ellison Greenslade states the following results of 2011, "Officers all across the Force and, together, we took five hundred and forty one. (541) illegal weapons out of the hands of criminals in The Bahamas."

We don't manufacture these weapons in The Bahamas, it's even illegal to possess or sell a handgun in my country. Yet these weapons can easily be purchased in the US legitimately, and then they turn up on our streets.

It's no secret that the majority of weapons, that end up on our streets are used for the protection of drugs. Yet we are not a drug producing nation, rather drug runners only use our islands because of our close proximity to the US which is their ultimate destination. Therefore, it goes without saying, if the US government can make it much more difficult for firearms to leave their boarders, then they would also make it difficult for drugs to land on their shores simply because cash and guns are what keep drug dealers in business.

However, I was charged for the two guns, the attempted murder in the mall, and the armed robbery. I was still a juvenile, so I went back to juvenile court where I was remanded for the charges. A few days later, I was hauled back before the juvenile court and was sentenced for six months for violating my probation.

Back To School

"My father used to say that stories are part of the most precious heritage of mankind." —Tahir Shah, author of Arabian Nights

   It was during my second trip to prison, that I was polished and perfected into a harden career criminal. I initially shared a cell on the upstairs 'G' Block with two inmates. One was named Carlton; he was a sentenced inmate. I had met him at the Detention Center during my first trip to prison. Our other cellmate we simply called Kobna, who was in my age bracket. Both of them were from the South Beach area in Nassau. It was from each of these individuals I would learn something that would help shape and mold my criminal career.

Carlton was once a disciple of an individual called Bobo Wade. He was a Rastafarian who was notorious for robbing and taxing drug dealers. It is said that he would catch a ride to the race tracks on Sundays, where drug dealers would gather to race and show off their new flashy toys. However, by the time Bobo Wade was ready to head home, he would be driving a way in one of those drug dealer's flashy toys. If they wanted their toys back, well they had to pay him for it.

Bobo Wade was killed by police officers, in the late 80's when I was working at the service station. I could remember that day so well. I was working the pump when scores of police vehicles went speeding down Blue Hill Road heading south. Then 15 minutes later they were followed by an ambulance, along with more police vehicles with sirens screaming in the same direction. A co-worker of mine commented, "Boy, it looks as if something big is happening in the south."

Some two to three hours later, a few police officers driving together pulled up on the pump in a private vehicle. The driver got out and slam his door, then he loudly exclaim, "We finally got that SOB, we got him"

I didn't know who the individual was that he was referring to, but from the sound of it this fella was big. Days later, I would learn that the person who was killed by the police was Bobo Wade, even though it was my first time hearing about him he was revered and feared on the streets. Now in prison for the second time I'm learning more about him, from someone who personally knew him.

I would also learn about other heavy hitters from the South Beach area like Collins Bastian, Morison Cunningham and Eugene 'Gene' Symonette [who today is in a Cuban prison cell for drug trafficking].

Gene was one of the most notorious robbers, that The Bahamas ever knew and he was down with the Rebellions. He was smart, bold and resourceful as they come. They related to me the following story. Gene needed a motorbike getaway driver, for a high profile and daring armed robbery. He selected one out of their area who they called Spicky. They committed the arm robbery, but before they could get away Spicky was shot off his bike by a police officer. Here's where it gets interesting, Gene didn't run away and leave Spicky to fall in the police hands. He turned around and opened fire on the officer, pushing him back to look for cover. He then got Spicky off the ground who was unconscious and drove away with him to safety. Spicky told Carlton, "When I first woke up after being shot, I was in the back seat of a vehicle on the beach with an IV line in my arm, and I blacked out again. When I woke up the next time, I was in a hospital room in Miami Florida."

Yet Gene was a quiet and regular looking individual that one would never suspect of being involved in such crimes. They say that he was really fond of children and the children in South Beach all loved him. It was Gene who Kobna ran with, and it was Kobna who would sharpen my skills on committing armed robberies with each story he told. Kobna's brother is the former Florida State University football standout Kamari Charlton, and ironically, their mother taught at R. M. Bailey during the time I was there.

Gun Shot in Prison

"We have made no progress in reducing the number of substance-involved inmates crowding our prisons and jails." —Joseph A. Califano, Jr., Chairman and President of The National Center on Addiction and Substance Abuse (CASA) and former U.S. Secretary of Health, Education, and Welfare.

It was during my second trip to Fox Hill Prison, that I first saw and experimented with marijuana. I know that some people may find it hard to believe because one would think that in prison, these contrabands would be hard to come across. But in prison, if one has the cash and knows the right set of people, one can get just about anything one wants.

For a lot of the inmates, if you can get your hands on marijuana, then you are saying something. So an average of two or three times a week, my cell mates would get their hands on marijuana, trying to get high. I say "trying" to get high because the dope in prison is normally weaker, and at the same time, they would be looking out for officers. A few times, they asked me to try it, but I would always decline their offer. Kobna himself found it really surprising that I never smoked marijuana or drank alcohol. He once asked me, "If you don't drink, smoke dope, or do other drugs, then how it is that you could commit all those serious crimes?"

Nonetheless, one day they blazed it up and asked me to try a gunshot. I didn't know what that was, but it sounded tough and I liked the name. They demonstrated to me how it was done. Carlton would take a long pull on the joint, and then hold it in his mouth. He would then turn the joint around, with the lighted end of the joint facing his mouth. He cupped both of his hands around the joint, with the joint being held in the middle by his forefinger and thumb. At the end of his cupped hands, where his pinky fingers were, there was a small opening. Kobna would put his nose at this small opening, then Carlton would blow the smoke out of his mouth onto the lighted part of the joint. As this happened, Kobna would inhaled the smoke as it passed over the joint and exited the end of Carlton's cupped hands. The idea behind this is a simple one: one would get an instant and immediate high, because the smoke goes directly to the brain.

Liking the name of this way to inhale marijuana, I agreed to try it. I put my nose at the end of Carlton's cupped hands, and as he blew, I inhaled it deeply. Then I stood up to walk to the back of the cell. Carlton told me, "Now, don't let it out quickly. Just hold it in for a few seconds."

When I got to my little makeshift bed, which was about five feet from Carlton, I blacked out. It felt as if I was in a plane crash. There is just no better way I can explain it. I felt and heard the impact of three hard thuds. When I came to a few seconds later, I was on my knees facing the wall where the foot of my bed was. I knelt there for a while trying to figure out, what in the world just happened? Through my fogginess I heard laughter, which was coming from the front of the cell. When I turned and looked, it was Carlton and Kobna, who were both on the floor laughing their hearts out. Now this was really confusing, because I'm there wondering what's the joke, and why were they laughing so much? Not knowing that the joke was on me.

After they caught themselves and were able to speak, they told me what had happened. Apparently, after I had inhaled the marijuana and took the few steps to reach my bed, my legs buckled from under me, and in coming down, my head hit the wall three times. This was the three thuds that I felt and heard; it was my head bouncing off the wall of the cell. I indeed got high that day, but thankfully, it was short-lived because I came crashing back down to earth. Now, please appreciate that the cell size in Her Majesty's Prison is only six feet wide and ten feet long, which meant I didn't do much walking. It goes without saying that I never experimented with marijuana again.

The Making of a Monster
"You can't create a monster then whine when it stomps on a few buildings." —Yeardlyy Smith the French-born American actress

During my first trip to prison in 1992, I never made a conscious decision to shoot or rob anyone. But after spending seventeen months at the University of Yamacraw [which is the name that some inmates have given to Fox Hill Prison], this time I had chosen to make a career out of crime. I had already demonstrated what I could do. It's no more guessing if I had the nerve and the will to pull the trigger. But worst of all, not only could I pull the trigger without any remorse; I could now do it in such a way that the evidence would not point in my direction. This, to me, is one of my definitions of what a monster is. It is a person who has the ability and the means to commit a violent crime at will. He doesn't fear being caught, because he knows how the system works: if there's no evidence-then he has no case to answer to.

Once I decided to make a career out of crime, I became sponge-like. With my naturally quiet personality, it was sometimes easy for the other inmates to forget that I was there. As a matter of fact, they really didn't care because this was their self-proclaimed moment to shine. They would proudly speak about their criminal deeds, their conquests, and their moment in the media. I've never heard so many masterfully delivered stories as I did in prison. Our oral tradition is alive and well; sadly, it's only alive in our prison system. In prison, I learned more about our out islands than I ever did in school. These storytellers were masters of the spoken word, for they would have everyone's attention and I greedily took everything in. The really good ones were so often caught up in dramatizing their action points that they would be drenched in sweat at the end of their action adventure movies. With the telling of each story, I would eventually become more like them as Proverbs 27:17 states, "As iron sharpens iron, so one person sharpens another." NIV. My mind was now opened up for learning, but I was learning and taking in the wrong things. While in prison, I also became an avid reader. I read more books in those seventeen months than I had read in my entire eleven years of schooling. While other inmates craved a cigarette to smoke, I craved another book to read. Many times, I would go on the gate to inform other inmates in the two neighboring dorms that I wanted to exchange a few cigarettes for a good book. However, the majority of those books were violent crime novels, which also further enhance my education on crime. It was the 17th century English novelist and dramatist, Henry Fielding, who wrote, *"We are as liable to be corrupted by books, as by companions."*

This was how I spend the majority of my seventeen months, learning from the mistakes of others through their stories and reading books.

These storytelling sessions were, in fact, teachable moments for me, directly from the mouths of hard-core criminals and gangsters. These individuals, more than anybody else, were my true teachers, and I became their most attentive student. Patrick F. Fagan and his researchers add to this point by stating, "Prisoners have openly admitted that they found themselves in prison because they were sloppy in their lives of crime and had not perfected their skills. Through mutual exchange of ideas with one another in prison, where they have plenty of idle time to talk and think, they will sharpen their abilities so that they do not make the same mistakes again. Prisons become literal training grounds for more professional criminals. These men become even more hardened and brutal in having to endure the system. Prisons do not restrain, but actually foster crime. "

I also notice while hanging on the blocks that the stories were basically the same as they were in prison where proven gang members traded war stories back and forth with each other. There were guys like Hours, Gray Eyes, Scrooge and Owen, who could take a fight and turn it into a Hollywood blockbuster movie. These settings more than anything else were the training ground for the inexperienced gang members. During these colorful storytelling sessions, they learned what and what not to do in a fight, as well as the type of action and bravery required and expected from all of them. They learned what to say and what not to say when they were arrested. The goal of these real-life story sessions were quite similar to any police department, from the FBI to Scotland Yard and every military organization around the world - these story telling moments were used to pass on valuable lessons learned the hard way in the field.

So for us green, inexperienced, and ambitious young men who had this desire to please, we took everything in. These storytelling moments, or the trading of war stories, were in fact teachable moments for us. These were crucial lessons to be absorbed and imitated—Gang Violence 101.

Franco also contributed to this point by saying, "The young fellas who are hanging around me today, in truth, I know what they are hanging around me for. They are interested in the guns, the bulletproof vests, and the war stories because that is what they come up seeing and so this is what they want to be."

Peer Pressure is Often Unspoken

"We have more to fear from the opinions of our friends than the bayonets of our enemies." —Shelby Foote

When I was growing up, just hearing the term "peer pressure"— I always envisioned somebody trying to force another to do something against their will or belief. I admit this is sometimes the case, but the majority of the time, peer pressure is often unspoken. It is what we say to ourselves internally that causes us to give into the external opinions, forces, and pressures from others. It is more of a struggle within to live up to the views of others, in order to gain their respect and approval.

Case in point: while on remand at prison in 1993, I spent the majority of that time in the 'P' dorm in the Detention Center, which is awaiting trial facility for persons on remand. There was an individual in our dorm with dreadlocks. I wouldn't call him a Rastafarian, but just someone with dreadlocks. Nonetheless, he had this weird tendency after his bath to exit the bathroom, take off his dirty pants, and put on his clean pants by his bunk bed. He did all of this in his underwear rather than just taking his clean pants with him when he went to shower, like all the inmates in the dorm did. The other inmates always got on his case each time he performed his peep show, calling him ill names and raising the question as to whether or not he was straight. I never got involved in their verbal spats, because a lot of my time was spent reading a novel of some kind.

However, one day, the prison officers came in the dorm to do their twice-daily count. This was before the 2:00 p.m. change of the guard. I was just getting ready to exit the bathroom, but stood still for the count; it is customary when a count is going on to stay where you are and keep still. However, our friend Mr. Peep Show stood by his bunk getting ready to change his pants. As the officer came in to do his count, I realized that it was officer Burrows, who everybody just called 'Big B' because of his size, 'Big B' was cool with everyone. As 'Big B' passed, Mr. Peep Show was in the process of doing his thing, when Officer 'B' said to him, "Don't move."

'Big B' continued on with his count, but I guess he picked up some movement from the corner of his eyes, because he spun around and said to Mr. Peep Show, "Didn't I say not to move?"

Then me and my big mouth interjected from across the room, "Look here Bey, sit your sissy self-down! You can't see Officer 'B' is counting?"

Mr. Peep Show shouted back to me, "That's your ma [mother] who is a sissy."

The other inmates in the dorm went silent with anticipation, without a doubt they knew that this was going to be a fight. Without even thinking about it I shouted back, "I gon' show you who is a sissy right after this count."

When 'Big B' was finished counting, instead of leaving the dorm, he turned around and looked at me. Everybody else did the same thing. They all turned and looked at me. The other officers standing at the gate waiting on 'Big B', did the same by looking at me. It was like, "Okay, you said it. Now do it."

So here I was, eighteen years old in prison, having never learned how to win the battle in my mind. I was now bound up by my own words. If I did nothing, then I would be the sissy. Without thinking or any sort of direction from me, my feet started to carry me toward Mr. Peep Show's bunk. This was now a fight.

This individual and I had been in the same dorm for about a month, and had never even spoken with each other until now. When I got to his bunk, without saying a word, we started to exchange blows. There was no anger or animosity between us. It was a dry, emotionless fight, but that didn't lessen the impact of our blows. We both were trying to inflict maximum damage on each other. However, in a matter of seconds, the fight was all over, for I eventually knocked him to the ground somewhat dazed. Officer 'B' then came and snatched him by his collar, pulled him to his feet, and said, "Let's go." He was taken out of the dorm and placed in another dorm downstairs, and a few minutes later they sent for his possessions.

The next day, one of the prisoners from the work crew [the work crew consisted of sentenced inmates who come over from medium security to keep the area clean and also serve the food to the inmates on remand], called my name with such authority that I thought I was in trouble.

I thought that he was told to inform me to pack up my stuff to go to maximum security. But when I got to the gate he looked me up and down, and with a sly grin on his face he asked, "The fellas downstairs want to know what you beat homeboy up with?"

I was first of all relieved to know that I wasn't being transferred to big jail. But I was puzzled and even repeated his question. "What I beat up homeboy with?"

He explained, "Everybody wants to know if you used a can of sweet milk, because homeboy's face is really swollen up pretty badly."

The only thing I could've done was laugh, and then I said, "No, man, that was a straight up fistfight."

The other inmates who stood around the gate with me proceeded to fill him in on the fight, telling him how it all went down. To be honest, I didn't even know what had happened because it all happened so quickly, and I didn't look at him when it was all over.

I walked to my bunk, feeling somewhat smugged to know that the damage my fist did, could pass for an unopened tin of sweet milk. However, I thought to myself, "Just suppose the results were reversed? I would now be the laughingstock of the Detention Center. Those who were laughing with me today would've been laughing at me, all because I was unable to resist their silent stares."

From the time I was in primary school, the calling of someone's mother always evoked a fight. They could speak ill about our fathers all day long, but the minute something ill was said about our mother, oh, that's a fight. This is something I share with my son from time to time. Don't let anyone play you like a puppet on a string. Don't let what someone else say cause you to act foolishly. You are only going to end up in trouble. So what if they refer to your ma in an improper way. They don't know your mother. Even if they did, what are you going to prove? Yes, they may say something nasty about her or me, but don't let what anyone say to you give you a reason to fight. If you do, it is a sign of weakness on your part because you were unable to control yourself. Then I would quote to him Proverbs 12: 16 *"Fools show their annoyance at once, but the prudent overlook an insult." NIV*

Chapter 11
THE ULTIMATE LESSON FROM PRISON

"Loose lips sink ships."

It was during my second trip to prison, where I would learn the ultimate lesson from a rival gang member named Jackson Clarke. Jackson was an up coming general in the Gun Dogs gang from Bain Town. Both he and another Rebellion general called Rugged were charged with the same murder case, even though they were from different gangs. Apparently, a shooting took place in a nightclub and both of them were identified as two of the three shooters.

We were downtown in the Central Police Station, all of us having come down from prison together. Another inmate was passing our holding cell, escorted by a police officer. The inmate then stopped in the front of our cell to say to Jackson, "Boy, they gave me twenty-five years." After he left, Jackson gave us the run down of the guy who was just in front of the cell. His name was Jimmy, and he and Jackson were in the same cell at prison. Jackson said, "Do you know that Jimmy was just several days away from freedom?"

Apparently, Jimmy was serving a short prison term in First Offenders. This is the part of prison mainly for those individuals who are soon to be released. However, he had a tendency of getting in small, petty arguments, and his way of trying to win these arguments was to tell people, "You don't know me, you don't know I done kill before."

This was his national anthem while in prison, but Jimmy would then go on to make the ultimate mistake. One evening after the prison was locked down, Jimmy and a small group of inmates had just finish smoking some jailhouse dope. After they were all high as a kite, Jimmy told his dope buddies who he had killed. Unfortunately, he couldn't keep out of those petty arguments, and one day he got into a heated quarrel. This time it was with one of his dope buddies, and he went on to repeat his famous line, "You don't know me, I done kill before."

However, this person was on a work release program, and of all places, he was stationed at C.I.D., the section of our police force responsible for investigating such crimes. His dope buddy readily passed the information on for the murder in question was an unsolved one. So just days before Jimmy was due to be released from prison, C.I.D. officers came to the prison and took him for questioning. The long and short of it was when he came back to the prison a day or two later, he was charged with murder.

I learned two crucial lessons from this: Firstly, never talk about a crime with someone who was not there. Committing a crime for me was like a love affair. The information was sacred and something to be jealously guarded. The crime was only to be discussed with the person with whom I had committed the act with. With anyone else, it was strictly on a need to know basis. Yet I knew of many individuals who would sit down and just rattle off everything they did. This was something I never did, and whatever information I would've passed on, it was with individuals I knew I could trust.

Secondly, after Jackson told us the story, I recalled Jimmy's face and the anguish that I saw there. His expression was that of a defeated man. I made up my mind right then and there: I'd rather be beaten to death by the police during an interrogation any day, than to spend twenty-five years in prison wishing that I didn't fold up under pressure. I was not going to become one of those professional jailhouse storytellers. I would rather be dead and resting in my grave. There would always be a lot of people alive who could tell my stories far better than I ever could.

My Second Fight in Prison
"Getting involved in an argument that is none of your business is like going down the street and grabbing a dog by the ears." —Proverbs 26: 17 GNT.

Even though prison can be a very dangerous place, I learn if you could keep out of people's way and out of idle chatter you would avoid a lot of unnecessary problems. In the dorm that I was in, the number of inmates range from 20 to 30 who were all on remand for mainly non-violent crimes. I guess the only reason I was allowed to stay at the Detention Centre was because of my age. We slept on wooden bunk beds which were made by sentenced inmates.

After about four months of being in 'P' Dorm, I moved to a bunk bed at the very back of the dorm to get far away from the Television set which was to the front. I preferred to be at the very back of the dorm where it was quiet and more conducive for me to read my novels without interruptions. I can remember on several occasions after reading a book all day, when I made my way to the front of the dorm to watch the evening news, a couple of the inmates asked me if I had been to court because they didn't see me all day. Ironically, each time I was asked this question it was on a Saturday, a day in which our local courts do not convene.

I have come to appreciate that prison is just like the free world where you have different classes of individuals. Those with money hang together, however, in prison one is befriended for the sake of property (goods/products) that are sent to us by our family members. There was an individual by the name of Keith who went out of his way to befriend me, and move himself on the bottom bunk bed where I slept on the top bunk. One day Keith was playing a card game with a small group of inmates. In the dorm the inmates usually occupy their time with card games, board games and dominoes. After their game a heated argument arose between Keith and another young man who was much bigger than Keith. At first I did not pay much attention to the argument. I figured that they would just get tired and the argument itself would come to an end. However, the young man that Keith was arguing with his voice kept getting louder. I lied there in my bunk watching him and wondered to myself, 'Why does Keith always get himself in these petty arguments?' This one he was not going to win and I could tell that he knew it. However, the young man in question kept raging on, and he looked as if he was about to attack Keith at any moment.

I reluctantly came down from my bunk with the intention of being a peace maker. If Keith was sharing bunk with somebody else, he would have been on his own but because we share the same bunk, and often share our property together I decided to intervene.

I said to both Keith and the young man in question, "Look man that was only a card game. You'll don't have to carry on like this."

Keith agreed with me by saying, "This fella just can't take his loses, he's making noise over a silly card game."

The young man in question then turned his attention on me, and then started to argue as if I was the one who told him that he couldn't take his losses. His anger had now shifted away from Keith, and was fully directed at me. Keith realized that he was in the clear, quietly slipped away and went and sat on his bunk, leaving me there on my own trying to calm down this young fella who was working himself into a full blown rage.

I kept quiet while this chap was raging on, because I realize there was no reasoning with this guy. So I let him blow off his steam, believing that after a while he would calm himself down. However, he took my silence for weakness, and as he was arguing he kept walking up and down the dorm really working himself up. By this time the dorm was absolutely quiet everyone's attention was on us. I'm standing there wondering how in the world I got myself in this mess.

I look back towards our bunk and saw Keith making himself a bowl of cornflakes, yet here I am taking the brunt of his problem. It was now obvious that this guy and I were going to fight, because he was not going to calm himself down. And to be truthful, I was somewhat intimidated because this fella was taller and much thicker than I was. He was now getting ready to walk past me again, but as he did so he made the ultimate mistake. He suddenly threw his hand in the air as if he was going to slap me. I guess he did so to gage my response, but it had the opposite effect because without thinking I reacted and attacked him. I honestly cannot say exactly what all happened, because I somewhat went into a blind rage and when I caught myself, I heard him screaming, "Okay you win, you win, okay you win."

He was up against the wall, my hand was around his throat and I had been slapping him repeatedly. After he said," I won", I release my grip from around his throat and backed off from him to see what he was going to do, but he just walked past me and went into the bathroom. I stood there waiting for him to come out, so we could start round two. I was ready to continue this fight. The Dorm was in complete silence. You couldn't hear a pin drop. After he did not exit the bathroom right away the Bosun of the Dorm, Mario Deveaux went into the bathroom and came back out a few seconds later laughing.

He said to me, "Man that fella isn't coming back out. He is in the bathroom sitting down with his head in his lap. It was at this time the entire dorm erupted in laughter, and one by one the inmates came up to congratulate me by shaking my hand.

Some of them were saying "Boy Deal, I thought he had you, because all that noise he was making a while ago, and you were just quietly standing there."

The inmate that I had fought with never came out of the bathroom that night. I was told some two hours later that he was in their filing down the end of a tooth brush on the concrete floor. This meant that he was making a jail house shank in an attempt to stab me. By this time, it was probably after eleven' o' clock at night and the prison was already locked down, and I did not want to call the officers just to say that this fella was in the bathroom filing down his tooth brush. However, that meant that I was not going to sleep that night, because I did not want to be awoken by having something rammed into my midsection.

At first there were five individuals who were telling me, "If he comes out of the bathroom with this jailhouse shank, they had my back". As the night wore on and we got into the early morning hours, one by one they drifted off to their beds starting with Keith. So around two 'o 'clock in the morning I stood there on my own again wondering how I got myself in this mess. I looked at Keith who was fast asleep. It was then that I promise myself, "I would not fight anyone's battle again, if they are not going to be at my side throwing blows with me."

Here I am, having intervened on someone's behalf and the person whom I reach out to assist he's off in la, la land. I'm standing on guard and cannot sleep, because there is a mad man in the bathroom sharpening down his tooth brush to stab me. Fortunately for me, I was used to pulling morning especially when I was on the road committing shop break-ins. When the guard changed over, I heard the prison work crew. I called one of the inmates and ask him to call Inspector Anthony Hines. I had never dealt with Inspector Hines before, but from my time being at the Detention Center I knew that he was an officer who dealt with everyone fairly. Mr. Hines came to the gate and I told him what had happened the night before. I was honest and up front with him. He called for the young man who was still in the bathroom at this time perfecting his toothbrush.

Inspector Hines asked him, "What are you doing in the bathroom?"

I thought that I was being honest, yet this guy blew us all away with his honesty. He quite calmly said to Inspector Hines, "I'm filing down a toothbrush to stab him," pointing his finger towards me.

Inspector Hines, who is originally from the Caribbean Island of Barbados, put both of his hands in the air as if to say, 'I can't believe this.' He shouted to one of the officers downstairs, "Bring the keys mon, bring me the keys now, mon."

The young man was taken out of the dorm bareback and bare feet. Just five minutes later I saw a prison officer escorting him handcuff to maximum security. It was then that I went to sleep vowing to myself to never be put in that position again. I promised myself to never carry someone else burden, if they are not prepared to help me lift it.

How Crime Can Often Ruin a Family
"The wrong we over look, is often the burden we will later carry."

I believe that the toughest part about prison for me was not the horrible and deplorable conditions that existed at Fox Hill Prison. Instead, it was the absence away from my family. This more than anything else was the most unbearable part. This was the toughest part I had to overcome. At one point, I had to remind myself constantly, "Drexel, your family is just beyond those prison gates. They are right out there. You are still on the same island with them, so just ride this out."

When I reached the one-year mark of my time behind bars in prison, on a night when everything was still and quiet, I wept and wish that I was charged with a petty shop break-in case.

During the thirteenth month on remand at Fox Hill Prison, just like before, my court appointed lawyer, Mrs. Joan Ferguson, convinced my mother and me to have me plead guilty to everything. She reasoned that the offenses happened while I was a juvenile, so I would be sentenced as a juvenile. My mother agreed to this, but she refused to let me plead guilty to the attempted murder charge. I guess to her, the crime of attempted murder sounded too serious for me to plead guilty too. There was just no way for her to determine how the courts were going to deal with me pleading guilty to such a crime. Yet my lawyer knew what the outcome would be, and that outcome was just six months in prison.

Yes, it's amazing what a minor can get away with in our judicial system. Our courts do not allow a minor to be charged as an adult, even though they might be accused of committing adult crimes. Ultimately, the court was unable to prove the charge of attempted murder against me, but it took almost an additional five months for them to do so.

Yes, I was arrested with the gun, but first of all, the police never did any ballistic testing on it to say with certainty that this was indeed the gun that shot the person in the mall. Secondly, of all of the witnesses that were called to testify, none of them was able to place me at the scene of the crime. So reluctantly, the magistrate had to dismiss the case against me. I pleaded guilty to the rest of the charges. They had caught me red-handed anyway.

Having been on remand for more than seventeen months, once I pleaded guilty, I was given six months for each offense. Each six-month sentence ran concurrently with each other. (This meant they all started together rather than starting one after another.) Therefore, I was released from prison that same day, because my seventeen months on remand was far more than my six-month sentence. So by law, the judgment handed down had to be counted as time served, which is a common practice. I was released by the juvenile court at the age of nineteen.

This time when I came back to the streets, I knew that I was a changed person. In fact, I was now a predator who would be dwelling among humans. I entered the system as a troubled youngster, and the system spat me back out as a monster. My mind was firmly established in a life of crime, and it was highly unlikely that I was going to change. Those seventeen months in Fox Hill prison were like a training ground of some sort. I was not only capable of pulling the trigger, but I also knew how to clean up my tracks behind me.

The law is a simple thing, and it basically works the same way in most judicial systems around the world. If an accused person is unable to be identified, or if the physical evidence to connect the accused person to the scene of the crime is lacking, then it becomes quite difficult to get a guilty verdict. So with that in mind, after months of fine-tuning and honing my skills, I left the "University of Yamacraw" with my bachelor's degree in crime, and my intern work would now begin in earnest. This was now my chosen life—my calling, as the religious community would say.

Upon my release, I quickly discovered that things were pretty rough at home. The telephone was disconnected and the cupboard was bare. My mother was also renting out one of the bedrooms for additional income. My sister Vanessa was no longer living at home, and was pregnant with her first child Leon whom we all call LJ. He would be the only one of my twelve nieces and nephews whose face I would see before losing my sight.

I was released on a Tuesday, but by that Sunday, I had run into a little more than three thousand dollars. I simply fell back on what I knew best, which was shop break-in. In all my years of shop break-ins, this was the largest amount of funds I had found in a building since I started, but there would be a whole lot more to come. I gave my mother sufficient funds for herself, and to reconnect the telephone service. Then my sister Quannie and I went out that Sunday morning to buy groceries for the house.

When I gave my mother the money, I told her that this is what I was going to do for a living. I asked her not to worry about me, because I believed that I have this thing down pat. What does a mother do when her only son tells her that he has chosen crime as a career? What could a mother say to her child to persuade him otherwise? What does a mother do when her child gives her money that she knows he didn't work for? To top it off, things are rough—the telephone is off, the cupboard is bare, and she is behind on her bills.

I have discovered in life that it is easy to condemn the action of others, especially if you haven't been there yourself. Looking back now, here's what I can honestly say: my mother should have turned my cash down. She should have said to me, "Drexel, as much as I love you, I cannot just stand by and watch you destroy your life because you will also destroy ours at the same time. I know that I could use the funds, but keep it to find a place of your own."

However, when she accepted the cash that day, she was also accepting my chosen lifestyle. At the same time, unbeknownst to her, she was also signing my own death warrant. As noted in Proverbs 19:18, my mother became a willing party to my death. After she accepted the money, this meant that she would also accept anything I bring home.

Case in point: the stolen goods she wouldn't allow me to bring in her house, to the point where she would toss me out, now little by little those same stolen goods started to make their way back inside our home. I am not talking about simple and small items; rather, I'm talking about valuable appliances, two thousand-dollar stereo systems, a VCR for each room in the house, plus more. I only brought home the best, and everything was always brand-new. It was the 16th century Spanish Jesuit, philosopher and author of, *"The Art Of Worldly Wisdom",* Baltasar Gracián, who stated, "Never open the door to a lesser evil, for other and greater ones invariably slink in after it."

Yet, these were things we didn't even need, because my mother did a good job in providing for us all. She had quality stuff of her own; my mother always had good taste in furniture and appliances.

Now here's the sad part: when I lost my sight some 18 months later, my mother held at least four patio sales [same as a garage/yard sale] to get rid of all those stolen goods. During those patio sales, she had to raise money because I was no longer bringing home an income. Even the stuff she had bought legitimately, she was selling them as if they all were stolen by letting them go for very little.

The point here is this: when we accept or turn a blind eye to our children's wrong deeds, then we as parents will help bear the load of their punishment. It's pretty simple, the person who is contented to overlook a wrong, must also be contented with one day carrying its burden.

Shop Break-ins Were a Means to an End

" Any time you take a chance you better be sure the rewards are worth the risk because they can put you away just as fast for a ten dollar heist as they can for a million dollar job." — Stanley Kubrick the American film director, screenwriter and producer.

I had no problems being charged with petty crimes, for I was not seeking status, rather I was seeking only cash. As far as I was concerned, the police could have arrested and charged me with petty cases all they wanted. I had no problem being charged with shop break-ins and stealing. I could live with that; to me they were small cases. It was these lesser crimes, I noticed, that the police gave very little attention in winning in the courts. Rather, they focus their resources on getting convictions in the more serious cases that they still often lose. One time, Denny, his younger brother Donny, along with Troit and I left a nightclub downtown together. We then broke into a popular appliance store in the Palmdale area. While inside the store, unknown to us, we had set off a silent alarm. The alarm led to police and security guards surrounding the building. Fortunately for us, I had covered our tracks as to how we got into the building. I knew from experience that if an alarm goes off, and the police or security guards comes to investigate but can't see any telltale signs of forced entry, they would usually just leave, considering it a false alarm or a glitch in the system. So we were determined to ride them out, thinking they would eventually just leave after a while.

We were on the upstairs portion of the building, so Donny came up with this bright idea to open the upstairs door to get a peek at the scene outside. He said that when he did so, a police officer pointed a shotgun at him and told him not to move. Donny quickly shut the door, locking it, and ran to let us know what had just happened. I had now resigned myself to being arrested. My only concern was how the police were going to do it. Were they going to send dogs up at us, or were they going to come in themselves with guns blazing?

Troit, on the other hand, was horrified at the prospect of being arrested and charged for shop break-in. He couldn't deal with that, the idea of him being a top gangster from East Street and Lizzy being arrested and charged with such a petty crime. It was below him and could damage his reputation. However, I preferred shop break-in over a street crime any day, especially those ones where money was found on the premises.

So on that night I began to make up a bed for myself—nothing else I could have done; might as well get some sleep. However, Troit wasn't having that. He was determined to get away. He found some unused hacksaw blades and quietly began to saw at the steel bars. He then found a phone in an upstairs office, and then called Ricky, a Lizzy Rebellion who had transportation. Troit got Ricky to drive to where we were, and look around the building outside for us. Ricky had agreed to return home within an hour to receive Troit's second call. At this time, cellular phones were not main stream. When Troit called Ricky back, he told Troit that he had not seen anyone around the building, and nothing looked out of place. Once we got the word that the outside was clear, we now debated who would go out first. Everybody was reluctant to be the first to go down, especially after Donny said that a police officer had pulled a gun on him. Since this was my plan I agreed to go down first, to confirm that the coast was indeed clear. I was somewhat puzzled as to why the police would just leave us in the building, so I went down thinking to myself, that this was probably a trap to lure us out. However, much to our relief there was no trap, and we were all able to get away. Troit left vowing never again to break into another store.

Denny and I were completely un-fazed, because this was what we did. The next night Denny and I went back, and raided the very same store.

In all of the petty street armed robberies that I had participated in, the most I ever got was about six hundred dollars.

Compare that to shop break-ins, I've stolen thousands of dollars and that didn't even include the stuff I could sell. Now what was the minimum sentence for a street armed robbery? It was fifteen years the last time I checked not to mention that I personally know of individuals, who spent that kind of time and more for less than two hundred dollars. On the other hand, the maximum sentence for a shop break-in was only eighteen months. There was just no comparison. During my research I was surprise to stumble into a news clipping, which made me aware that I was not the only gangster with such a mindset. Under the heading, 'Counterfeit Goods Funds Violent Gang Activity' - this news piece was featured on KABC-TV Los Angeles News, and done by one of its reporters David Ono on February 10th 2010. Mr. Ono reported, "LAPD investigations show that gangs are deep into the counterfeit goods business, enabling gang members to fund illegal activities. It takes low risk but yields high reward."

"They're making more money selling pirated CDs and DVDs than they would selling narcotics," said LAPD Senior Lead Officer Randy McCain. "They make a lot of money and they make the money faster."

"We've found it tied to murder, extortion, human trafficking, insurance fraud," listed Kris Buckner, a former L.A. County Sheriff's deputy. Buckner now trains law enforcement personnel on how to spot and investigate counterfeit goods. In the past couple of years, we've seen a huge surge in gang members, 18th Street, MS-13, 42nd Street Little Gangsters," said Buckner. "Why? It's all about economics."

"They're now trying to run their organizations like Fortune 500 companies. They need to raise revenue, but if they're out there shooting each other, doing drug sales, their potential to make higher revenues is actually lower," explained Buckner. "So every time you buy a fake Fendi or a knock-off Chanel, you could be putting cash in the pockets of some of L.A.'s most dangerous gangs, including the Mexican Mafia."

This was why I couldn't care less about being arrested for shop break-ins, there's nothing macho about being charged with a serious indictable crime. Unlike me, Troit had never spent seventeen months on remand for a serious indictable offense, to do so one would wish that one had been charged with a petty case. He didn't know that those high profile cases were sometimes the most expensive, longest, and hardest ones to win. He didn't know yet, but he would soon find out, that those cases were also stressful and burdensome on your loved ones. Troit would soon learn this the hard way. Just a few months after this incident, he went on the run for murder. He was caught several weeks later and charged for the offense. He was subsequently convicted for the offense and sentenced to death by hanging.

I began to notice that whenever things were rough for me, I always turned to shop break-ins, and it was these petty and minor crimes that always lead to more serious and violent crimes. I would purchase guns with the funds found in those stores, and those guns were then used to commit any number of crimes from armed robberies, to drive-by shootings and more.

However, this is what the 'Broken Windows Theory' crime fighting concept is all about, which was made public by the social scientists James Q. Wilson and criminologist George L. Kelling back in 1982. They reason, "If a window in a building is broken and is left unrepaired," they observed, "all the rest of the windows will soon be broken." So too, tolerance of small crimes would create a vicious cycle ending with entire neighborhoods turning into war
zones. But if you cracked down on small crimes, bigger crimes would drop as well." Shop break-ins were more or less my trade; this was the one thing I was extremely good at. Once inside a building, if money was on the premises I was going to find it. There was no store that I was unable to get into. Once I made a small penetration of a building, just enough to see inside and to get a smell of the interior, this in itself was enough to motivate me to get inside. After getting into a couple of difficult buildings, most times I would be drenched in sweat. It was for this reason I used the Bible to justify what I was doing. I would wipe the sweat from my forehead, and then I'd quote to myself Genesis 3:19, which states, *"By the sweat of your brow you will eat your food."*
Yes, I knew what I was doing was wrong, but by quoting scripture, I felt justified in what I was doing. I wasn't stealing anybody's stuff; rather, I worked hard for whatever I got. But as William Shakespeare wrote, *"The devil can cite scripture for his purpose."*
The problem is this: whenever we start justifying our wrongs, what we are in fact saying is that we have done no wrong. If another person were in our same position, he or she probably would've done the same thing. It was the Russian Novelist, poet and the Nobel Prize winner in literature Alexander Solzhenitsyn, who stated, *"It is in the nature of the human being to seek a justification for his actions."*
The justification of a wrong can never make that wrong right. There are a lot of individuals who are on death row today, and if one listen to some of the reasons why they did what they did, one could sometimes identify with them or even sympathize with them. But at the end of the day they are still wrong, and that's why they are where they are today. I like how Joyce Meyer puts it, the Charismatic Christian speaker and bestselling author she stated, *"Justified means just as if you've never sinned."*

Chapter 12
The Birth of the Rebellions

"We had a genuine love for each other, and we loved being around each other, and in the gang was where I felt love. This is where my heart was and I was not putting anything before the gang." —Troit Lynes, former death row inmate of Her Majesty Prison

In the next two chapters, we will look closely at the conditions which gave birth to the Rebellion Raiders and many other gangs. Even though today the gang is not a shadow of its former self, but in the early '90s it was the most revered, feared, and respected street gang in The Bahamas, boasting of close to ten thousand members. We will first look at the rise of the Rebellions and, in Chapters 15 and 16 we will then look at its fall.

Why did the gangs flourished during this particular time in our country's history? More importantly, why did they flourish when the traditional family unit was declining? There's a huge lesson to be learned regarding the value of the family, for when the traditional family unit of a father and mother is compromised and laid aside, then our young ones will violently rebel and buck against society.

To get started on the right foot, I'm going to let Troit Lynes a.k.a. Taco introduce the major players who started everything. I believe that Troit is the most qualified person to do so, for he was the first member of the Rebellions to be convicted for murder and sentenced to death by hanging. In my interview with Troit, he said, "Everyone who I called my friends, persons who I used to hang out with, these were the individuals who formed and made up the gang known as the Rebellion Raiders. So when the gang was formed I was automatically a part of it, because it was formed by my friends. I didn't have to go out and join the gang.

When I was growing up, there were three guys I looked up to in my area. One was KC [a.k.a. Barkley because of his Resemblance to the NBA player Charles Barkley]; he was the father of the Rebellions. Everyone in the gang and the community at large respected him. He was a no-nonsense fella. I also looked up to Scrooge [would become the leader of the gang after KC's death]. He was more or less my next-door neighbor. I used to live just two doors down from him. There was also Ada, who was the individual who came up with the name 'Rebellions.' I wanted to walk more in their footsteps. I wanted to be like them."

I asked Troit, "What was it about them that made you want to be more like them?"

Troit said, "To be truthful, I used to feel good in their presence. I used to feel wanted in their presence. I used to feel appreciated in their presence. In their presence, you can sit down and talk and you can feel that they appreciate you."

In the bestselling self-help book of all time, which is *'How To Win Friends And Influence People'*, written by Dale Carnegie he quoted the successful businessman Charles Schwab who stated, *"The way to develop the best that is in a man is by appreciation and encouragement."*

In my interview with Scrooge, he confirmed Troit's point by asking me, "Do you know the reason why fellas liked hanging around me? It is because I made them feel appreciated and respected. If you were a scary fella but you are good at stealing cars, then be good at that. This is where your respect is coming from."

He then asked me, "Do you remember the fella they call Skid?"

"Yeah, he's dead now," I said.

"You're right", answered Scrooge, "but he was an A-1 thief. Skid could have gone in the premier jewelry store on Bay Street, slip behind the counter, remove the key from off the hook, open the closet, and steal a whole band of watches. That's how good Skid was, and that was where he got his respect. You have to respect a person for what he can do, and you can't judge him to the fella who shoots ten people who feels nothing, goes to jail and come out and shoots ten more. You have to make people feel that whatever you are good at, we appreciate and respect you for that."

It was the American author Ralph Marston, who said it best, *"Truly appreciate those around you, and you'll soon find many others around you."*

Scrooge continued, "We had a lot of fellas who were in the crew. They were scary and I knew that. In every crew, you have your top fellas and you have your scary fellas. It's like on a job where you have 20% of the people bringing in 80% of the results. So you have certain fellas in the gang for different things, and that's what you have to look at. You can't look at everybody out there in camouflage as somebody who will do damage, and at the same time you can't take them lightly."

Supt. Allerdyce Strachan adds to this point by saying, "A lot of those young men were just looking for love, and they got that love from Scrooge. They were not perhaps able to get it from home or from no one in the community. So instead of holding on to Scrooge, they could hold on to me. That was the way I looked at it. If Scrooge could get a young boy to follow him, I should have been able to get one to follow me as well so why can't I as a police officer do the same? I found out by reaching out to them, a lot of them did not realize what they were doing. Some of them were saying that they were a part of the Rebellions from the time they were nine years old."

It was the NBA legend Ervin Magic Johnson who stated, *"All kids need is a little help, a little hope and somebody who believes in them."*

Supt. Strachan stated that these individuals were looking for love, which echoes Troit's quotation used at the opening of this chapter: "We had a genuine love for each other, and we loved being around each other and in the gang was where I felt love. This is where my heart was and I was not putting anything before the gang."

I asked Troit, "What do you mean when you say, 'You were not putting anything before the gang'?"

"My life was the gang, and I wasn't putting anything or anyone before it."

Troit then went on to explain his point further by saying. "I could remember a good friend of mine. We grew up on the Fort Hill together like brothers, [the Fort Hill is a part of Mason's Addition a rival gang area of the Rebellions]. So even though this friend of mine was living in Mason's Addition, I was convinced that he was not hanging with the Mason's fellas nor mingling with the enemy.

But there were persons in my gang who had reasons to believe otherwise, that this friend of mine does be hanging with the Mason's group. I could remember clearly when my gang members told me this, and me being loyal to the gang, I went up to the Fort Hill, collected him and put him into a vehicle, and brought him through Strachan's Corner. I told him brother, if you joking, you gon' get it. When I took him down through there, a few fellas put couple of big slaps on him, but I only allowed them to go so far. This was how committed I was to the gang. Whether it was a good childhood friend or a relative, you cross my gang, you cross me."

Gangbanging Was our Drug

"I have absolutely no pleasure in the stimulants in which I sometimes so madly indulge. It has not been in the pursuit of pleasure that I have periled life and reputation and reason. It has been the desperate attempt to escape from torturing memories, from a sense of insupportable loneliness and a dread of some strange impending doom." —Edgar Allan Poe

In my interview with Apples from Lizzy, he said something that I always knew to be true for me when he stated, "Gangbanging was our drug." As I've said already, I knew that this was true for me, but I never expected it to be true for him as well. He went on to explain, "Looking back, I have come to realize that the gang lifestyle back then—the fame, the respect, and the recognition—was stronger and powerful than any drug. We were serious with what we were dealing with. It was like a do or die situation."

I remember listening to Apples on a radio talk show some time ago, sharing his personal story. He was asked by the host, "Do you think that drugs and alcohol were a major factor, as to why you and so many young men were attracted to the gang lifestyle?"

Apples simply answered, "No."

There was a slight pause by the talk show host. I guess that this was not the answer he had expected. However, to Apples' credit, he realized that the host was surprised with his answer, so he illustrated his point. "A lot of the young men who I was gangbanging with, we never use to drink nor do drugs. One day, a young lady I was interested in invited me over for lunch. This was during the time I was deeply involved in the gang. Her parents were not at home, for this was in the middle of the day. This young lady had cooked a nice dinner that she set before me on their dining table. However, to my surprise, after I had finished eating this wonderful meal, she came and put a half point of gin on the table in front of me as to say, 'I know that you are a gangster so here's some gin to wash your meal down.'"

To this day, this is a widely accepted perception that most people have of gang members. I do admit there were some of us who use to smoke marijuana and drink, but this was not the norm in the Rebellions. As a matter of fact, Scrooge had a no-nonsense approach to dope smoking.

Apples then said, "A lot of us who were from Lizzy in particular, those who were in the front line of leadership, we were not drinkers or smokers. We liked to party and have fun, go to the dance/nightclubs, and we would take our tool [gun]. If we see fellas we had to deal with, then we dealt with them. When you look at it, Scrooge was never a drinker or a smoker. I knew he would drink his Guinness every now and then, but other than that, that was it. Then there was Troit, he never used to drink nor smoke. And I could call off a lot of fellas who never used to drink nor smoke, and yet they were die-hard gangsters."

Then he stopped and asked me, "Do you used to drink and smoke?"

I just smiled and answered, "No."

Satisfied with himself, Apples said with passion, "My point exactly. When we were gangbanging out there, that was our drug. It was the lifestyle itself that got us high."

I was almost tempted to remind Apples that this was my interview, but he was indeed right. We were addicted to the thrill we got from violence, for every brawl was different, every shooting was more glorious than the one before. Violence was like a sport for us. We were not only trying to break the record of others; we were also looking to break our own records from our previous violent deeds.

Again it was Camila Batmanghelidj the founder of the charity, 'Kids Company' in London, she stated, "Children who have been genuinely loved will not get a high from humiliating others, they will not seek to express their terror in terrorizing… These children are emotionally cold and nihilistic; they don't feel anything unless it's the excitement of pursuing their prey and the release of victimizing someone else."

Scrooge also added to this point. "I never smoked marijuana or any other drugs in my life, and many people find this hard to believe. As a matter of fact, do you remember that the fellas couldn't hang around me smoking marijuana?"

However, Troit would provide some insight about the drug we were all on when he said, "When I went to prison and came out, it was like another stripe being added to my shoulder— another notch of respect on my belt. On the streets, you cannot get a name until you do something. You have to prove who you are by doing something outrageous, like shooting someone from a rival gang. It allowed others to see what type of person you were, and established the fact that you were ready for anything."

He continued, "Back in the day, what we were looking for was for someone to have our backs. So every time I did something and was recognized for what I did, it gave me more nerves to continue. After the deed was all said and done, and we were hanging on the blocks, everyone is praising you and talking about what you did. You all should have been there. You should have seen how Taco rushed up on that fella and dealt with him."

Troit now reveals this drug and its harmful effects, "Those praises were like drugs that eventually poison the mind, and gave you more inspiration to do things to have more people talking about you. People recognizing you as one who isn't scared, one who is ready to do whatever is needed.

No one ever wants to go to prison. I never wanted to go to prison. I just wanted to be recognized as one willing and ready for a battle anytime. So each time I got into a problem and got locked up, and when I came out, the fellas on the street knew I was not telling the police anything, which added more to my creditability and respect."

Troit Continued, "I used to actually hear guys who I respected and looked up to say, the only fellas they would do things with and they would call three names, and my name was among the three. These were individuals they know they can trust. These were individuals who won't tell the police anything."

Note: When Troit stated he never wanted to go to jail, the truth of the matter is every young man growing up on the street and getting into mischief, his aim is not prison. It is just that the need to be recognized and respected is greater than the fear of being arrested and going to prison.

The Making of the Rebellion's

"It's so easy for a kid to join a gang, to do drugs... we should make it that easy to be involved in football and academics."
—Snoop Lion

In my interview with Ada, he said, "The event that changed my outlook on life into one of crime and violence and the gang lifestyle was one day a mob surrounded our family home. My older brother, Tyrone got into a fight where he ended up stabbing several fellas in the process. He ran back in the area, and some twenty or thirty fellas came with knives, baseball bats, cutlasses, and guns. You name it, they had it. They came around our house, and I had my little brother and sister in there with me. The mob outside was saying that they should just pull down this door and kill this girl. For me, that was my turning point. Prior to that, my friends and I was just into breakdancing."

Ada went on to speak about their different groups. "There were always several different groups in our area. The guys I used to hang out with were into breakdancing. Scrooge's group used to call themselves the Truck Boys. They used to go wandering around the neighborhood stealing sea grapes and guineps [local summer fruits]. Then there was KC, who was a bit older. His group was into playing basketball."

Scrooge now explained how he got into the crew. "I never understood why, but the best of girls like gangsters. This was something that was always odd to me. Here, you have fine working girls who are involved with someone who isn't working, just sitting on the blocks all day with a big gun in his waist. For some girls, they like that. I don't know why."

In the same newspaper article headlined, 'Galloway Boys are back on the street' that I quoted back in chapter eight, which was published in the Toronto Sun of Canada, and written by Chris Doucette. He again quotes Dr. Anthony Hutchinson, a former gang member who adds to Scrooge's point. By explaining what happen when he pulled a gun out in school. "Some guys from school were laughing at me, so I pulled it out and they quickly stopped laughing, and girls were suddenly interested in me because I was the bad boy." Scrooge continued, "When I came out of school and got my first job, I remember saying, 'Here I am, a young man working and with a car, yet I cannot get any fine girls. There were guys who were older than me and were not working, just sitting on the blocks all day playing dominoes or playing basketball yet they are getting the finest girls in the area. To top it off, she also has a nice job, and I'm wondering how this could be?' This was how I got into the crew. I said, 'let me hang with these fellas to see how they do it. How do they go out there and get these fine girls when I can't get none?' Even up to this day, I still don't know how fellas who don't work, who are not interested in nothing in life, yet have some of the finest women. I am still trying to figure this one out." Author and youth Pastor at Bahamas Faith Ministries International [BFM] Dave Burrows who is better known as the Roughneck Pastor, because of his troubled past with drugs and many run-ins with the law. Pastor Burrows adds to Scrooge's point. "I believe one of the biggest challenges that females face in the Bahamas is dealing with a dysfunctional male population. Too many young males in our country do not have any ambitions. They don't want to go nowhere. You have a lot of females trying to achieve things in life, but they get hooked up with males who are basically delinquent. Males who are aimless, with nowhere to go, and it hampers their ability to have a decent family or create a good life. Because for many of them, they end up with a guy who ends up in jail or they have children for him and he disappears."
Scrooge continued by saying, "So I was sitting down hanging with the fellas them just for the girls, because really and truly this was bugging me. How could these fellas have the finest girls in the community, and they don't work, they don't have any money. Anytime something has to be purchased they would say, 'Man, Scrooge, throw the blow; buy this and buy that.'"

"So we were sitting on a car one day. They were out to a disco the night before and this fella got chopped or stabbed. I didn't know anything about it until the fellas came around looking for KC the next day. These fellas just yuck out their guns and started busting shots, and everybody just break off running for their lives. Afterwards I mumbled to myself that these are some crazy fellas. They just came shooting for no reason. The funny thing about it is this: guns were not even that common on the streets then. We're talking around 1987, 1988. I believe the fella who fired those shots at us, goes by the nickname Dog and he lives in the US now."

Scrooge continued, "I said to Ada, 'What kind of thing this is? I mean, these fellas came and just started shooting.'

That sent a whole new way of thinking in my mind. Prior to that, I was just a person going to work, coming home, and chilling. I just happened to be sitting there one day. They didn't know me and they didn't care who I was. I never used to even be with KC and them. I just happened to be there that day. If I had known that those fellas were crazy like that, to come shooting at whoever they saw, I wouldn't have been there hanging with KC and them. After that, my whole mindset changed. It was either shoot or be shot."

Taking Their Stand with the Purchase of a Gun

"The general who wins the battle makes many calculations in his temple before the battle is fought. The general who loses makes but few calculations beforehand." —Sun Tzu, The Art of War

Scrooge talked about the problems they inherited. "The mischief and fights we got into with other areas were passed on to us from the older guys like KC and them, who were going to nightclubs and getting into fights. These were the fellas I was looking up to. So the problems they got into at nightclubs brought guys from different areas looking for them during the daytime. When they opened fire on us, that was when I realized—these fellas are willing to get at KC and them by shooting anybody. I then said to Ada that we have to put up together and buy a gun, because this is ridiculous. You could lose your life like this. So that was how I got involved in the crew.

Ada and I made the decision that we will save and put up our funds together to try and buy a handgun. The first weapon we purchased was a little .22, and back in those days it was only your .22s, your .25s, or a .38, which was the biggest handgun on the streets then. So the next time a scene happened at the dance and these fellas come around, we now had a .22. It wasn't long before some fellas came looking for K.C. and them, and that same little .22 came through for us. I guess just hearing the sound of shots busting back at them scared them and they started to run even though they came firing on us first. We now had them running and we were all running behind them with this little .22.

We kept busting, busting shots at them. When we came back and sat down on the truck, it was like a feeling out of this world. We were like muddoes [local slang for surprise or amazement], we just ran those fellas, hey. That's good, that's good so from then we started to go to the dance with the bigger fellas. Even though KC and those were into a lot of fistfights, we realized you can't fight that kind of fight with the people who they were fighting with. It can't work like that. That's why for the most part they were always losing. So when we came into the picture, we just turned it around. We started to fight fire with fire. If those other fellas could have guns, we decided that we are going to have guns also."

Scrooge continued by saying, "Once we started to fight KC's and those wars, we decided that we might as well go out and have fun with them. So they accepted us even though we were much younger. They were around 21, 22, and 23, and we were like 16, 17, and 18. So when we defeated those fella's who came around looking for them, I guess they said you know what these little guys are capable of hanging with us. They seem to be ready to accept whatever came their way. That was how we got accepted by KC and them. It was like a good feeling to go to a disco with these big fellas, because 10 to 1 most of us couldn't get into a disco but they were respected by the doormen at the discos they frequented, so to us it was like a big thing. Hey, we were at the disco, we were in the nightclubs. They introduced us to the nightlife; on the other hand, we took it to a whole other level."

Scrooge went on, "I thought to myself, 'If we just ran those fellas from our area and we are now going to discos, we better be ready at all times.' One thing I always told the fellas when I was thugging, 'I ain't going no place where my gun cannot go, and if it can't go, it has to be close.' So I always ensured that we had a gun on the scene. There was always a little fella who would be with us, but he would be standing a little ways off by himself strapped, so if any scene kicked up in the clubs, it was always us on top of the situation just by having a gun right on the scene, where we would be in control of the situation. Even before KC died, I had said to Ada and them, 'You know what? We done conquer this going out to disco thing, so let's just chill on our blocks.'"

Ada revealed how the Rebellions obtained their name. "One day I was watching the cartoon She-Ra, and the episode that was on was called 'She-Ra and the Mighty Rebellions.' At that time, the gang was already formed and was on the move. We were already getting involved in territory fights. This was when the Syndicates was out [the Syndicates was the first street gang ever to be established in The Bahamas; however, they were put out of business by the Rebellions]. One day we were on the wall, and guys were throwing out different names. I told them that the best name for this gang would be the Rebellions. To this day, I'm sorry I ever came up with that name, because I'm getting tired of seeing that name on the walls throughout Nassau."

The Rebellions' First War
"Do not protect yourself by a fence, but rather by your friends." —Czech Proverb

We continue with Scrooge who said, "Our first major war came about from going to Junkanoo practice in the Mason's Addition area, [Junkanoo is the ultimate Bahamian cultural festival]. We went on the park in Mason to watch the Junkanoo practice and somehow something started up where we ended up fighting with the Mason's fellas. They had guns, but we did not have any with us this night. They had the upper hand and they won that first battle. That was the first crew we ran into. It wasn't really a crew because they were not organized. It was just a bunch of fellas hanging together on the park. And when you get into mischief with one, you get into mischief with all. So even though we lost, we learned from that. It was the whole area that had risen up against us because we were from another area. They ran us from around their park, but we learned a good lesson."

Scrooge said, "We came to realize that we lost that battle only because they stood together as one. So if we could stick together like how they did, we could do the same thing as well. We were stronger than them and had some experience under our belts, from the various fights we had gotten into at the nightclubs. So we really started sticking together even more, and looking out for each other.

"The next time we went to watch the Junkanoo practice, even though we were on their park, we were ready," said Scrooge. I guess they figured they ran us so easily the last time that they would now keep us from around their park. When they tried that again, it did not go their way this time. We ended up running them from off their own park and out of their neighborhood."

"When we came back home on our blocks, here again we were happy. To us, that was one of our first real victories—to actually go in someone else's area and run them out of their own area. It was only like thirteen or fifteen of us. Even though we were few, we felt like we were carrying a lot of weight. Now it was time to go to Junkanoo. We ran into these same Mason's fellas again, which was a starting trend of the different areas sticking together. So we are going to Junkanoo minding our own business, walking up East Street Hill but the fellas in Mason's Addition ran us right back down the hill where we couldn't even go to Junkanoo, at least not from that route."

Scrooge then said, "Here again this was another lesson for us, because what the Mason's fellas were in fact saying to us was, 'You fellas didn't remember that you just run us from off our own park. Now you have the nerve to walk over East Street Hill?' We lost another battle but learned another important lesson. 'You can't assume that nothing is dead because you won, unless you are sure it is dead.' So we got run down the hill. A few persons ended up getting burst in their heads with bottles and rocks."

"Now after Junkanoo, we were sitting down talking about the whole ordeal. Ada said to me, 'Boy, Scrooge, these Mason's fellas, they're starting to be a problem.' I said to him 'Boy, that's how it looks.' Then Ada started to run down a list of issues that we were having with them. It seems as if we can't go on the park to Junkanoo practice, or anything they are having on the park. We can't travel over the hill to Junkanoo. It's like we can't pass them in peace. In the middle of this same conversation we were having about the Mason's fellas and the problems they were giving us, out of nowhere came this big crew of Mason's fellas, who came just shooting at us. We had to run out of our own area from them into another area to talk about these guys. They really were our biggest, biggest problem, I could say, especially at that starting point."

"As a matter of fact," said Scrooge, "we were not really looking at ourselves as a crew. We were just looking at ourselves as a couple of fellas hanging together. But those Mason' fellas had an idea of what a crew was about. They probably were a crew established in their own mind and in their own neighborhood. Even though the potential was there, they never branched out. They just wanted to be left alone. As to say, 'We who live in Mason's Addition—don't mess with us, and everything will be cool.'

I quickly realized that was what they wanted. But I realized we had to make a statement by going back at them."

He continued, "So, Ada and I started talking to the fellas through our corner. We pointed out to them what we all were up against by saying, 'You saw how those fellas came shooting at anyone who they saw so whoever they catch will be beaten badly, you might as well join up with us and let's make a move around there and see who we could catch. I had to do a lot of talking and putting my words together to convince the fellas to fight back."

"All of that talking paid off, because we were able to put together a nice-sized crew. It was at least thirty or forty of us, and we had two guns. I could remember clearly a .22 and a .38 that wasn't working properly. You had to line up the bullet in the chamber with the hammer of the .38 before you pull the trigger, but it used to make a loud bang. To be honest, back in those days that was all you needed, for something to go 'bang' to get fellas running. The rest of the fellas who was with us were carrying bottles, rocks, baseball bats, knives, and cutlasses."

He then said, "We made our move on them around 8:30 to 8:45 p.m. and caught them totally off guard because they had underestimated us. They thought we would never come back at them, especially how they came in our turf and ran us out of our own area. We caught a lot of them on the slunk [a local term for just loafing around. At least fifteen fellas who didn't get chopped up got stabbed or burst with bottles and rocks. We actually did them worse than they did us, because when they ran us out of our area they came through firing a lot of shots, but everybody got away. Nobody was injured."

"When we crept up on them, we only had two guns and the most shots those guns had in them were three shots each compared to when they came at us. I don't know who was arming them because they had shots to waste. For some reason, when we caught them this time, that put a little fear in them—so much so that we didn't get any response back from them. We rightly felt as if we were even, and we left it at that."

"I then said to Ada and the rest, 'You know what? We don't have to worry about the Mason's fellas, because all we have to do is obey their simple rule, which was not to mess with them and they will be out of the picture.' We quickly realized that was what they wanted, and left them alone. These were a bunch of crazy fellas, but all they wanted was to be left alone. When you look at it, they don't go to Junkanoo and they don't really go anyplace. They are not affiliated with anybody; they just keep to themselves in their own community. As tough as they were, once we respected their simple rule, they would be out of the picture.

I then told everybody," Scrooge said, "since all they wanted was to be left alone then let's leave them alone. It is not as if they want to conquer and take over our whole area, but if you trouble them, there will be some consequences. So the word got passed down to everybody that Mason's fellas and everyone associated with them—leave them alone. This simple acknowledgment of what they wanted worked for them and us because we respected what they wanted."

"But us, we wanted more, we got greedy," said Scrooge. "I said to our fellas after everything had settled down, those Mason's fellas could've control East Street as tough as they were—and they really were some tough fellas. They had some name-brand fellas in their crew who could have really done some damage if they had hooked up with other areas. If they wanted to, they could have been a force to reckon with, but they only wanted to be left alone and to live in peace in their area."

The Rebellion's Fight with the Border Boys

"One man with courage is a majority." —Thomas Jefferson
Again we pick up this continuing story with Scrooge, "We decided okay, one down; let's go to the next area on East Street. From our experience with the nightclubs fights, and dealing with the Mason's fellas, it would just be a cakewalk. We went over to Hay Street, the Border Boys' area, where we ended up taking their area over, at least for a while. It was more like a park thing. Every area had a park and they used to have their festivals on the park. We would just go out there and take the park over. We were a lot more organized when they were not, and we were battle tested when they were not. We would harass their females, whereby we were daring the fellas to do something about it. We were running that area for a while, but the fellas then took a stand against us. I guess they decided, 'you know what, we need to fight back against these Strachan's Corner fellas who are coming around here and doing whatever they want to do, and we are not doing nothing about it.'"

Scrooge went on to explained, "This all came about because of one person, Nelson Mandela Cooper. It was him who had sparked some fire in those fellas to fight back. The Border Boys' first attempt was successful, because only a few of our fellas were on the park and they ran them off. When we heard about it, we went back and chopped a few fellas, gun-butted a few, and put them back in check. But this Nelson fella was just unruly, and for the most part, it is always just one person. Even though he got beaten the worst, he still wasn't going to play dead.

"Nelson was their turning point. They rallied up and they rallied up big—at least some thirty or forty fellas," Scrooge said. "Back in those days, thirty or forty fellas were some big numbers. Don't forget, this was about the same size of our crew. They fought back against us strong. It was not as if they overpowered us. But what they did was put us in a position to realize that it wasn't safe to go in their park unless we were going full force, and we didn't want to go full force in an area every time. So we left their area alone because it seemed as if they wanted the same thing as the Mason's fellas wanted, which was to be left alone."

In 1996, some weeks after giving his life to Christ, Nelson went in the Mason's Addition area to share his faith. As he was leaving the area to go home, somebody opened fire on him, shooting him in his neck. He died some days later in the hospital. No one was ever charged with his murder. Every year in the month of July, Pastor Carlos Reid and his group 'Youth Against Violence', puts on a basketball tournament in the memory of Nelson Mandela Cooper. Their slogan is, "Shooting hoops instead of Guns."

The War with East Street Top Drug Dealers
"The wicked covet the catch of evil men." —Proverbs 12: 12 NKJV.

It's rather interesting to note, that even gangsters expect drug dealers and major companies to give back to the communities that they profit from. This was what led to the third war undertaken by the Rebellions, which was between drug dealers Stinky and his brother Robert, who were Ada's half-brothers.

Ada now picks up the story here. "I was working for my brothers selling drugs, and I was making some good money. However, my brothers were trying to get me to sell out on my friends, and to turn my back on the very same fellas I grew up with. They were telling me that I needed to stick with them and make this money, and forget about those fella's I grew up with. My main reason for not considering their offer was that I saw how they were treating their workers. They got them to turn against their friends and family members. On the other hand, if these workers were to rip something or to come up short, they used to beat their workers half to death. At the end of the day, I had to choose between my brothers or my friends, and I chose my friends, for these were my true brothers."

Ada concluded, "I didn't push the war between my brothers and the Rebellions, because that war was going to happen. It was just a matter of time."

Scrooge picks up the story here by saying. "Stinky and his brother were doing quite well for themselves selling drugs, and one day KC said, 'You know what? These fellas are selling drugs and they are making a lot of money, but they are not doing anything for nobody.' So this whole mood and animosity kept growing to the point where I had to ask KC, so what you gon' do?"

Scrooge said, "KC replied, 'Man, let's talk to these fellas and let them know, if they are going to be selling drugs in our area making money, then they need to do something for us.'"

"KC and I went around there. He was the respected person among the older fellas and I was the respected person among the little fellas. We went around there to Stinky and them and said what we had to say. Not long in our conversation with them, I realized that they were going to work with us. They didn't look down at us as to say, 'Who the hell you guys think you are trying to tax us?' Rather, they were talking pretty nice to us and then they asked us, 'So what you'll want?'"

Scrooge continued, "I guess they saw our wars between the Mason and the Hay Street fellas, and knew that we were not a bunch of bad fellas, but that we could cause them some problems. The kind of business they were in, they did not need any problems simply because they were into making money, and we were just into making a name for ourselves. It would be a no-win situation for them to go to war with us so they told us, 'We can't give you money all the time, but we could give you something and you can start something the same way we did.' That's when KC asked them, "What you'll going to give us?' They said, 'We could give you a kilo of cocaine and a pound of herb [marijuana], and you could start the same way we did.'

KC was like, 'Man, that's good, that's good.'"

Scrooge then said, "That very same night, KC went to the disco with his fellas and them to celebrate, and that's when he was shot and killed. He and I were supposed to go back to Stinky and them to pick up this kilo of coke and this pound of herb the next day. When KC got shot and died, I guess they felt like this little fella, we don't have to respect him. KC is now gone. When we made that deal, it was only because of him. This other person, Scrooge, we don't have to fear him."

"I then laid the case on the table to the fellas. You know, before KC died, we had talked to Stinky and them where they promised us a kilo of coke and a pound of herb, but now they are going back on their word all because KC is dead. They probably feel that they don't have to respect me, but they already promised us something and now they are going back on their word. We have to do something. Ada jumped up and asked, 'What do you want us to do?'"

Scrooge said, "I asked Ada, 'Man, they are your brothers. You want to go up against them?' Ada replied, 'Man, they ain't doing nothing for me, so let's do it.' I was like, 'Okay, let's do it.'"

"We went around there with a nice-sized crew, and we break out all the glass and windshields of their cars and trucks. They were in their yard just watching the destruction, and that ran them hot. They came through the corner, but we were ready for them, having experience with other fellas running us out of our area before. We knew where the best spots were for us to fight them. It was almost impossible now to beat us in our area. When they came around with all the guns they had, they didn't know where to shoot and who to shoot at. They didn't know where we were. We only had a couple of shots and one gun. We would bust a shot from behind a house, run around the next way, and bust another shot. Then we'd run around the next way and bust another one, and to them it sounded like it was a whole bunch of fellas with guns."

Scrooge went on, "Even though they had us outgunned and way more ammunition than us, we were able to outsmart them because we knew our area. After a while of not knowing who to shoot at, and who all were shooting at them, they just freaked out and broke off running back into their area."

It was Sun Tzu, the ancient Chinese military general, strategist, philosopher, and author of the bestselling book *'The Art of War'*, which was written more than 2000 years ago. Sun Tzu stated, *"Hence that general is skillful in attack whose opponent does not know what to defend; and he is skillful in defense whose opponent does not know what to attack."*

"So we considered that a win," said Scrooge. "A few days later, they sent a message with Ann, one of the girls living in our area. 'Tell Scrooge we need to talk. This isn't making any sense, because you don't have anything to lose, but we have too much to lose.'"

Scrooge continued, "When we went around there, a lot of us stayed hidden in the shortcut, and I asked Crazy Horse [another one of the gang's lieutenants] and two other fellas to go and see what they were saying. As soon as Horse walked into their yard, all I heard was gunshots starting to go off. Horse ran back with a limp, shouting, 'I got shot, I got shot.'"

"It was a setup," Scrooge said. "They couldn't beat us in our area, so they drew us onto their turf, where they could have the upper hand. They had us outgunned, but not outmanned. I guess they had some fellas in there who they were paying to do whatever when we showed up. I told a few of the guys who were through the shortcut, 'You go get Horse.' They ran out and got Horse, lift him up, and went running through the shortcut with him. We started to make our way back into our area, and the fellas who shot Horse started to come through the shortcut at us. But I was able to keep them at bay, because I was busting back at them."

"We managed to make it back in our area without anyone else getting shot. When they shot Horse that was a major blow for us, because this was the first time any one of us had gotten shot before. During all the time we were having our little battles, there was never any serious injury. We took him to the hospital. Now it was an all-out war with Stinky and them. They set us up; they couldn't be trusted no more."

Scrooge continue, "Later that night, we went back around there and bust couple shots at them. But they were waiting and they bust couple shots back at us. Everyone was alert and ready. Then Stinky and them went to the Mason's fellas as well as the Border Boys. They got them involved by paying them off. They put them in the front line to fight with us, because the Mason and Border Boys did not have anything to lose and we did not have anything to lose either. Our backs were now against the wall. We were now warring with the Mason crazy fellas, the Hay Street fellas we were harassing, and now they have a chance to get even with us, plus still fighting against Stinky and them.

Scrooge concluded, "We were up against all of them, and for the first time without K.C. It was then I realized that we were up against too many fellas and now the odds were greatly stacked against us. We were outmanned, outgunned, and we were scraping money to keep buying ammunitions. I knew we had to try and branch out if we were going to be able to defeat them."

Again General Sun Tzu puts it this way, *"He who knows when he can fight and when he cannot, will be victorious."*

Chapter 13
When Underdogs Unite

"When spider webs unite, they can tie up a lion." —Ethiopian Proverb

With their backs pushed against the wall from three different groups, the Rebellions were outnumbered, outgunned, and out-resourced, and KC, their revered and trusted leader was dead. Their enemies were basically right in their backyard; they knew that they had to get help. But where could they find battled ready fellas to link up with in the middle of a war? It is interesting how they would overcome this hurdle and go on to become the largest street gang in The Bahamas.

There's an important lesson here that gang members are teaching us. It's a lesson for the family, a lesson for the church; it's a lesson for our communities and our nations. As the seventeenth century English novelist and dramatist Henry Fielding wrote, *"What's vice today may be virtue tomorrow."* There's only one way to win the war on crime, and it is by coming together. When one looks at it carefully, it's also Biblical. As God himself once said, *"If as one people speaking the same language they have begun to do this, then nothing they plan to do will be impossible for them." Genesis 11:6.*

Once again we turn to Scrooge as he filled us in on how the Rebellions dug themselves out of this hole. He began, "I knew we had to make something happen, and we had to do it quickly, or we faced extinction like the Syndicates. One day, Troit came to me and said, 'You know what, Scrooge, there's a whole crew of fellas in Elizabeth Estates [Lizzy] who are ready.' So I asked him, 'Troit, are you sure a whole crew is in Lizzy? Troit responded, 'Yeah, a whole crew is up there.'" Scrooge said, "I told Troit and others, we need to make a move that way and see what's going on. When we went up there on their park, it was a whole crew of fellas just like Troit said, and I mean a real crew. I told them, 'You all might as well link up with us because we are at war.' So the first area we branched out with was the Elizabeth Estates fellas."

Troit explained his role connecting Lizzy with East Street. He said, "I had an aunt who was living in Elizabeth Estates, and when things got hot between Mason's Addition and Strachan's Corner [Troit was then living in Mason's Addition], instead of going home, I would go and stay in Lizzy by my aunt until the heat died down. While I was staying in Lizzy, the young men in the area always looked up to me. They admired me and the way I conducted myself. I was viewed as a leader. The young men who carried the weight at that time, the leaders in Lizzy, I was down with them and we were cool. One of the things I did for them was to provide them with an easy access to guns. When they needed to do something, I would tell them to check me because through my connection on East Street, I always had access to guns. It was because of this that I helped them to step up their game to the next level."

Even though Troit was still in school, he explained how he was able to get his hand on a gun. "It was due to the way I carried myself that I was able to borrow a gun from someone like Scrooge, when many other individuals who were a part of the same gang were not able to borrow a gun from him. Scrooge was the kind of person who was not going to put a gun in anyone's hand, because they must have the right temperament. They cannot be careless nor do stupid things that would cause his gun to get thief or lost. Neither someone who would cause unnecessary problems, nor a person who like to just show off was unable to borrow a gun. You must be someone who would first of all protect his gun, and at the same time be able to deal with anything that came up. Likewise, if something was to happen where you were to get locked up, you would not call his name." Troit then goes on to say, "I was either in the 9th or the 10th grade at school, when another gang member and I put our funds together and purchased our first gun. The leaders at that time believed so much in protecting the name and the reputation of the gang, that I along with one or two other individuals who were still in school who were trusted, responsible, and ready were given weapons to take to school to make sure that if anything arises, the matter would be dealt with properly. They made sure that even if their presence were not there during a fight, we were in a position to properly defend ourselves."

We now pick up the story with Shelton Burrows, a.k.a. Apples, who was one of the leaders from Lizzy and who has also made it out of the gang. But Apples came from a community that was divided against itself. The front part of Elizabeth Estates was warring with the back part but then the front part linked up and joined forces with the guys from Fox Hill.

Apples provided me with some history on how the front and the back ended up at war with each other. He said, "We all grew up together riding bicycles in the area, and the split or war came about as a result of bike parts. Some guys from the front stole some bike parts from the fellas from the back. This resulted in one or two fights, which eventually led to Elizabeth Estates being subdivided into a front part and a back part, and it just started to get worse. The lines were drawn."

"I, who lived in the back, couldn't go in the front, and those who lived in the front couldn't have ventured to the back. So it started very small, from a fistfight to cutlasses and knives, and eventually those fellas from the front part started hanging with the guys from Fox Hill. All of us attended the same school, which was L. W. Young on Bernard Road, so when the front linked up with Fox Hill, we who was living in the back of Elizabeth Estates were greatly outnumbered. We had to fight our way to school in the morning, and we had to fight our way out of school in the afternoon. With that linkage between the front and Fox Hill, they were much stronger than us."

Apples now explained that both the back and the front had a link on East Street to the Rebellions. "Berto [who was the head of the front, today he is in Cuba serving time for drug smuggling] had a link with Rugged [a general in the Rebellions], because Berto used to live off East Street and him and Rugged were tight (close friends). Fatty, who was the leader for the back, and I, also used to live off East Street in the Plato Street area, and we were close as a result of that. Then there was Troit. He had an aunt who used to live in the back, and so all of us became good friends."

Apples continued, "Rugged, who was older and had more rank than Troit at the time, tried to get Berto and the front part of Lizzy to link up with East Street, but that couldn't happen because the front had already aligned themselves with Fox Hill. Then the Fox Hill fellas were in bed with the Kemp Road fellas, and East Street and Kemp Road could never have gotten along, so that couldn't happen. To top it off, Troit was going to C. I. Gibson at the time, which is basically in the Kemp Road territory, and he was having problems with those Kemp Road fellas. Whereas we, the fellas in the back had no ties and so it was easier for us to link up with East Street."

Now this was shaping up to be rather interesting, because here you have two groups who were basically fighting a losing battle. This was something that didn't register with me during my interviews, but both of these groups were the underdogs. The Rebellions and the back of Lizzy were facing the same thing, for not only were they outnumbered, but also their enemies were both in their faces. Lizzy's enemies were pushing from the front, and the Rebellions' own were pushing from the rear. So they were being pushed away from each other and not toward each other.

On top of that, these two communities were not even nearby each other. Lizzy is situated at the eastern end of our island, and the Rebellions, whose base was on East Street, were more centrally located. This meant that they were some six to eight miles apart. If you asked me, this wasn't much of an alliance, especially when both of their enemies were in the front and in the back of their yards. As a matter of fact, in the day of trouble, even scriptures state, *"A neighbor living nearby is better than a relative far away."* Proverbs 27:10.

On top of that, they didn't even have a vehicle of their own. They were hitching rides just to link up with each other. So how did they overcome their enemies and go on to become the largest gang in The Bahamas and in the English speaking Caribbean?

We turn back to Scrooge for more information, as he continues to explain the linkup with other areas. He said, "Then there was Biggie and Smallie [identical twin brothers who were only distinguishable by their size]. Biggie and Smallie were now living in the new subdivision called Flamingo Heights in the Carmichael Road area.

They told me, 'There is also a strong crew in our area, and these guys are not into nothing. All day long, these guys are on the park playing basketball, talking foolishness, and slamming down dominoes."

Scrooge continued, "So we drove out to Carmichael Road, where we were packed into two cars. When we got there, I stepped out on the court where they were playing basketball. I stopped the game when I pulled out my .44 revolver and bust a shot through the basketball, and one through the backboard of the rim. After which everybody was standing there dumbstruck, with their mouths open just looking at me. It was as if they had never seen anything like this in their entire lives. But for us, we were already living this lifestyle on East Street, where shots were being fired constantly, and people getting shot was just a way of life. Once I had their attention, I gave my little speech. I told them you guys might as well join up with us. There is a whole crew of you guys and it's a whole crew of us on East Street. It was as if these fellas from different areas were just waiting for this, because no one else was going around to them. No one else was telling them that they were needed, only us."

It was Dr. Jawanza Kunjufu, an educator, publisher and the author of over 25 books including his national bestseller, *'Countering the Conspiracy to Destroy Black Boys'*. Dr. Kunjufu quotes a notorious gang leader who stated, *"We will always get the youth because we know how to make them feel important."*

In my interview with Ms. Iris Adderley she said something quite similar, when she stated: "One of the things we haven't taught our people as a nation, that this is their country. We haven't told them that this Bahamas belongs to them. Whether it succeeds or fails it is entirely up to them. WE haven't told our people that they are valuable. I sometimes pass little boys playing in the road and I would stop my car and say to them: 'Excuse me baby, do you realize how valuable you are? Do not play in the road, if anything happen to you that is going to hurt us. Because you might be our Prime Minister one day."

Scrooge continued, "The good part about these areas that we were taking over, was that all of them had parks where a lot of guys were just hanging out playing basketball. So I used those parks to make a good first impression with my gun, then I followed up with a speech presentation. At the end of the day, we were able to win over the entire park, and eventually their community."

Here again linking up with Carmichael Road was nothing major, if you ask me, because these two communities were separated by more than eight to ten miles. Carmichael Road is located on the southwestern part of the island. But again, let's turn to Scrooge to see what happened.

He said, "After we had linked up with Elizabeth Estates, they came down one Friday afternoon. It was about forty or more of them, and more than forty of us. With the crew being so big, we decided to go around by Stinky and them for a little action. They had one or two guns among them as well, and we had three guns with us, so altogether it was about ninety of us, with four or five guns in the crew. When we went around there this time, the damage and destruction was even worse. We broke up all the glass on their vehicles again, and we were able to shoot a couple fellas this time. No one got locked up for that incident, because with a crew that size you don't know who did what.

I guess that Stinky said, 'Hold on, hold on, this is not making no sense.' So he cut the Mason's fellas and the Border Boys off by telling them to stay put in their area, because they didn't had anything to lose. Even though we were at war with Mason and the Border Boys, we were directing our efforts at Stinky and them. As the holy scripture puts it, "Without wood, a fire goes out." Proverbs 26: 20 GNT.

Scrooge continued, "So Stinky and Robert came to the reasoning table again, but this time it was only for peace simply because we were starting to be a problem for them. So this time when we went to the reasoning table, it was nothing about drugs. It was just for peace sake. When we talked again they said, 'Look here, let's put this down. If you get in trouble and need a little help, you could call on us.'"

Scrooge continued by saying, "Out of all the other gangs that were around, you could always have come to the reasoning table of the Rebellions without being fearful and present your case, and whatever is decided at the reasoning table you know that is what it will be, whether it's war or peace. Unlike the other gangs that were around, you didn't even know who to talk to.

Scrooge continued, "After we talked and everything was agreed upon, they told me that they were having a party and to bring everybody down. So I told everybody that the warring was over with those fellas, and Stinky and Robert were throwing a party on the beach. The party was held on a beach out west, so we went out there. It was like a hundred of us, and they also invited the Mason's fellas and the Border Boys. They had a lot of beers and food, because you know, they had the money. So you are looking at more than two hundred fellas, and everybody is partying like a war never took place, and that was the end of the war on East Street."

However, Scrooge would go on to say something rather interesting, when he said, "Through all of those different wars, we came to understand each other. The Mason's fellas just wanted to chill in their area and be left alone. The Border Boys basically wanted the same thing. Stinky and Robert just wanted to be able to sell their drugs and make their money. But us, we were on a mission to take over the whole town."

Isn't it sad, that these neighboring communities were only able to know each other better through a gang war? But couldn't this have been better achieved through sports and other structured activities on their parks? As Scrooge mentioned, every area had its own park, but there were no structured activities and no positive outreach programs being conducted on them. The young men in the community were left to languish and to figure out how to best use their time, their talent, and their energy on these parks.

It was the criminologist James Allen Fox who stated, "Too many children are coming out under socialized and under supervised. They have too much free time on their hands. Literally time to kill."

LeBron James, who is regarded as the best player in the NBA today, said something quite similar, "Sports carried me away from being in a gang, or being associated with drugs. Sports was my way out."

How are we providing a way out for our young men today? What way out are we going to provide for our young ladies? What plans do you have, to reach the young people right in your community? How effective are our outreach programs, are they reaching the youth, running them or missing them entirely?

Now, what's the lesson here? First, when two underdogs come together as one, they don't become a stronger dog; rather, they become a lion, and in this case a rebellious one as with East Street and Lizzy.

Second, as stated in Genesis 11:6, they were all one, even though the two communities were miles apart. Yet there was a common understanding among them, for everybody was on the same page. Lizzy took on the Rebellions' war, and the Rebellions took on Lizzy's war, which led to the front and the back part of Lizzy eventually uniting.

Third, they went at the root of their problem rather than taking on the branches. As Scrooge indicated, they didn't go at the Mason or the Border Boys, because those two groups also had nothing to lose, and were probably in it just for the fun. Rather, they directed their limited resources at the root by targeting Stinky and Robert, who were funding everything. These were the individuals who had everything to lose. Whose vehicle were they going to destroy in Mason's Addition, or even in the Border Boys' area?

How the Rebellions Grew Into Thousands

"They come from dysfunctional families lacking role models. Whatever they don't get in the family structure they are trying to get from the gangs." —FBI agent Mark Becker, head of the FBI special gang task force in Gary, Indiana.

There are three additional things that the Rebellions did that really brought thousands of young men into their gang. These three things are well documented as to why young people join gangs and they are: support, identity, and excitement/risk-taking. We will now look at the practical application of these three areas and see how the Rebellions put them into practice.

Support:

I asked Scrooge, "How were you all able to get so many young men to be a part of the gang?"

He said, "That question was put to me by a lot of pastors, and I mean by some of the biggest names in The Bahamas. They all wanted to know how I was able to get so many young men under control with no money, no future guarantees, and at the end of this road you are going to get so much, but to be honest, I don't know myself. Let's use Lizzy as an example. There were so many different gangs they had to pass before they got to East Street. They could have linked up with any one of them, and the same thing with Carmichael Road, Nassau Street, Regency Park, and so on."

Scrooge continued, "But here's what I can say. The groups in different areas that were affiliated with us knew one thing for sure, and that is that they could trust and respect the base. When you look at it, people want to know they have someone in their corner for the worst. If they got into a situation that was above their heads, they know that we will come down there with them, hang with them, wait on their problem with them, and deal with it for them. This was why they respected the East Street fellas, because the East Street crew always proved themselves to be a real backup."

Jim Parker, the executive director of the Do It Now Foundation, wrote a pamphlet entitled 'Street Gangs: The View from the Street'. Mr. Parker wrote, "In many ways, gangs are the human equivalent of the 'safety in numbers' herd-survival mechanism seen throughout nature. But gangs do more than just protect members; they drive up the ante so high that challenges to members are reduced."

Identity:

To show how identity is important in the lives of young people, Ada explained how the name "Raiders" was added to the gang's name. He said, "Now the name 'Raiders' came about because I was trying to separate my group from Scrooge's Truck Boys. I didn't know that the name was going to go this far. It was as if everything I did which was negative seemed to be going somewhere, but when I was trying to do something positive, I didn't get anywhere. When the name 'Raiders' was picked up, the gang became known as the Rebellion Raiders."

Everyone I spoke to seems to agree that this also brought with it a dress code, which was the wearing of the Los Angeles Raiders [now the Oakland Raiders] clothing. This was when the Rebellions just exploded in membership, simply because we now had an image, an identity—one in which we never had before in our lives.

It was the US Congressman Dave Reichert who stated, "Gang violence in America is not a sudden problem. It has been a part of urban life for years, offering an aggressive definition and identity to those seeking a place to belong in the chaos of large metropolitan areas."

The Rebellions were the first gang in The Bahamas, to come up with a popular logo/brand in the wearing of Raiders clothing. However, other neighborhoods gave birth to their own gangs using popular sporting team images as their official colors and name. You had the Hoyas Bull Dogs out of Kemp Road; the Coconut Grove area took on the name Nike, which became their clothing of choice. Miami Street took on the name Hurricanes, and wore Miami Hurricanes clothing. However, when you look at it closely, because of the lack of involved fathers, a lot of us were simply lacking an image and a positive identity of ourselves.

Excitement/Risk-Taking:
Scrooge also agreed that adding "Raiders" to the gang's existing name of "Rebellion" was powerful and that was when the gang really began to grow in size. But he also talked about the excitement and risk-taking that came about through the East Street wars. He stated, "The numbers really grew when we were at war, when all the fellas who used to be inside their homes watching TV saw that the action movies they were watching inside were actually happening outside, and so they came out of their homes to join the fun, because even though we were firing real guns, it was all a game for most of us." When you look at it carefully, it was through these risky and dangerous behaviors that they found acceptance, approval and respect among their peers. The identity, support, appreciation, acceptance and approval that we were unable to get from our fathers, we got from each other and the gang. Therefore, it goes without saying, that the answer to street gangs is involved fathers. The Edmonton Police Service of Alberta, Canada, gave one of the reasons why young men join gangs on their website as:

"The excitement of gang activity, which often involves violence, danger, and outward expressions of cultural biases, coupled with the acceptance given by fellow gang members, provide the social support and community involvement that are often lacking in the lives of young male gang members."
Ada continued, "Looking back on it all, I believe when we were on the streets coming up, we were simply looking for somebody to look our way. Even though guys were getting killed, the gang continued to grow. I heard some older folks say one time, 'As soon as two or three of them get killed, this gang will go to the dogs.' Each time one of us got killed, it hurt, but, that made us stronger."

In 1992 when I joined the Rebellions, a member named Terrence had just been shot and killed. I went with Whitey and two others to view the body at the funeral home. Whitey then started reminiscing, by saying "It was just last week, Friday, Terrence and I was in the barber shop. I was asking Terrence should I get this hawk drawn in the back of my head?

Terrence laughed and said, 'Yeah, but I wouldn't go anywhere with you.'" (The hawk was the symbol of the Gun Hawks.)

I remember looking at Terrence's body as he lied there in his casket and I asked him in my mind, "I wonder what you would say to me if you knew I just joined up with the Rebellions? Realizing the situation that you are in, I really want to know what you would say about joining a gang."

It goes without saying that Terrence never answered me back on that day. However, here's what I can say about joining a gang, and this is from 22 years of in depth knowledge on the matter. Joining a gang is like sky diving without a parachute. Oh, at first it's all fun, as you take on gravity in a thrilling and exhilarating free fall towards earth.

The truth is, anything that is risky and dangerous always starts out as fun. But the odds are always stacked in gravity's favor, for you will eventually come face to face with the earth, and mother earth always wins those battles. The same thing can be said about being in a gang. There are often only three outcomes which are: long term imprisonment, permanent disability which can also be accompanied with imprisonment. Let me just say, that this one is a real bummer.

Being imprison is tough on the hold, but to do so disabled is even much worse. I've experience this twice and the difficult part about it is that you're at the mercy of everyone. Then there is the third outcome, and you guessed right, its death himself. I know it is said that death will eventually knock on all our doors one day, however, by being in a gang you're actually banging on deaths door, and this is something he doesn't take to kindly.

Having looked death several times in the face, I could tell that this brother really likes stocking his victims. I guess it's where he gets his kicks, so to be interrupted or preempted really gets him angry. For he cuts down those who interrupts him, and to the perpetrator who does his bidding he cuts them down as well.

I guess this is why hardcore gangsters die violently. Case in point: twin brothers named Eric and Derrick from Yellow Elder were charged with Terrence's murder. However both of them are now deceased. Derrick was violently gunned down in Miami Florida, and his twin brother Eric was brutally gunned down some year's later just minutes away from his home.

I remember that there was a phrase someone came up with that stuck: "Rebellions don't die; we multiply."

However, in the following chapters the deaths are about to multiply. As death turns his attention on us who were interrupting him, and those who were doing his bidding when we started to rebel, which was our way of protesting against society. For we were demanding the immediate attention of our fathers, but what we got instead was much more than we had bargained for.

Scrooge goes on to give some additional reasons, as to why so many young men were joining the Rebellions. "One thing I always used to say: Being a part of the gang was like being a broke millionaire. In that I mean you can have anything you want, do anything you want and you can get more women than you can ever want. It's like another world you can't see, and you can't even imagine."

ACP Hulan Hanna also talks about this next world by saying, "They live in a world that was created by somebody else, or they create a world for themselves. It can be a world of violence, a world of antisocial behavior, a world of crime."

Taking Control of D. W. Davis High School
"Opportunities multiply as they are seized." —Sun Tzu

Scrooge then explained how they were able to further strengthen their base, and eventually taking over D. W. Davis School which was a strong hold for the Rebellions for many years. He said, "Back in the early days when there were only thirty of us from Strachan's Corner, I said to Ada, 'It's thirty of us, and we all are from just one corner. But we have the whole of East Street.' [East Street itself is seven miles long, and it's the only road that goes from one end of the island to the other.] To which Ada replied, 'You're right, ya know. We have Gibbs Corner, Thompson Lane, Fritz Lane, Toote Shop Corner, et cetera.'"

Scrooge said, "So just by targeting the guys through the surrounding corners, we were able to bring in more than three hundred guys into the fold alone. Then Ada came back to me and said, 'You know what, Scrooge? We have thirty guys in this school, twenty in the next school. We need to start concentrating on schools.'"

"This led to us having a stronghold on D. W. Davis," Scrooge said, "and that hold still exists to this day. We tried with other schools, but we were not able to duplicate the success of D. However, we had guys in every junior and senior high school in Nassau, and even in a lot of the private schools as well."

So how did the Rebellions get control of D. W. Davis School? Franco helps us with this. "There was a group of older fellas that came into 'D' from Mason's Addition looking for us, and we had to run for our lives out of the school. I believed one person was caught and chopped with a cutlass. So we had a meeting through Strachan's Corner later that evening where we made the older guys aware of what took place. We brought the problem to the table for a discussion on the matter. At the end of our discussions, it was decided that they would let us carry a .25 caliber pistol to school for our protection, because when those fellas came to the school, it was not only the Mason's Addition crew, but it was also the Border Boys, the War Kings, and Hoyas from Kemp Road. Scrooge selected me to carry the gun, because I was the most senior person in school then and I was already keeping his guns hidden at our house."

Franco continued, "Now, you know, Scrooge always had a plan, for he told me, 'Let your girlfriend keep it during school hours, and only if there's a problem then go get it from her and deal with the situation.' This was to ensure that I didn't get arrested with the gun, but at the same time, we were positioned to protect ourselves. Everything was fine for the first couple of weeks. Somehow, the word got to the rival gangs that we were coming to school strapped. So they never bothered us again. This led to us always having the upper hand in school.

My girlfriend's class was just opposite mine, where we could've looked through the window and see each other. So this day in school it was all nice and quiet. Classes were in and everybody was focusing on their classwork, when from out of nowhere a gunshot rang out, shattering the silence. I was trying to figure out what was going on, because only us that I knew of had a gun in the school. So I looked across to my girlfriend's class to make sure that she was safe, only to see when her teacher bolted from the classroom, screaming and running to get to the office. By this time, everybody was now looking at my girlfriend's class. When I looked at my girlfriend and our eyes met, her face said it all. She had this shocked look on her face, and I knew then the shot came from her. I knew I was in trouble, but at the same time, I couldn't allow her to be caught with the gun. I dashed out of my class and ran across to her classroom, where I snatched the gun and ran out of the school. My girlfriend later told me, that she was playing with the gun in her skirt pocket when it just went off. I was eventually locked up by the police for it, and I explained to them that it was a firecracker that went off in the class."

I asked Franco "For the most part, the police knew that you were keeping the guns for Scrooge. How is it they never caught you?"

Franco answered, "Well, they caught up with me once, but by the grace of God and pure luck I slipped out of that. One time, they came and picked me up from school and they had me on the head [red-handed].

They said to me, "Mister, we hear you keeping these guns for this Scrooge and this Franz fella. We need to search your house."

Franco now said in a serious tone, "When they picked me up, I had all of the guns then—our entire armory, plus ammunition. I'm telling you, Deal, they had me cold. But at the time, I was a juvenile, and you know that we knew the system. I knew that they couldn't search our house without my mother being there, so when they pulled up by our house, I played the fool on them. I said to them, 'Officer, I have to wait on my mother to open the door.'"

Franco continued, "Fortunately for me, they couldn't wait around for my mother to come home from work, but they had me dead in my tracks. If they had just opened that door, they would've had me and all the guns for the crew. After that, we said that someone was talking and so we stashed the guns different places."

It is interesting to note that while D. W. Davis was known as a school under the control of the Rebellions, but it was one they fought for. There were always constant fights for control. On the eastern side of the school was the Kemp Road area, and directly opposite the school gate to the north was Culmersville—the No Mercy Dogs. Directly behind the school to the south was Apple Street, and the Union Village fellas or the War Kings. Then there were the Mason's Addition fellas attending the school as well, so all five of these gangs were unified against the Rebellions. To the western side and beyond was the Rebellions' turf.

Scrooge commented about the decision to have a gun stationed at 'D'. "Giving these lil' fellas a gun was important to keep the name of the Rebellions strong, because whenever the name drops, it's only a matter of time before someone kicks your door in."

Giving the Rebellions a Say in Prison
"When we understand the needs that motivate our own and other's behavior, we have no enemies." —Marshall Rosenberg

We now turn to Scrooge once again, to see what the Rebellions did to neutralize the Gun Hawks in prison. He began by saying, "When I first went to prison, I made the best out of it. From the streets, I was hearing reports of Rebellions going to prison and getting do in [beat up]. Our fellas had no say, couldn't even open up their mouths. When I went up there for the first time, I turned that prison into a place that everyone could say that the Rebellions were running it after that. I wouldn't say I did it alone, but I help set the groundwork to give the Rebellions a say in prison."

"Now fellas could have gone to prison and don't have to worry about getting do in," said Scrooge. "I did this by reasoning with the gang leaders from the Gun Hawks, who were basically running prison at that time. You know those fellas were in the game way before us, so their crimes were more serious than ours because they were charged with drugs and big scale armed robberies. They only started gangbanging when we came out, and then Shaney took a gun off one of their boys.

"I told Bitto, 'It's the system that we all are up against, and it's the system that has us all in here.' Through those conversations, we were able to resolve a lot of petty little issues. Prior to that, the worst thing you wanted to do is end up in prison as a Rebellion. Now when you go up there they would say, 'He's a Rebellion, he's coming this way.'"
Scrooge continued, "Like when I was in prison and I heard that Franz was coming up. The minute I heard that he was in Central Police Station, I started to make a space for him. There were two other persons in the cell with me. I told them, 'You all have to go. Someone important is coming up from East Street.' They started complaining, 'But we don't want to go anywhere.' I gave each one of them a pack of cigarette and shipped them out, making room for Franz."
Scrooge then said in earnest, "When I was on the streets thugging, I wanted loyal people around me. I made my crew aware if you're going to bleed, I will bleed, too. If we have to go to prison, then we are going to prison together. But one thing about us: if someone is locked up in prison, whatever it takes, we gon' get that person out."
He provided me with an example by saying, "When Rugged got locked up for gun butting Mickey Mouse, and he went to court, they remanded him on the charge because he was already on bail for murder. I told his lawyer to just ask the judge for one hour, because I'm going to bring the complainant to court who wants to drop this case. The lawyer asked for the case to be put down for an hour, and the judge said, 'okay, she would give him just one hour.'"
"Now Donald Davis School was having their sports day, so we had to go to the sports center and try and convince Mickey to come to court with us and drop the case. People could say, 'oh! you forced them, but you could only force a man right to the court door, but when he gets in there he could say whatever he wants to,'" said Scrooge.
I remember going around the court the next day with Rugged, and as we were heading up the steps to the parking lot, Rugged asked me, "Deal, did you see the way CID officer Anthony Ferguson looked at me?"
I said to him, "Yeah. He looked somewhat surprised."
Rugged just chuckled. Afterwards he said, "He caused me to be remanded to prison on yesterday, but by two o'clock the case was dropped and I was freed."

We Were Running Communities

"Never doubt that a small group of thoughtful, committed citizens can change the world. Indeed, it is the only thing that ever has."— Margaret Mead, anthropologist

I put the question to Scrooge, "It is said back in the day at its strongest point, the Rebellions had some 7 to 10 thousand members, but in your estimation what do you believe the numbers were?

He said, "Really and truly, it is hard to estimate because it could be more than 7,000, 8,000 or more than 10,000 because we were basically running entire areas and communities. When you are running a community, it is difficult to put a number on that, and you can't just count everybody you see because some people are behind in the shadows and usually it does be the people behind in the shadows, that are doing the most damage."

The point that Scrooge made about running communities is so true because even though the young men were the ones who were doing the mischief, the adults in the community were down with us.

When I was staying with Scrooge on East Street, after the shooting in the mall, I was now on the run, during which time Whitey had given me a bag full of .22 bullets. Archie along with another Rebellion called Duff, and I had a heck of a time playing target practice trying to shoot birds out of trees. This time it was my turn and, as I lined up my sights on a bird to shoot, a lady push opened a wooden window, looked me in my eyes and said to me in an annoyed tone. "Why don't you all go somewhere else and fire that thing," gesturing to the gun I was holding in my hands.

She then continued, "I have two persons over visiting me, and we are trying to hold a prayer meeting. But you all are just here firing that thing, making a lot of noise, so go somewhere else." When she was finished speaking, she looked at me for a second or two to make sure that I heard her.

I somewhat manage to nod my head, as to say I heard you and will do as you suggested. She then slammed her window shut, with a loud thud. I'm standing there in a shooter's position, with both of my hands still wrapped around the gun. I'm completely dumb-founded, I must be hearing things. I'm absolutely stunned, because if I had heard correctly. What she just actually told us, "I have no problem with you'll firing that gun, but right now don't fire it here go somewhere else, because I have company with me." Even though she appeared to be angry with us, and asked us to leave her yard. Yet she was still down with us, we just happen to caught her at a bad time. I said, "Now, she's really cool."

If this was in my neighborhood, nobody would've said anything to me. I just would've seen a patrol car heading in my direction. I often wondered if she had prayed for me, or if they had prayed for us that day. It is quite obvious that this was a normal occurrence for her, because she was not trouble by the gun I was holding in my hands. Her only concern was the amount of noise we were making outside her window. This meant that if she had no one over at the time, then it would've been no problem for her.

Ada adds to this point by saying, "Every mother in that neighborhood was basically down with the gang. Everyone knew each other and they liked the protection. There were times I heard one or two of them saying, 'Boy, no one could come in this area playing.'

However, today, if you go around Strachan's Corner and Thompson Lane, it is a ghost town. Franz was giving me the joke the other day, that two Joneses [local term for a person strung out on drugs, normally crack cocaine] does come around there, and terrorize the area at nights. I had to laugh. I said to him, 'things really gone to the dogs.' Even though we were destructive in the gang on one hand we were positive on the other. Our most destructive behavior was when we were out of the community warring."

Scrooge agreed with Ada by saying, "We really had a close netted structure to rely on for anything, you could have gone by anyone house and get something to eat. Whatever they were eating, they would've fed you, and all the mothers would've treated you just like they treated their own. What the gang also did, it provided some level of protection for a lot of the working adults in the neighborhood. They knew that their houses were safe, when they went out to work and didn't have to worry about anyone breaking in to their homes."

The Public Terrorist Rebellions
"Names are an important key to what a society values. Anthropologists recognize naming as 'one of the chief methods for imposing order on perception." —David S. Slawson

The Public Terrorist Rebellions were situated through Milton Street, some four to five blocks headed south from Strachan's Corner. What is so interesting about their gang name is that it came about as a result of a criminal case. The second man in charge of this crew whom we simply called "S" shared with me before I lost my sight how they got the name Public Terrorist.

He said, "A group of us were downtown on Bay Street. It was some twelve to fifteen of us with nothing to do. We had just been in a fight with some Kemp Road fellas. It really wasn't anything to talk about, because we quickly ran them off Bay Street. Feeling pumped up about what we had just done and looking for more action, we started running in the middle of Bay Street, screaming and shouting "Rebellions!" and "Raiders for life!", making a real nuisance of ourselves. About nine of us were arrested by the police and charged with public terror and disorderly behavior. So in fact, we were given our gang name by the police, and Milton Street became known as the Public Terrorist Rebellions."

I interviewed Galen Nordelus a.k.a. "Ninja," who was once the leader of the Public Terrorist Rebellions before making it out of the gang.

Galen said, "From the age of nine, I was on the streets. This came about because I was being rude with my parents and I was moving things without their permission, like money. So my stepfather didn't like what I was doing and he didn't like me, so he eventually put me out on the streets. My mother was always sick, and my father—I never met him." Galen related, "While I was on the streets, I used to sleep in old abandoned vehicles. However, I would eventually go on to be adopted. How this came about—I used to hang out at the end of the corner every night, and one particular night I just happened to fall asleep on the corner. There was a lady's son by the name of Ricardo who woke me up, and he said he will ask his mother for me to sleep in the house that night. He took me inside their home, and his mother Mrs. Green made sure that I took a hot bath. To tell you the truth, that was the first time in my life that I had ever bathed in hot water with Dettol [a liquid disinfectant made in the UK]. The next morning they took me to the police station, wherein the police took me home to my parents. They spoke to my stepfather, who denied the story I had gave to the police. Soon after the police had left, he ran me again from out of the house. This went on for at least about two times. It was then that the Green family decided to keep me."

"So how did you get connected with the Rebellions?" I asked. He said, "As I roamed the streets, I used to see how the brothers used to stand up for each other, and I wanted to be a part of that as well. When I used to see the brothers go out to steal bicycle parts, I used to go behind them. They would always try and run me, but as I got bigger they couldn't run me any longer. This was way before there was ever a gang. "After the gang got started I moved to Milton Street, [At one point, Milton Street used to war with Strachan's Corner]. So when I went to live down there, I was able to bring an end to the war between Strachan's Corner and Milton Street, and the brothers from Milton Street ended up joining the Rebellions," said Galen.

One of the people Galen used to look up to was K.C. Galen said, "I used to carry and keep his guns. This really boosted my image and standing in the gang."

He then recounted what happen after Shaney had taken the handgun, off someone from the Gun Hawks. Galen said, "The next day, several of them came looking for Shaney to get their gun back, and these guys were really armed—from handguns to machine guns. They were going through the area trying to find Shaney. Somehow, one of them came through the corner with a .45 in his hand. I was by myself. When I saw him, I immediately pulled a gun from my waist and squeezed the trigger, but nothing happened. So I pulled another gun from my waist, and squeezed the trigger and again nothing happened. However, by this time, I had already spooked him, because he was running back bent at the waist. But at the same time, he pointed his gun back and fired off a lucky shot that hit me in my left arm."

Galen continued, "I guess it really shocked him to see this lil' fella pulling out two guns on him."

The individual who shot Galen was a twin named Jeremy. They were able to resolve the matter when Jeremy gave Galen a Rolex watch to drop the case. Some five or seven years later, Galen would help him escape from jail. Galen picks it up here. "I came down from prison with a makeshift handcuff key that I was going to use to escape if they had refused to give me bail. It so happened that I was given bail and was just brought back in Central Police Station until my release warrant came down from the courts. In the process, I was put back in the holding cell with the other inmates that I had come down from prison with. I in turn gave the handcuff key to one of the twins, Jeremy, the same person who had shot me years before.

"Later that night," continued Galen, "a group of us was chilling on Milton Street, and you know, I had the floor, having just been released from prison earlier that day. As I am talking about my trip to prison, I kept hearing this psst sound. So I stopped and asked the fellas, 'Did you all hear that,' but everybody said, "no". So I went on talking and I heard the sound again, but this time someone else heard it as well, and they told me that the sound was coming from through the shortcut. I walked over to 'S,' who I knew was strapped, and pulled a 9 out of his waistband. When I walked through the shortcut, there was Jeremy wearing a camouflage trench coat that came down to his ankles. The trench coat was opened, revealing a machine gun strapped around his shoulder. When he saw the gun in my hand, he laughed and told me, 'Put that thing away.'"

"Surprised to see him standing there, I asked, 'what you doing through here, bey?'

He answered me by saying, 'I just came to tell you thanks a lot for that handcuff key. I truly appreciated that.'"
Galen concluded, "I learned the next day on the news that he had escaped out of a moving bus that was heading back up to prison, in spite, of armed police escort."
Jeremy was on the run for more than two years. He was later captured on the island of Jamaica, where he was working as a taxi cab driver.

We Were Mainly From Single Parent Homes
"The proliferation of gangs in this country is a result of boys missing their fathers." —Patrick F. Fagan Ph.D.

At the end of my interview with Mr. George Mackey, he said something that caught me totally off guard. He asked, "Do you know something?" I had just started to cut my recorder off, but I stop and allowed it to continue recording. I was glad I did, because Mr. Mackey's remarks are the foundation from which this book was written. He continued, "The gangs filled a void in society, and the void was the absence of family life. The gang became a family. For some of those guys in the gang that was the only family they knew, because when their mothers had them they were too busy having children for other men. Some of them never knew their daddies. Their daddies never look back after they got their mothers pregnant, and those guys just grew up and they couldn't relate to nobody.

When they had their problems, who could they have talked to? Nobody would listen, so they gravitated together and form a gang."
It's rather ironic, but in 1976 according to our Department of Statistics numbers this was the defining year, that children born outside of wedlock surpassed those born in marriages in The Bahamas since we began to keep record. This was the year after I was born, but less than 16 years later the verdict was in for it was us who made up 85% of the membership, in all of the gangs in The Bahamas. The gang problem that was gripping the US, the UK and the rest of the western world in the late 80's and early 90's was as a result of one thing: the breakdown of the family.

Professor of Political Science at Howard University Stephen Baskerville, stated, "Virtually every major personal and social pathology can be traced to fatherlessness more than to any other single factor." He continued, "Fatherlessness far surpasses both poverty and race as a predictor of social deviance."

I've come to learned in my almost 40 years of existence, that the best way to confront a problem is simply to prevent it from developing into one from the onset. By strengthening families is the most effective way that we can fight crime, teenage pregnancy, youth gangs, drugs and alcohol abuse among our youth. The truth is it's the breakdown of our families that is fueling our social ills. As journalist, author and public policy researcher Karl Zinsmeister, who also once serve as chief domestic policy adviser, and Director of the White House Domestic Policy Council under President George W. Bush stated, "We talk about the drug crisis, the education crisis, and the problem of teen pregnancy and juvenile crime. But all these ills trace back predominantly to one source: broken families."

In my interview with Ada, he talked about the makeup of the homes on East Street by saying, "The majority of us were from single parent family homes. You could have counted the fellas on your fingers that had a mummy and a daddy at home."

Patrick Fagan and his team of researchers, at the Heritage Foundation reported the following, "The Douglas Smith and G. Roger Jarjoura, in a major 1988 study of 11,000 individuals, found that "the percentage of single-parent households with children between the ages of 12 and 20 is significantly associated with rates of violent crime and burglary." The same study makes clear that the widespread popular assumption that there is an association between race and crime is false. Illegitimacy is the key factor. It is the absence of marriage, and the failure to form and maintain intact families, that explains the incidence of high crime in a neighborhood among whites as well as blacks."

I asked Ada, "So how involved was your father in your life?" He laughed aloud, and said, "That's a good one. I've seen that man but only twice in my life and I'm now thirty-two years old."

"So you don't know whether or not he's alive?"

"I know that he's alive and doing well. The last time I saw him was a couple of years ago."

"Realizing that your father was not involved in your life, how involved are you in your son's life?"

"I'm there for my son 24/7, because I don't want him to take the road we took. I believe if I had a father around, I would've learned plenty things. There was no father there to tell me look here son, this is the wrong way to go. When we were coming up, we learned through trial and error," Ada said. Geoffrey Canada is President and CEO of the Harlem Children's Zone, and author of the book Fist Stick Knife Gun: A Personal History of Violence in America. Mr. Canada stated, "Boys who grow up in homes with absent fathers search the hardest to figure out what it means to be male." When you look at it, us men who grew up without our fathers' involvement in our lives, we often go through life with a limp in our psyche. We are unsure of ourselves, and are like drunken men staggering and groping around in the dark. As we try to figure out, what it means to be a true man. Some of us will eventually figure it out, but we would have used up a lot of time in the process. Time that could have been better spent building on our fathers' successes, and avoiding the pit falls and ditches that he and his father fell into. This is why we are unprepared for the real world, because we are unsure of ourselves and the steps we must take. While at the same time there are others, just breezing past us along the way. So it becomes easy for us to just follow and emulate them, because it is easy to follow someone when you don't know the way.

Ada continued, "The older guys in the neighborhood were our father figures. Even though they were doing foolishness we looked up to them, and they looked out for us. When we would be out playing and it was getting dark, they would tell us now don't be out here too late, because you know that freaks does come out at night."

Ada then shares something that happened to one of the young fellas, when they were all growing up. He said, "There was a young boy who grew up with us, an older guy in the neighborhood sodomized him. When word got out what was done to him, we watched the older boys we looked up to beat that older guy really bad. The police had to come and escort him out of the neighborhood."

Ada continued, "One time when I was much younger, someone tried to break into our house. I remember being afraid walking through the yard. Lil John and couple of his friends were passing through, and he said to me, 'Look here, shorty, don't be scared to walk around here, because you live around here. If we ever catch that person who tried to break into you'll house, you will hear about it.'"

Ada said, "What Lil John said made me feel good, even though that was a scary night for me and my younger siblings. But they were assuring me if they catch that person, they will deal with him severely."

In my interview with Franco, he said something similar, "I didn't have any father to reach out to me. The persons who tried to steer me in the right direction, were the persons on the street and I still went the wrong way."

Then he said, "Everything starts from home. If the father isn't there, then the friends are going to step up to influence the young boy astray. This is where the problems come in, because in my community the majority of the children do not have any fathers in the home. I can only speak for my community. This is why with the young guys who do hang around me, I always do my best to encourage them. I have already lived the negative side on the streets, so I prefer to encourage them on the positive side - to encourage them to get a job, save their money and to do something for their families."

Here again Patrick F. Fagan and the Heritage Foundation stated, "High-crime neighborhoods are characterized by high concentrations of families abandoned by fathers."

In my interview with Apples, he shared with me, "Before I was born my father disowned me. You know those ones who get the females pregnant, and then say the baby is not theirs? He rejected me, told my mother that I am not his child, so I never had a relationship with my father." Apples also shared with me the makeup of the families that existed in Elizabeth Estates at that time. He said, "90% of us came from single-parent homes who were in the gang. There was just a small 10% who had a mother and a father in the home. For a lot of us, we did not have that father or authority figure who could have intervened on our behalf. Where we could have said, 'You know, daddy, Johnny tried to rob me or Johnny just slapped me', and our father could have either taken us to the police station, or went to school with us to address the issue. So we had to defend for ourselves."

Apples continued, "I knew a lot of fellas who live in Lizzy and never got involved in some of the stuff that we were getting into. This was because they had a strong father figure at home, so they couldn't have gotten involved. The few of those who did end up in the gang even though their father was in the home, their father was just there as a provider, but he was not directly involved in their lives. The biggest challenge a lot of the guys face who were in the back, a lot of them were not initially a part of the gang. However, because they were living in the back they were often taxed in school or wrongfully accused with hanging with us. And after a while some of them got tired of being picked on for no reason, they just decided to link up with us as a source of protection." Apples then said, "I am surprise to find out as I'm talking with the young fella's today, who goes to L. W. Young that they are dealing with the same problem we had with the Fox Hill fellas growing up. The Fox Hill fellas know that L. W Young is in their turf, so they are trying to tax these fellas each and every day just because they live in Lizzy. So they have two choices either they continue to get tax, or you resist it which leads to a fight." The point Apples made is so essential, that I just have to say that the Lizzy's gang could've been avoided. Let's go back to something Apples said earlier, where he talked about what brought the split in Lizzy. It was a simple issue surrounding some stolen bicycle parts that led to a fist fight. For the love of god, you mean to tell me that some level headed adult male couldn't intervene to resolve the issue? As Apples mentioned before this incident, everybody was cool with each other. Elizabeth Estates is a good size area for riding bikes and that was what they were all into. However, what happen instead, because nobody intervened to bring this simple matter to an end. Therefore, they came of their bikes, and stop being boys but became gangsters, thugs and murderous.

One afternoon two of my young men were walking through the Hay Street area, to make it to the youth program that Troit and I were spear heading. When a young man from the area pulled alongside them on a bicycle, produced a knife and asked Andrew for his phone he was holding in his hand. When they got to the meeting, Mikey, who was walking with Andrew told me what had happened, I was in rage. I didn't show it, but I was angry none-the-less. Andrew was saying that it was no big deal it's just a phone, and he was trying to tell us don't worry about it. I politely pulled out my phone and called ACP Hulan Hanna because I was determined to get that cell phone back. Within 5 minutes there was a patrol car outside the church door. The officers took Andrew and Mikey to look for the young man in question. However, about 10 minutes later they came back and said, "We didn't spot him." The officers told them they would keep looking for him, based on the description Mikey and Andrew had provided to them. To their credit, they kept looking for this young man, because before the end of our meeting the officers came back to say, the young man and the cell phone was at the police station. The young man in question was known to the police, he had just recently been put out of school and was being raised by his grandmother. After our meeting we went to the Quackoo Police Station got the phone, and left without pressing any charges. To this day I am still thankful to ACP Hulan Hanna, and those two police officers who kept looking even after they had dropped Andrew and Mikey off.

Looking back now I could see that our biggest mistake that night, was not attempting to reach out to the young man who had robbed Andrew of his phone. It was quite obvious that he was also in need of help, but I was so relieved to get Andrew's phone that I never looked backed.

Chapter 14
The Ultimate Bahamian Cultural Expression

"A people without the knowledge of their past history, origin, and culture is like a tree without roots." —Marcus Garvey

The same day I was released from prison in November of 1994, I went through Strachan's Corner. Some of the gang members were shocked that I was actually out of prison. When one looks at the seriousness of the charges that were against me, it was easy for one to conclude that I should've been spending a long time behind bars. Yet within seventeen months, I was a free man. Let me correct that: I was a free hardened criminal. I went in wayward and unsure of myself, but when I came out, I was quite sure of where I was headed. This was when my criminal career took off; this time it was deliberate, cold, and calculated every step of the way.

I was released on a Tuesday, but I didn't see Scrooge until that Thursday evening. He had been working with his older brother John, installing drywall on Paradise Island. The next day, he took me downtown and purchased me three name-brand pants and shirts to go along with them, a pair of the white 1995 Air Jordan tennis shoes, and then put a gun in my waist.

In my first interview with Scrooge I asked, "Was this something you were doing to keep individuals who came out of prison loyal to the gang?"

I asked him this question because I knew that he had done the same thing for Franz, who had also been released from prison that same month, two weeks before me. He had shot a Border Boy. I remember quite clearly Archie telling me, "Scrooge is going to fix you up like he did Franz."

Scrooge answered, "I wouldn't say so. You see, to reach that stage what you had reached, it had never been reached before. You had reached a stage what took people years to reach."

My release from prison in November was one month before Junkanoo. This is the one event that the Rebellions look forward to each year. It's almost like a family reunion for us. Junkanoo is the top native festival on the Bahamian calendar, and nothing surpasses it. According to Dr. Nicolette Bethel, an authority figure on Bahamian culture and Bahamian history, she stated, "Junkanoo, for Bahamians, is the ultimate national symbol. A street festival of West African origin held at Christmastime, it represents poverty and wealth, discipline and rebellion, competition and cooperation, creative genius and physical prowess."

I couldn't wait to get out to Junkanoo, and it would be my first time going there with the Rebellions. The 25th of December came within a blink of an eye, so after dark on Christmas Day, we started to assemble through Strachan's Corner. Others were making their way there from all over the island, by the time it was 11 o'clock at night, there was a sea of people, mostly young men who had gathered through Strachan's Corner. Shortly after midnight, we began to make our way to Junkanoo. Even though the crowd was huge, this was just the beginning for there would be a lot more to come. We walked onto East Street and headed north toward the hill. There were so many of us that we were causing a traffic jam. After going through the various police checkpoints, we arrived at our destination on Shirley Street. This was our area directly in front of the Bank of The Bahamas (the building is now occupied by the Register General's Office). It is also opposite The Bahamas Financial Center, where I did plumbing during my summer break of grade 11. Once we had peacefully made it to our area, we saw another huge group of Rebellions who were already there from different areas. Then the hand clasps and the hugs began. As I said before, it's like a family reunion, for some of us haven't seen each other in months, in my case close to two years. The crowd was really huge now, and it would be some time before the first Junkanoo group made it onto Shirley Street. After all the hand clasps, hugging and catching up with fellas from other areas were done we got restless. With nothing else to do except wait, boredom started to set in among us. We became like junkies who needed a fix, the only thing was that our fix came from violence. So Scrooge suggested, "Let's make a run on Bay Street."

This was something I was definitely down with. Some thirty-five of us went on this mischievous mission. In a nutshell—we would be going directly into our enemies' stronghold. Normally when people go to Junkanoo, they tend to go with their neighbors and others from their community. This meant that just about every community had their own spot along the parade route. For example, Kemp Road and the Fox Hill fellas would normally be in front of Hoffers Shoe Store on Bay Street. The Bain Town fellas would normally be in front of John Bull, formerly The Nassau Shop on Bay Street. The East Street fellas, the Rebellions—our post was Shirley Street. This was a bold and daring move. It's like going into the heart of your enemies' territory on a night they are there in strong numbers. The only difference is that you are unarmed, but so are they. There is such a strong police presence during the Junkanoo parades, and different checkpoints one has to go through. It's an almost impossible task to take anything illegal to Junkanoo. The safest thing to do is just leave everything illegal over the hill and enjoy the parade.

Knowing that we would be greatly outnumbered, Scrooge himself handpicked the thirty-five of us to go on this run. We didn't need anyone with us who scared easily. At the same time, we didn't need large numbers for this run. We made our way down Shirley Street and on Elizabeth Avenue, which is one of the many streets that connect Shirley and Bay Streets. Once on Bay Street, we had to go through an additional checkpoint. Once everybody made it through, we went on our way. The sidewalks of Shirley and Bay Streets were normally crowded during Junkanoo, so it is always a slow process to pass. On top of that, there were thirty-five of us. However, it wasn't long before we made it to the Kemp Road and Fox Hill area. There were easily three to four hundred fellas there. Once in their midst, one might think we would just pass through quietly, but not us—we were the Rebellions. This is how we built up our reputation, by doing daring and stupid things like this. Once in their midst, we took it over by jumping and shouting "Raiders in the place!" and "Rebellions on ya case!" This startled and surprised them. A silence fell over the entire area. It was as if they couldn't believe it. They had no response for us, simply because they didn't think we would do something stupid like this.

Some of their younger members that weren't battle-tested ran and leapt over the barricades to get out of our way. They ran across the street to safety. Those who didn't run away stood still because they were too shocked to do anything but look. When they did come out of their shock, they tried to surround us by blocking our path. But we were already in motion; we had momentum going for us. We easily pushed right through their human barricade, knocking a few of them to the ground as we passed.

Their crew across the street started to throw cans and plastic soda bottles at us. By this time, the police were also pushing through the crowd to get at us. We were now making their jobs difficult by venturing into the Kemp Road and Fox Hill fellas' territory. Two or three of our fellas were arrested, but we kept moving and shouting "Raiders!" as we went along the sidewalk. Even though it was crowded, people got out of our way.

We ended up in front of the Gun Dogs, but there was no war on with them, so we passed through and made it back to Shirley Street without incident. We had put ourselves in harm's way and risked being arrested, but when we reached our spot on Shirley Street, it was like a celebration, a homecoming, so to speak. The message had been sent to the Kemp Road fellas: "No territory is off limits for us. Regardless of where you may be, we don't care, we would look for you, until we find you."

Once we were back on our turf, we were greeted like war heroes returning home. Everybody wanted to know what happened on Bay Street, and we all had our different versions to tell.

Some gang members that had not been there were trying to convince Scrooge to go on another run this time including them in. He almost gave in, but later decided against it.

I cannot speak for everyone who was on that run with us, but for me it was like a high out of this world.

We hoped that the Kemp Road fellas would not be stupid enough to venture on our turf, because we were out in full force. However, they stayed in their area and Junkanoo went on without another incident from us.

Looking back I can now see that we were all young, naive, and reckless with the risks that we all were taking simply because, we were trying to fill a void in our lives, that could only have been filled by our fathers.

During my second trip to prison, a rival gang member from the original Gun Hawks who goes by the street name Lil Nugget (ironically, I would later date his sister Ophelia) he said to me, "When people told me how many members the Rebellions had, I thought that they were joking, until I saw them for myself. One morning, I saw them leaving Junkanoo. They were coming down East Street Hill. Some were already at the bottom, yet the crowd of fellas went straight to the top of the hill. It was as if there was no end to their numbers, because there were still more fellas coming over the top of the hill."

Even though the other gangs were represented fully and out in strong numbers themselves, nothing was able to rival the Rebellions' numbers. We numbered easily in the thousands. According to Scrooge, "Junkanoo was always our biggest showing in terms of numbers. However, that crowd is made up of different communities throughout the island and the members' families. Somebody has a cousin who is a Rebellion and so they come to Junkanoo with him, and sometimes they also bring a friend or two. Usually, once that cousin or his friend experienced that thrill and excitement by being with such a large crowd, he would then join the Rebellions' fold. More importantly, it allowed them to join without the initiation ritual. In effect, they joined by way of Junkanoo."

Even though there might be a few minor incidents, we all generally behaved ourselves, especially since thousands of police officers were stationed throughout the area, and walking the parade route consistently. Nobody wanted to be locked up during Junkanoo, for we all wanted to see and enjoy the entire parade. ++

This is our national festival. Despite our gang affiliations, and the rival between different communities, yet it is all our heritage for we are all one people. It is something that resonates deep within us, and much deeper than any gang allegiance.

[5]

The Vibration Within

"A nation's culture resides in the hearts and in the soul of its people." —Mahatma Gandhi

---

[5] ++appendix

Our Junkanoo festival takes place in the cool and dark hours of morning, which is around 2:00 a.m. This is on December 26th the Boxing Day holiday, which was carried over from our time during colonial rule. Junkanoo also occurs just one week later on the first day of the New Year. It provides locals and visitors alike the opportunity to ring in the New Year in celebration

I know that the experience itself is different for everyone, but for me, the thing that stands out about Junkanoo is the drummers' section of the "A" size groups, where there are hundreds of people beating drums made from goatskin, or what we simply call goatskin drums. When the drum section of the parade marches to where you stand. , it is an out of this world feeling. You just don't hear the pulsating drumbeats; rather, you feel it deep down in your soul. It is a thunderous sound that emanates from without, and it works its way inside you, becoming a part of you. Once you stand in front of those drummers, you cannot even hear yourself, much less the person next to you. It's even difficult to understand your own thoughts. The ground itself also conspires in this ordeal, for you can feel the pulsating rhythm vibrating through you from the ground up. The drum section of these "A" size groups is like a mini moving earthquake that takes a hold of you.

I had never gotten this close to the drummers' section before, and I was overwhelmed by the experience itself. Physically, I knew I was on Shirley Street, but mentally, I was hundreds of miles away. I was totally lost in the music. Some people like the vibrant colors of the costumes; for others, it's the choreographed female dancers. Yet others like the music, which consists of the brass section, the cowbell section, and the drummers' section. But it's the drummers' section that captivates me, the feeling of that pulsating rhythm vibrating through my body. It's more like a spiritual cleansing of some sort. Just like water renews, replenishes, and cleanses our bodies, one can feel the drumbeats doing the same internally. If I ever was high at any time in my life, it's when I'm standing in front of those drummers. I don't care about anything then; I'm just locked up in the rhythm and everything around me is in slow motion. Here you will find energy, passion, anger, love, but most of all freedom—the freedom to lose yourself in the music. I guess this is why drums are becoming a popular therapeutic method.

Is it any wonder for us blacks living in the Caribbean, that reggae music appeals to us because of its strong bass drumbeat? We might have been stolen from our motherland and kept in slavery for centuries, but they couldn't take away our drums and the firm connection we have to them. According to music therapist Jamie Blumenthal, "The drumbeat is the human way of imitating the heartbeat. Remember that a mother's heartbeat is what a baby has heard and felt for the first nine months while in the womb. We never lose our response to this comforting sound. Even Alzheimer's patients will respond to the beat of a drum when nothing else will reach them."

The Kemp Road Fellas Attempt to Get Even
"Hatred is something peculiar. You will always find it strongest and most violent where there is the lowest degree of culture." —Johann Wolfgang von Goethe

After the Christmas/Boxing Day Junkanoo, we had already made it down East Street Hill with no incident when two Rebellions namely Marley and Geo and some others pulled up alongside us on East Street. Marley told us that the Kemp Road fellas were on Collins Avenue waiting for us. Marley said, "I thought that was you all. I was wondering what you all were doing there. When we stopped to find out what was going on, that was when I recognized that they were Kemp Road fellas. I told the driver 'to let's get out of here. It's a big crowd of them. It must be seventy-five to a hundred of them on Collins Avenue."

Collins Avenue was more or less our territory; the Kemp Road fellas were basically in our backyard. I guess they had seen the small number of us that pushed through their ranks on Bay Street. Maybe they thought that they could take us on and surprise us by waiting over the hill. They made several mistakes in their reasoning: first of all, they were waiting at the wrong hill. They should have known that East Street fellas would come over East Street Hill and not Collins Avenue Hill.

Secondly, they thought that our numbers were few. They didn't know that those of us who had been on Bay Street were all hand-selected and proven fighters. Thirdly, and chief among their mistakes: they came too close to the base. It now was a matter of honor to protect our home turf, and so when Marley told us about their presence, again a handful of us ran from East Street to Collins Avenue to meet them. We went through Gibbs Corner, crossing over into 6th Terrace. This was where we met them.

I guess they realized that they had chosen the wrong hill to wait for us, because they were now heading home. Once we were close enough, Owen, my partner from high school, and another Rebellion name Duff, shouted at them. The Kemp Road fellas then turned around to confront us; this was what they wanted.

Just as Marley had told us, there were probably more than a hundred of them. This time there were fewer than thirty-five of us. Our fellas didn't even bother to make that run from East Street to Collins Avenue, which was not a short run. On top of that, the Kemp Road fellas were not a serious threat; they were not a challenge, so to speak. They had an impressive number of members, but that was it. As a crew, they were not organized and were considered just bottle and rock throwers. When they saw us, they turned around and came charging and throwing rocks. They pushed us back over Collins Avenue and through Gibbs Corner, but they didn't venture further than the Super Wash Laundromat. There we were for about a half an hour, just throwing rocks back and forth at each other. We didn't have to look for rocks; we just simply threw their rocks back at them. In spite of their numbers, they didn't advance. They had a once in a life time opportunity to really run us out of our area. But they just played it safe, not wanting to venture any further on to East Street. Sensing that they were half stepping, we started to push them back over Collins Avenue. A patrol car finally pulled up. One of the officers got out and fired a shot in the air.

"Do you see their numbers?" I asked while pointing at the Kemp Road fellas and then I said, "You need to fire a shot in the crowd, and if you don't want to do it, then let me do it."

The officer ignored me, while his partner radioed in their location and requested backup. I turned my attention back to the matter at hand. Even though the police were there, we kept throwing rocks at each other. We continued to push them back. By this time, the road was littered with rocks. Vehicles were turning around and going in the opposite direction to avoid our rock war.

While turning around to look for more rocks, I saw three fellas running toward us. I didn't pay them any mind, because I thought that they were with us. Not until they were about to pass me did I look up only to see Boy Hoy, the Leader of the Kemp Road Gang. It was too late for me; he had already extended his hand. He clotheslined me with his momentum and speed and I hit the ground hard when I fell. I quickly got back to my feet, trying to find a rock or something to burst one of them. By the time I found one, they had already blended in with their crowd.

After a while, we simply got tired. We'd already had a long run before we met up with them. So we headed for Strachan's Corner, leaving our Kemp Road opponents and their police escort alone. Shortly after assembling in Strachan's Corner, I discovered that I had lost my gold rope chain. Scrooge had lost a gold ring and a bracelet that he had just purchased. Now we were angry. We'd been pulled into throwing bottles and rocks, which at this time was beneath us. We stooped to their level and their game, and looked silly in doing so. As a matter of fact, we came out the losers, because they came right into our backyard. Even though none of our fellas had been injured, now those fellas have something to brag about.

We were just formulating a revenge strategy, when the police came through Strachan's Corner and Thompson Lane in full force. There were several cars and a police bus. I said to the others, "I guess it's time for me to go."

As soon as I made it home, I heard someone outside blowing a car horn. When I looked outside, it was Olds in his brand-new Honda Accord. Olds was a member of the gang by virtue of living in the area where he grew up with everyone. He was not involved in the day-to-day activities of the gang. He had a good job and I was surprised to see him willingly taking us on a drive-by. Scrooge was in the front passenger seat, and Owen was in the back. When I got to the car, no one had to tell me what was up; I knew what was up. Scrooge said to me, "Get that thing and let's go for them."

I dashed back inside and retrieved the .380 pistol that Scrooge had put in my hand, and then jumped in the back seat of the car. Olds took off following Scrooge's directions. It didn't take us long to find the Kemp Road fellas. They were coming out of Culmersville, one of their allied territories, and crossing over Mackey Street. The only problem was that the police were still escorting them but this time there were two patrol cars where before it had only been one.

I was annoyed with what the police was doing, so much so that I angrily said, "Now, this isn't fair. These fellas greatly outnumbered us and yet the police came at us full force through Strachan's Corner. Now they are protecting these fellas by escorting them home, as if they are little girls."

This just confirmed who the police considered to be a more serious threat. The police official who had made that judgment call saved a lot of lives that morning, when they escorted the Hoyas Bull Dogs straight to their territory, while clamping down hard on the Rebellions. Just by that decision alone, they narrowly escaped becoming the headline news of the next day's papers.

We were not only angry, but their crowd was so big that it would not have been difficult for any of us to miss. We could easily have squeezed the trigger with our eyes shut and still hit a few of them.

We then drove down farther on Mackey Street, where we saw five to seven guys from Union Village. This is another one of the allied territories that the Kemp Road fellas had linked up with. Scrooge instructed Olds to stop alongside them, but before Olds brought the car to a stop, I opened fire on them. However, I was only able to get off one shot that missed them entirely, and then the gun jammed on me. At the sound of the shot, Olds pushed the pedal to the metal and drove off. Scrooge tried to get Olds to stop, but Owen told Olds to go, and I was there trying to unjam the gun. I later learned from Owen that the leader of Union Village crew (the War Kings) was there. His name was Brent Sands; he's now deceased. He had also attended R. M. Bailey with us. It was a good thing that the gun jammed when it did, and Olds drove off at the same time. I had only been out of prison for one month, yet I had picked up right where I left off. If Olds didn't pull off when he did, Owen and I would've been arrested for attempted murder and other serious offenses because they knew us from school.

Taking the Troops into Battle
"Take time to deliberate, but when the time for action comes, stop thinking and go in." —Napoleon Bonaparte

We couldn't allow what the Kemp Road fellas did to go unanswered, because they basically came in our backyard and made fools of us. Scrooge just wasn't having that, and so for the next several days he questioned members of our gang who were more familiar with the nature of the Kemp Road fellas. He wanted to know everything about them: how were they organized, who were their top lieutenants, where did they hang out on Kemp Road, which route did they take to get to Junkanoo?

At the end of this questioning process, Scrooge sat down with a handful of us, and there he proposed several scenarios. One of those options was a drive-by on Kemp Road, or we could catch them before they made it out to the New Year's Junkanoo parade. He then asked us for our input, and we all added our two cents to this plot. It felt good to be a part of such a discussion. This was new to me, and it felt good to be a part of such a discussion. I told them that I liked the idea of catching them before they made it out to Junkanoo. There would be more of them, making it difficult to miss. This was my reasoning. At the end of the day, we all agreed to the idea of ambushing them. We chose the area of Hawkins Hill and Canaan Lane for this ambush. I was tapped to head this operation, because I was more familiar with this area.

It was my responsibility to cut down as many of them as we could, before they made it to Junkanoo. I relished the honor that Scrooge had bestowed on me. I felt like a soldier heading into battle. On the night in question, it was Owen, Marley, and I, all of whom had attended C. I. Gibson. The school itself was basically at the front door of Kemp Road. Even though Geo had never attended C. I., he was also there with us. Our getaway driver was going to be Damien, a schoolmate of ours from R. M. Bailey School.

I stationed Geo and Marley on Bay Street, while Owen and I were positioned on Shirley Street. These were the two main routes to get from Kemp Road to downtown. The plan was that once Geo and the others saw a good-sized crowd coming their way, one of them was supposed to come and alert Owen and me so we could join them on Bay Street. Otherwise, if Owen and I saw a crowd coming our way, I was going to get Geo and Marley to join us on Shirley Street. Once we were all together in one place, then all hell was going to break loose on them. With three handguns amongst us, we would be able to inflict maximum injury to our enemies.

Damien waited for us at the top of Hawkins Hill, ready to go. Once we did our deed, we were going to run the entire length of Canaan Lane. This was a good run; it was like running the 400-meter dash, but we were good for it. Canaan Lane was a dead end; it ended at the top of a hill. But there was a track road, a walking trail, which came out on another dead-end corner on Hawkins Hill. This corner was directly opposite Michael's Corner, where I used to hang out on Hawkins Hill before I went to prison, so if the police pursued us through Canaan Lane, they would come to a dead end, giving us ample time to get away.

Owen and I were in the shadows on the corner of Canaan Lane and Shirley Street. It's hard to believe that only three years prior, both of us were kicked out of school together. I had already been to prison twice, and would go back twice more. Owen at that point had not been to prison yet, but he would eventually get there. Both of us were strapped, waiting to cut down some of our very own, individuals who probably were just like us and grew up under similar home conditions. Even though Owen grew up with his father, yet his father was a former bad boy/ drug dealer, and Owen would eventually walk in his father's footsteps.

If everything went as planned, one or two of the Kemp Road fellas would be leaving Shirley Street in a body bag. However, I have discovered that when it comes to crime, nothing goes as planned. Just fifteen or twenty minutes after taking our positions, Owen and I heard a gunshot on Bay Street. We looked at each other, trying to figure out what in the world just happened. I took off running to find Geo and Marley, with Owen close behind me. I wondered what went wrong—why did they fire a shot without bringing us in on the action?

As I crossed Dowdeswell Street I ran into Marley, who told me that Geo fired a shot at twenty or more of our enemies, but the fellas ran away. I then took off to find Geo. I arrived onto Bay Street from Hawkins Hill heading east. I didn't see Geo anywhere, but I did see a small group of fellas looking for him. This meant that when Geo fired his shot he ran and hide. I pulled out the 9 from my waistband, which was a black Smith and Wesson with 17 shots in the clip, and a shot was already in the head [chamber]. When they saw me running toward them, they started running away. I open fired on them as I ran. Even though vehicles were passing face-on, and there were also people in the service station yard, I tuned them all out and just focused my attention on the fellas running away. I was in the zone, and everything was moving somewhat slow. The only noises I heard were my heart beating in my chest, and the spent shells hitting the ground after each shot. I fired eight shots at them before cutting through Scotia Bank's parking lot and on to Dowdeswell Street again. This time I was in full throttle. I knew that I had to get off the scene quickly. There was a police traffic station about 150 yards down the road and I had just fired eight shots on Bay Street, which is the capital of commerce for The Bahamas.

When Plan [A] Falls Through
"Great ability develops and reveals itself increasingly with every new assignment." —Baltasar Gracian

I made it to Canaan Lane where I ran my heart out. Within a few short minutes, I had reached the dead end, and ran through to the next side. I burst out of the track road to our designated pick up spot, panting and out of breath. To my horror, I saw no getaway car and no Damien there waiting on us. I looked around in disbelief to see if the others now realized that we were on our own. But when I looked behind me for the others, I got another shock: there was no one behind me. They were not even close, because I couldn't even hear anyone thrashing around in the bush. This meant that they were far behind. I was just about to go back for them, realizing that we still had some time on our side. Then I heard a dreaded familiar sound, it was a patrol car siren in the distance.

Right then my mind was flooded with the unpleasant memories, of discovering that patrol car behind Bullet and I after robbing Snack Food. There was no question about it now—I knew that I had to go. I didn't know how far away the rest were, but that patrol car was getting closer by the second. I looked around one more time at the track road leading to Canaan Lane, and again I saw and heard no one. Everything had gone wrong on this mission, and everybody was now on their own in getting back to East Street. I checked the gun in my waistband, just to make sure that it was firmly in place. Then, without a second to spare, I took off. I ran harder and faster than ever before. I ran down Hawkins Hill like a bat out of hell, using the downward momentum from the hill to propel myself even faster. In record time, I was safely through Strachan's Corner. Some five minutes later, Geo and Marley came strolling through the shortcut wrapped up in their own conversation. When they saw me, they stopped, and Marley asked in surprise, "What are you doing here already?"

In response, I asked them, "What you mean, what I'm doing here already?"

Instead of answering me, Marley went on to asked me a question of his own, "Bey, we caught a ride here from Canaan Lane in a 280ZX, so how it is you still beat us here?"

I thought to myself, 'No wonder why they came strolling through the shortcut looking as if they hadn't broken a sweat.' Marley went on to explain their own ordeal. Apparently, they caught a ride from Canaan Lane with Horse—one of the individuals I used to play ball with through there.

I asked them, "Have you seen Owen?"

They looked at each other for a second, and Marley then said in surprise, "We thought Owen was with you."

Just then, we heard several branches snap through the shortcut. Right away I knew we were going to have company, from the noise alone it sounded like several persons were making their way towards us. I reach for the nine in my waist band, but before I could pull it out to my shock I saw who it was. For goodness sake, it was Owen. He was staggering out from through the shortcut. He looked haggard and beat up and he was panting and completely out of breath. It was as if his legs were about to give way at any moment. He sat down without saying a word to us and then he started fanning himself with one hand, at the same time opening his jacket with the other. We all just stood there looking at him, unable to say a word. I didn't have to wonder about his ordeal in getting here, it was quite obvious that he had a rough time.

He looked up at us, and finally said with deep anger in his voice, "You'll don't know, you'll don't know what I been through to get here. I had to hop a lot of fences with the police hot on my trail. If it wasn't for Peacock and them who showed me the way, I would've been locked up."

Owen then turned his anger on me and asked, "Why in the world you left me?"

I then told all of them of my ordeal in getting away from the scene, only to get to our designated pickup spot and discover that Damien was not there. I had no other choice but to foot it out to East Street and run the hardest I ever ran in my life.

Marley told of Geo's and his adventure, with Geo chiming in at times. It was obvious that they had the smoothest ride in arriving here.

Owen then asked incredulously, "So Damien was not there waiting on us?"

I took in a deep breath, and said, "No, he wasn't. I guess all those shots on Bay Street must have spooked him."

Owen then hung his head down, and started to shake it in disbelief.

We all basically agreed that none of the Kemp Road fellas were shot on Bay Street. Even though we didn't accomplish our mission as planned, we all made it back in one piece and with all of the guns. Looking back on that night, we each faced a unique challenge that we overcame, especially after our getaway driver abandoned us. We all improvised, adjusted, and used the few resources we had at our disposal, such as when Marley and Geo flagged down Horse and convinced him to drop them off on East Street.

With my knowledge of the area combined with my natural running ability, I made it to East Street in record time. Owen, who was not familiar with the area, got assistance from Peacock, who lived in the area and who was able to guide him safely to East Street. Peacock put himself in harm's way by assisting Owen, because if he was caught, he would've been charged along with Owen.

Yet, this has always been Owen's strength: his ability to get others to follow him.

Marley secured the weapons, and we went to the New Year's Day Junkanoo Parade. It is a common Bahamian tradition to bring in the New Year at church, something I have done many times with my family when I was younger. But on New Year's morning of 1995, we were looking to bring it in with a bang, with the shooting of several Kemp Road fellas.

However, life is really a funny thing; the same way I brought in 1995 it was also how I ended it. This time the tables were turn around, and it was I who was running for my life being hotly pursued. But I was not as fortunate as those Kemp Road fellas were. After being fired upon six times, one of those shots connected with my body, putting me in the hospital to bring in 1996, but I'm jumping the gun again.

We met up with everybody on Shirley Street. There was a great anticipation in the air upon our arrival. Immediately, we were surrounded and everyone started asking us how many people were shot. Marley, Geo, and Owen mainly did all of the talking. I stood in the background listening. I was in a somber mood; for me, there was nothing to celebrate because no one had been shot.

Afterwards, Scrooge pulled me aside to get my take on what had happened. I simply told him that Geo jumped the gun, and as a result, no one was shot. I felt like a failure standing before him. Everyone's hopes were riding high on this mission, and I didn't deliver.

He said to me, "Don't worry about that. Those fellas got the message."

What he said was indeed true. We so often are caught up in the attention-grabbing headline news about a violent and senseless crime. However, on the streets the most important thing is the message. Yes, we missed our targets by not shooting anyone that night. Nonetheless, the message was loud and clear for all to hear: don't ever dis (disrespect) the Rebellions because we will hunt you down—even if it means going on Bay Street for you. With gang violence, often the intent speaks louder than the act itself.

Scrooge then smiled reassuringly and said to me, "I heard that you light up Bay Street. They now know we mean business." Those few words from Scrooge really lifted my spirit, so much so that I was able to go on and enjoy Junkanoo.

Several days later, Owen told me of a conversation that was overheard in one of the government medical clinics. A mother told someone of her son's ordeal going to Junkanoo only to run for his life off Bay Street. She said, "Those Rebellions caused my son and his friends to run into the police traffic station on their stomachs that night." I just burst out laughing. From the time I knew Owen, he always had a way of telling a story. You just had to sit up and listen; you never knew when the punch line was coming.

When Duty Calls

"Let your plans be dark and impenetrable as night, and when you move, fall like a thunderbolt." —Sun Tzu, The Art Of War

We were more or less contented to leave it at that. We'd sent the message loud and clear to the Hoyas Bull Dogs. Everything was fine until the Kemp Road fellas had an incident downtown with Melly, who was Scrooge's girlfriend at the time, and now his wife. Scrooge had told me about it, and I believe it went something like this. Melly and Sheniqua (this was the name of Bar's girlfriend at the time, Bar was a part of the inner circle, and also Marley's older brother) were downtown together when they ran into some Hoyas members who also had some females with them. The females from both sides somehow got into an argument. It eventually got physical, and the Kemp Road fellas was there egging them on. Once Melly told Scrooge of the incident, it was no longer a matter of honor but a matter of duty. We now had to go and get them. It was now personal. We knew where their hangout was on Kemp Road. Three of our top shooters were sent in after them for a drive-by annihilation. This time nothing was to be taken for granted; even the driver himself was strapped. According to our information, they normally hung out on Strachan's Alley, in the heart of Kemp Road. The driver was told how to find it and where to look for them. But it seemed as though fortune was with them again, because even though the driver was told how to find Strachan's Alley, he was not inform that it was a one-way street. He entered travelling in the wrong direction, where he probably stood out like a sore thumb.

I was told that midway through our enemies spotted our guys and started their signature bark, which never failed to irritate us. They would cup both of their hands in front of their mouths and start barking into them. Even if there were only twenty of them, but once they started barking it was a deafening sound. I must give them credit; while we had the guns and the Raiders clothing, they had the defining bark. Yet as the old African proverb goes, *"The dog's bark is not might, but fright."*

I was told, "Each time the driver attempted to stop so that our guys could get off their shots, the Hoyas fellas would run away. As our guys started to move on again, they would then reassemble and start barking in unison. Our guys got fed up and left. When they exited Strachan's Alley and came on to the main Kemp Road, there were two fellas walking toward them. One was wearing a Hoyas Bull Dog jacket, so three of the shooters opened fire on the individual in the jacket, hitting him several times about the body."

However, we would later learn that the young man, who was shot, was only a teenager who was still in school. He would go on to make a full recovery, yet his only transgression that night was wearing a Hoya's jacket.

Chapter 15
THE WAR WITHIN

"When there is no enemy within, the enemies outside cannot hurt you." —African Proverb

Now that I was back with the gang, I slowly began to realize that something was different. The gang was not together. There was an unspoken division that was at work. We were all still Rebellions, and if you were at war with one you were at war with all. Yet the unity was not as strong as it was before I went to prison. There was something missing, because fellas from different areas were not hanging out through Strachan's Corner as they once did. The camaraderie just wasn't there. It was as if each one was drifting to his own way.

I didn't know what was going on, but I sensed that something was wrong. The closeness, the trust, and the unity that was there before I went to prison were all gone. Ada touched on this in my interview with him. He stated, "I believed that the problem started over the greed for guns. You had individuals who were stealing and swinging guns from other Rebellions. Then all of a sudden, that drove up the demand for every pocket of the Rebellions to get their own guns. This is when the problem started. The fellas couldn't trust Strachan's Corner anymore. Now they needed their own guns to fight their own wars. They no longer had to respect and wait on Strachan's Corner. They could now go on their own moves. So as a result of the trust issue, and fellas being able to go on their own moves, there was no more control."

Adding to this increase for guns, some members started smuggling drugs into the U.S. and then from the money made from the sale of their drugs, they would purchase weapons and traffic them back in laundry detergent boxes. Just about every name-brand person from the different areas was acquiring his own gun. The Rebellions were quickly becoming like a runaway freight train. Prior to each area acquiring its own guns, everybody more or less depended on Strachan's Corner to bring the firepower to the fight.

In my interview with Apples from Lizzy, he shed some more light on what was actually going on during that time. I asked Apples, "One time ago every Friday and Saturday, there used to be a big crew of you all from Elizabeth Estates hanging on East Street. But somehow, that dwindled down. What led to that?"

Apples said, "We had a good relationship with Scrooge and those fellas through Strachan's Corner, but what happened, because we were coming down all fresh up jewelry and money in our pockets, it was like a little jealousy started to develop. It got to a point where they wanted to tax one of our boys who came down with us. Troit stood up and said, 'Hey that can't work, because you fellas are trying to disrespect me.'

Apples continued, "As a result, we started to distance ourselves from East Street. We were still all one, but we never used to hang up on East Street anymore."

In my interview with Ninja, former leader of the Public Terrorist Rebellions, he confirmed this and elaborated even more. "I used to be in control of a yard on Milton Street, where fellas could come there and sleep. If they came there with jewelry, money, guns, or drugs, whatever they came with in their possession under my watch, they always left with what they came with. There was no one there trying to take advantage of them, or trying to take their possessions. This was one of the main things that I stood for, but in other parts of the gang that trust was not there. They did not feel safe. Even though we were a part of the same gang, they knew that they could be robbed by their own fellow gang members." So this was what I came out of prison to: the gang was not together as before. Our unity was quite fragile, and was only being held together by a thread. To top it off, I started to drift away from Scrooge. What brought this on was a gun. As mentioned before, when I was released from prison, Scrooge had put a .380 pistol in my hand. This was after I had given him five hundred dollars from the funds I had stolen during a shop break-in. Three hundred dollars out of the five hundred went towards the purchase of a gun for me. Scrooge told me that Mitch (now deceased) and Beacon had been bringing guns back from the States, so he would talk with Mitch about getting something for me. In the meantime, he told me to hold on the .380 until he got me straight.

One day, I took the weapon apart to clean it, where I remove the clip from the gun, and sprayed it down with WD-40. I then did the same with the clip, by first removing all of the bullets. Then I opened up the clip from the top, took out the spring, and sprayed that as well. However, I didn't put the clip back together properly. This led to the gun jamming each time I fired a shot. This was why the gun jammed on me when I had fired at Brent Sands and his crew. I was told that Scrooge spent all day at Franco's place trying to fix it, and complained about me straight through, first about causing his .44 to be busted, and now messing up this gun. When I heard about what he had said, I was disappointed. He was just complaining about guns, which could be replaced so easily.

Shooting Scrooge
"A close friend can become a close enemy." —African proverb

I stopped hanging with Scrooge altogether. This was in mid-January 1995. We did not even argue; rather, it was a matter of principle. As said earlier, Beacon and others were now trafficking guns in from the US where it is alleged that because they were not giving Scrooge something out of every shipment, he ordered a break-in at Beacon's place. They found a gun and some other personal items belonging to Beacon. I didn't know about this, as I was no longer considered part of Scrooge's inner circle. As a matter of fact, if he had told me what they were going to do, I would have been in favor of it simply because the majority of weapons that Beacon brought in were not being sold to Rebellions, but other people from different areas that were actually warring with us.

Owen even argued this particular point: one of the guns that Beacon sold was to a drug dealer on Kemp Road. This person was not involved in a gang, but his younger brother was in the Hoyas Bull Dog crew so the gun ended up in his younger brother's hands, and he fired several shots at Owen while he drove through Kemp Road. Prior to this, the Bull Dogs never brought a gun to a fight. Now things had started to change, because Beacon was selling guns to individuals from different areas.

I heard about the break-in at Beacon's house from Jeffrey (who was also a member of the gang from Strachan's Corner).

As a result, from that day onward I started hanging with a different group within the Rebellions. This included Beacon, Geo, Marley, Troit, Jeffrey, Cat, Dog, and Bolo from Wilson Track, just to name a few. Sometimes we would pass Scrooge and them, and one could sense the tension mounting. It was just a matter of time before we clashed with each other. One day, three of us—Marley, Geo, and I—were through Thompson Lane, which is the corner just to the north of Strachan's Corner. Scrooge and his crew were chilling further up through Thompson Lane. We had just passed him and ten others, and Franco and Lil Pat (now deceased) were beating up another Rebellion from a different area. We just walked past without saying anything. Marley whispered to me to remain cool. Once we got to the middle part of Thompson Lane, Marley said to Geo and me, pointing his chin in the direction of Scrooge and the others, "You know, they are trying to send a message to us, as to say that we will be next." I said, "You're right, but that fella is innocent."
Marley then told me that my 9 that Beacon had just sent from the US, was hidden behind the house in the yard opposite us. Beacon brought this gun over free of charge for me when he learned that I had given Scrooge three hundred dollars toward the purchase of a gun. At least that is what he wanted me to believe, but I would later learn otherwise the real reason for the gun.
Marley then said to me, "Deal, we'll be right back. Geo and I are just going to check on something."
I stood there by myself, looking down the road in the direction of Scrooge's crew. I could see that the beating was more or less finished. The fella in question was from Pinewood. I never knew his real name or street name. I only knew that Scrooge was sending a message to us, and it made me angry. Why beat up an innocent person just to deliver a message when you could deliver the message yourself? Anger boiled up within me, and without even thinking about it, my feet started walking in their direction.
When I got close enough to Scrooge, I told him, "You wrong for that. You beat up this fella for nothing."
He explained, "Man, this fella does be hanging with those Swamp Dogs."
The Swamp Dogs was another rival gang affiliated with the Hoyas Bull Dogs from Kemp Road. The majority of the gangs we warred with all had a dog somewhere in their names. You had the Hoyas Bull Dogs, the No Mercy Dogs, the Gun Dogs, etc.

Scrooge then stopped suddenly, I guess after he realized that he was explaining his reasoning behind the beating. As if to say, "I don't have to explain nothing to you." He walked over to me and said, "This isn't any of your business. You need to keep moving on."

As I've said before, there were about ten of them with him. Franz sat on a crate with a dagger in his hand. He was stabbing the crate and looking at his handiwork. He acted as if he weren't interested in the little argument between Scrooge and me. The rest also acted uninterested. I thought, 'Now this is going to be a fair one-on-one fistfight.' Even though Scrooge was taller than I was, I felt as if I could take him on and show him a thing or two.

It got to the point that he took off his gold chain and I took off my watch, putting it in my pants pocket. I believe that I even started to bob and weave like Muhammad Ali. Just as we were about to slug it out, Franz leapt at me like a cat with the knife in his hand. The others quickly followed him. I forgot about Scrooge. All I saw was that dagger in Franz's hand. I spun around and ran back where I came from, with all of them behind me in hot pursuit.

I had no plans as to what I was going to do. It was then I wondered, why do I keep getting myself into these jams? Fortunately, Marley and Geo were coming out of the shortcut at the same time. When Geo saw me running toward them, with Scrooge and his crew behind me, he pulled out a chrome .357 magnum and pulled the hammer back. I ran straight to him and snatched the gun out of his hand. I was not leaving it to Geo to pull the trigger. All of these guys grew up together, and I was the only outsider.

When I snatched the gun out of his hand, it fired because the hammer was already pulled back. It made the thunderous sound that the .357 magnum is known for. Even though the sound itself was deafening, it was like beautiful music to my ears. Just a few short seconds ago, the odds were greatly stacked against me. Now the tides had turned. The odds were now stacked against them, and they knew it. When I turned around to face my pursuers, they were in an all-out retreat. All I saw were their backs.

With the gun firmly secured in my hand, I fired two quick shots at Scrooge and just like that, the road was empty— except for Franz, who didn't run. I turned around to see him and Marley struggling over the dagger. Marley was able to wrestle it out of his hand.

Franz started shouting at me. "You better get from around here, you don't live around here, don't come back around here again!"

I snatched him by his wrist, and he tried to pull away from me. He was still shouting at me but at the same time trying to break away from my grip. I pointed the gun toward his midsection and pulled the trigger. The gun again bellowed its thunderous sound, but Franz kept struggling and shouting at me. I realized that I must have missed him, so I fired another shot toward his stomach. But just like before I missed him again, for he kept struggling and shouting at me, so each time I missed him I got even angrier.

I also was fed up with myself for missing such easy shots. I brought the gun up, but this time for a head shot. I was about to put this brother to rest. Marley gripped my wrist and shouted to me, "No, Deal, no, Deal, there's too many people around here."

I was totally caught up in the moment when Marley gripped my hand and shouted at me. I caught myself and looked at him. He was right. People were standing and gathering around. I had come within a fraction of a second of going back to prison, but this time it would've been for the murder of one of my fellow gang members. I let go of Franz's hand, and the three of us ran from the scene. We made a brief stop in the hood, where I felt a burning sensation in my left calf. I looked down at my calf to find out why it was burning so much. There I discovered a four-inch long gash on my left thigh. It was about an inch wide and a half-inch deep. I then asked, "How in the world I got this?"

We were puzzled for a moment, and then Geo said, "That must have happened when you snatched the gun out of my hand."

Marley reasoned, "You know, Geo's right. The gun was fully loaded with six shots, and you only fired five shots. When you snatched the gun, it went off. You then fired two shots at Scrooge and two at Franz, and that's the five shots there."

When we checked the gun, he was right. There was one more shot in the chamber.

We asked Mickey Mouse, a member of the Hood Rebellions, who was in the hood in his D. W. Davis school uniform and bag, to carry the gun for us. He used his school bag for this purpose. We moved on from the hood and made our way into Wilson Tract, where Bolo lived. Bolo, Cat, and Dog were there, and Marley and Geo told them what happened. While we were in Wilson Tract, I felt a light stinging in the back of my neck. I rested my hand on my neck just to rub it, but it stung. I quickly pulled my hand away, and when I looked at my fingers they were wet with blood. I got up and interrupted their story, and I asked them, pointing to the back of my neck, "Why is there blood on my neck?"

Marley told me, "Franz did that."

Puzzled, I asked him, "What do you mean, Franz did this?"

Marley explained, "When you were running from them, Franz was right on you. So when you snatched the gun out of Geo's hand and turned around firing at Scrooge, Franz was now behind you. That's how close he was on your heel."

Geo then chimed in. "Franz could run boy. Not many people could outrun him!"

Marley continued, "Franz sneaked up in the back of you. At first, I didn't even see him until he was about to stab you. That was when I caught his hand with the knife, which only scraped you on the back of your neck."

I rubbed the back of my neck exploring the cut, at the same time admiring Franz's bravery. I discovered that the knife wound was just below my hair line.

After a brief pause, Marley said to me, "But I thought you felt when he did that, because that was when you turned around and fired those two shots at him."

They continued telling Bolo and the others what had happened, but I tuned them out. I thought about Franz and his defiance, and I said to myself in a silent salute to him, one gangster to another, "Yeah, dog, yeah you ready."

I knew then that Franz was my real concern and not Scrooge. Marley told me years later, in the preparation of writing this book, "On that day you shot Scrooge, someone came running to Geo and me and told us that you, Scrooge, and the others who were with him were going to fight. It was them who told us that we needed to hurry back. That is why, when you came running down the road with Scrooge and them behind you, you met us coming out of the shortcut the same time."

When my son Lowell was eight years old, one day he and I had just finished playing. Tired and exhausted, we were lying on the bed talking. He sat up in the bed and started to trace his finger over the scar behind my neck. He asked me with concern in his voice, "Daddy, how you got this cut behind your neck?"

I hesitated for a while, wondering how much I should tell him, or if I should even tell him at all. I decided to tell him some of it, leaving out the part about the shooting. So I told him, "I got that from fighting with one of my friends."

Lowell didn't respond right away. After a moment of silence and tracing his finger over the scar, my son said something to me that I had never even considered up to that point. He said, "Daddy, your friend tried to kill you!"

What he said to me caused me to pause. My son was indeed right. I had always looked at that event as the day I shot Scrooge. I never fully realized until my son said so that I almost died on that day as well, and not just once but twice. I was viewed as a champion for shooting Scrooge, but I was almost a dead champion. If Marley and Geo had not been there that day, as we say locally, "Dog would've eaten my lunch," which is a kin to saying I would've been in some serious trouble.

The truth is I probably would've been paralyzed from the neck down today, or even worse, I could've died. I was so busy focusing on Scrooge that nothing and no one else mattered. I might have had the upper hand once I snatched the gun out of Geo's hand. Yet life is so fragile and unpredictable, especially when you are in a gang or in a life of crime. It's like playing poker; you think to yourself that you have a good hand. However, it is only when you reveal your hand do you sometimes discover to your horror that someone else's hand is better.

However, Franco would later make me aware, that I came close to death not twice but three times on that day I shot Scrooge. In 1998 he and I were in the same cell at Prison, when he told me, "You know, that day you shot Scrooge, we had a nine stashed nearby. We knew that tension was building between us and you, and so we started to keep the nine nearby instead of the .380. So when you came up the road, after we finished beating that fella nobody bothered going for the nine, because it was only you one to all of us. But after you snatched that gun out of Geo's hand and fired those shots at us, I ran back to get the nine. We had it stashed in a mattress through the shortcut next to where we were hanging out."

Then he asked me in a serious tone, "You know, each time I jammed my hand in that mattress to find the gun, I couldn't find it? I was like, 'Where in the hell this gun is?' I heard when you were firing those shots at Franz, but I couldn't find that gun. It was only after you left did I found the gun."
While we were still at Bolo's place, Troit caught up with us. He had heard what happened, and it was him who told us that Scrooge had been shot in his hand. He also told us that Scrooge was at the hospital, and Franz and the others were with him. Here again, Marley and Geo filled him in on what had actually happened.

There's Never A Winner In A Street Fight
"A fight between grasshoppers is a joy to the crow." — *African proverb*

I had just started dating a young lady named Linda. She was from the US, and was in her last year at Aquinas College one of our local private schools. Her mother is an American, and she had married a Bahamian whom she had met here while on vacation. I phoned Linda and told her what had happened, and she pleaded with me to allow her mother to look at my leg wound, because her mother was working at Princess Margaret Hospital (PMH), the government-run hospital. I reluctantly went to see her. Linda's mother looked at the wound on my calf, and strongly recommended that I go to the hospital. I called home and spoke to Vanessa, who happened to be there. I told her that I had been shot and how it happened. Vanessa and Leon came to pick me up from Linda's place. Leon was Vanessa's boyfriend at the time, and is the father of my oldest nephew, who is also named after him - whom we just call LJ. Leon, who is also a police officer, suggested that I go to the police station first, since the injury was not life threatening. I could also be the first to make a complaint against Scrooge. As Leon said, "Sometimes the first to make a complaint in a fight like this is never charged." They dropped me off at the Nassau Street Police Station.

The officer in charge didn't allowed anyone to take a complaint from me, because it was a gunshot wound, even though not life threatening. They called an ambulance to transport me to the hospital. They told me that an officer would get my statement at the hospital once the doctors were finished with me. When the ambulance arrived at the police station, I told them to drop me off at Doctors' Hospital. This is the only other hospital on the island other than PMH, but it is privately owned. I had been told that Franz and the others were at PMH with Scrooge, and I didn't need a second encounter with Franz and Franco especially now that I am unarmed, when they probably would be armed. I knew by then that they must have heard that I had been shot as well. My admission to Doctors' Hospital was denied because I didn't have the proper medical insurance therefore, I had to be transferred to PMH. By this time, my mother was there, and I expressed my concern to her about going to PMH. One of the ambulance drivers, who realized that this was a gang feud, overheard this. When he realized that someone from the opposing side had also been shot and was at PMH, possibly waiting with his crew, he refused to transport me to PMH until they were notified that armed police would be at Accident and Emergency. Once they received that confirmation from their dispatcher, then they transferred me to PMH.
When I got at PMH, Scrooge's girlfriend Melly came to me and said, "Scrooge said to tell the police you don't know who shot you." I nodded my head in agreement. I didn't know what Scrooge was up to. He probably thought that Franz and Franco had caught up with me and shot me. Nevertheless, I didn't trust him on this one. As soon as the police came in to get my statement, before he even sat down, I bellowed, "Scrooge shot me!" The officer didn't even bother to ask who Scrooge was or what area he was from. By this time, every police officer worth his or her badge was familiar with the name Scrooge. I used that to my advantage, because who was I to the police in comparison with Scrooge? I was basically a nobody and Scrooge was considered a menace to society.
The officer asked me, "How did this happen?"
I told him, "Scrooge pulled a gun on me. Without even thinking, I panicked and reached for the gun. We ended up struggling for the gun. That was when it went off, hitting me in my left calf. Being in fear for my life, knowing the type of person Scrooge is, I fought even harder, and I managed to get control of the gun, and accidentally shot him in his hand in the process."

The officer then asked me, "Where is Scrooge now?"
I said in my head, "What a dumb question that is. You had to walk past him to get in the back here to me". But I said to him, "He's right out there, with a towel wrapped around his hand."
He jerked his head up from his legal pad, and asked with a look of surprise on his face, "You're telling me, that quiet fella out there is Scrooge?"
I thought to myself, "Bingo, you finally got it". Yet I was also surprised that an officer at CID wasn't able to recognize Scrooge. I smiled inwardly to myself and said "Boy, Scrooge, you are busted now."
The officer didn't even finish taking my statement. He just closed his legal pad, got up, and left the room. Several minutes later, the doctor came in and examined the wound on my calf. He said to me, "For the most part, it is a superficial wound. We are unable to suture it because it is too wide. It may look bad now, but as it heals the flesh will come up more to the surface."
I was released from the hospital with a prescription for some antibiotics. Scrooge was admitted to the hospital for surgery to his hand. As I prepared to exit the hospital, the investigating officer told me that I had to go with him to CID. They didn't handcuff me; they just put me in the back of a car and off we went. At CID, I sat there for two or three hours until they decided to release me without pressing any charges. I guess they said, "Ah, let those two kill each other, and we'll go pick up the winner."
Franco adds to this point by saying, "When a guy goes out there and kills somebody, he might look at himself as the winner. But in truth he's also a loser, because now he would be lost in the system."
Then he said to me, "If you were listening to the news recently, some people you know well are doing 45, and 64 years for murder. They might have won their fight, but they lost their lives to the system."

Therefore, when one looks at it carefully there's never a winner when it comes to violence. Let's just say the worse did happen on that day, and I had actually killed Franz. Yes, I would've been viewed as the winner, but at the end of the day I was also a loser. Oh, I would've been revered and feared by others because of my actions, but those same actions would've been my downfall. Now my problems would really have begun starting with the police and, once convicted, I would've been sentence to death. So in fact nobody would've won, because the last man left standing would also be executed by the state.

Victory at The Hands of the Police
"From triumph to downfall there is but one step. I have noted that, in the most momentous occasions, mere nothings have always decided the outcome of the greatest events." — Napoleon Bonaparte
The next day, I linked up with Marley and the others, and we went to a phone calling station. Where he proceeded to called Beacon who was still in Miami, and told him what had happened the day before. After a while, Marley gave me the phone. When I came on the line, Beacon was ecstatic with joy.
He said to me, "When I sent those guns down, I knew you were going to do something. I just knew you were going to do something."
I mumbled some words back to him in return, and handed Marley back the phone. I felt sick to my stomach. I wanted to vomit right then. I felt used and foolish. This brother wasn't interested in me when he bought me that gun. He was only interested in Scrooge, and I was just the hothead triggerman. To make matters worse, he stayed in the States just to make sure that he would be in the clear. I felt used and silly. So this was the main reason he bought me that nine; it was so I could shoot Scrooge for him. I would eventually, slowly but surely, drift off from Beacon.
A day after shooting Scrooge, Troit, Marley, Geo, and I ended up on Nassau Street. This area was home to another arm of the Rebellions called the Fighting Irish. We were there to watch a basketball tournament. Once we got there, the Fighting Irish told us that they had a big fight on the park the night before, where they ran some fellas from the Gun Dogs from off the park.

On that night, it was a celebration of some sort. The fellas were passing around Night Train, saying, "Drink up, everybody, this one goes to Deal for shooting Scrooge last night!"

I indeed did drink up, to the point where I really got drunk. It was the first and last time that I would get drunk. I remember Owen being in the park as well. Somehow, Franz, Franco and those found out where we were, and they came there looking for revenge. There I was, drunk, bareback and barely aware of what was going on. In all of that haziness, I heard Franz and Franco calling Owen to the car. They were asking Owen for the 12-gauge shotgun that they had loaned to him. Even though I was drunk, I mumbled to myself, "You guys came all the way out here looking for a shotgun? If you guys are looking for me, then here I am. Just shoot me and get it over with." However, little did I know, because I was too drunk, that the only reason they didn't open fire on me, was simply because there were armed police officers on the park. As a result of the fight the night before, the police were there that night just to make sure nothing happened. It would not be the last time that police officers would prevent me from being shot or possibly killed.

Troit and Marley told me later that they were ready for them if they had tried anything, because they were also strapped. Yet it didn't stop me from thinking how close I came to being shot or even killed. On top of that, the next morning, Marley and Troit told me how badly I had been carrying on. I'd stopped people's cars and attempted to pull them out of their vehicles. To make matters worse, I didn't remember a thing. I made a vow to myself right then that I would never get drunk again, and I have kept that vow to this date.

I spoke with Franco about that night, and he confirmed the details by saying, "We got word that you were on Christie Park, out there on Nassau Street. We went and hustled a ride. It was four of us. Each one of us was lock and loaded, Franz, Bar, Poe Skull and myself [these were the individuals who made up Scrooge's inner circle at the time]. When we pulled up, I saw you there with no shirt on, and Franz was about to shoot you, but I stopped him. I then pointed to the two armed police officers who were also out there on the park."

After getting no response from Owen, they drove off, but at the same time, someone fired two shots in the air from the car. The two police who were there did not open fire on them, because there were too many people out there. Instead, the officers radioed in the make, the description and the color of the vehicle they were in. As a result they were intercepted by a patrol car, while making their way back on East Street. This led to a high-speed chase throughout the island, where the police opened fire on their vehicle. In the process, Franco was shot once in the thigh, Franz was shot four times, and Poe Skull was shot in the hand.

Franco picked back up by saying, "As we were fleeing through the East Street area, we started ditching the guns in yards we knew. The intention was if we got away, we would double back and get the guns."

However, the police cornered them on Dowdeswell Street. Five of them were in the vehicle, and the three who were shot were transferred to the hospital. Bar, the driver Michael who they had caught a ride with, were not shot so they were taken into police custody. Fortunately for them, the hospital was just around the corner. However, Franco also credits the driver, Michael, for saving their lives that night. He told me some years ago when we were in prison together, "If it wasn't for Michael, I believe we would all be dead, because he really handled that car well. We had so many near misses that I can't even begin to count. To top it off, I honestly can't see how more of us didn't get shot up. When the police counted the bullet holes, there were twenty-seven bullet holes in the car, and I'm not talking about all the glass which were shot out; I am talking about just the bullet holes in the car."

The driver, Michael, according to Franco, was just someone who lived in the East Street area and was never involved in the gang. They just happened to ask him for a ride to go to Nassau Street. He never knew what they were up to. A simple ride to Nassau Street turned out to be the ride of his life.

Just like that, within little more than 24 hours Scrooge was shot, all of his guns were gone, and his entire inner circle was in prison. Even though we were warring at the time, there was no rejoicing because at the end of the day, we were still all Rebellions. It was a bittersweet moment for us. It was bitter because they were Rebellions. On the other hand, it was sweet to know that Scrooge had lost all of his guns. This in itself provided us with some breathing room, because we all knew that Scrooge wasn't going to take a shot, lie down, and give up his crown.

One of the guns landed directly in Archie's yard, a .45 semiautomatic pistol. This gun had originally belonged to Marley, but Scrooge managed to get it out of the hands of another Rebellion named Nair, who lived through Strachan's Corner, and was keeping it for Marley. According to Nair, he said, "Scrooge just walked up and told me: 'Marley said to lend me that thing.'"
This had happened just two weeks before the incident between Scrooge and me. So the word got out that Archie had the .45, which was the only gun that had survived the police chase. However, just two weeks later, Scrooge was able to retrieve the gun the same way he did with Nair, and in the process, the fellas from Milton Street beat up Archie.

We Were All Rebelling
"The thing worse than rebellion is the thing that causes rebellion." —Frederick Douglas

I believe that the biggest hurdle that we face as a nation and as a people, is how can we ensure that those conditions which brought forth the Rebellions and many other street gangs, never be allowed to exist again.
When I look at it carefully, by examining the interviews and the various social scientists' studies, it becomes easy for me to see that we all were just rebelling. Regardless of the area we grew up in or the gang we were affiliated with, or which part of the Western world we found ourselves in, we all were rebelling. We were rebelling and crying out for our fathers. We were rebelling against the home conditions that existed in our communities. We needed our fathers, but above all we wanted to be loved and accepted by them. Since we couldn't find it at home and in our respective communities, we created it for ourselves.
My research continues to amaze and baffle me. As human beings, we are geniuses. What we didn't get from the home, we find ways of getting elsewhere. It's evident, then, when one looks at the stats we don't have a teenage pregnancy problem and we don't have a street gang problem. I will even suggest that we don't have a drug and alcohol problem, nor do we have a crime problem rather, these are only the symptoms that we are experiencing, and the real problem is broken homes that result in broken lives. This is why the African slave Frederick Douglass stated more than 150 years ago, *"The thing worse than rebellion is the thing that causes rebellion."*

We know that Douglass was referring to slaves rebelling against their masters in his day and time. However, the principle found within is applicable to the matter at hand. According to the American Heritage Dictionary of the English Language, the definition of the word "rebellion" is "an act or a show of defiance toward an authority or established convention. Extensions of the expression include to fly in the face of danger and to fly in the face of providence, both of which carry a sense of reckless or impetuous disregard for safety."Because we did not grow up with our fathers, we became reckless with our lives and disregarded the lives of others as well. Therefore, the problem is not the gangs, so to speak; rather, it's the conditions that create them. It is the dismantling of our homes and marriages that create the right conditions for gangs to flourish. If homes could be put back together or prevented from falling apart, then these symptoms could be eradicated. We again turn to the article written by Eugene C. Roehlkepartain, titled *"What Gangs Give Kids That You Don't"* published in the June-August 1990 edition of Group Magazine. He stated, *"We're seeing a whole generation of young people reacting to two decades of neglect, poverty, and the scourge of the dysfunctional family."*

Prevention Is Still Better Than Cure
"It is easier to build strong children than to repair broken men." Frederick Douglass
In closing I would like to turn my attention back to Supt. Allerdyce Strachan, for she is better known among her colleagues as the officer who pioneered community policing in the Bahamas. It was her who reached out to us on East Street, when everybody else was avoiding the area like some plague had broken out. Looking back now I can better appreciate, that it really was a plague of some sort. It was the social plague resulting from the aftermath of the absentee father, that was sweeping through our nation and the rest of the western world.

Today, community policing is at the heart of the Bahamian government's Urban Renewal initiative encompassing a lot of Supt. Strachan principles, which is strongly promoted by our Prime Minister, the Right Honorable Perry Christie.

I asked her, "When the Rebellions were at its peak doing nonsense, everyone was trying to keep away from the area, yet you were going in, why were you going into that area?"

Supt. Strachan answered quite frankly, "Because I was not afraid. I felt like they are my people, they are my color. I don't know of anyone born after me that I should be afraid of, that was how I felt. I knew I could've walk through Strachan's Corner, sit down and felt at home, and their parents also accepted me.

I came to the conclusion; these kids just need someone to show them some attention. They just wanted to belong, that was what a lot of them were looking for. So I said to myself, if I could assist them I would, and that was what I did."

One day I was through Strachan's Corner just hanging out, and they must have picked up Scrooge earlier for a pep talk, so they were now dropping him back home in one of their police vehicle. Supt. Strachan was in the back seat talking with him, while a male officer was driving. So I asked her, what were some of the things you used to say to Scrooge?

"I used to tell him it is not worth it," she said "You are hurting people. You are only going to end up in jail for the rest of your life, or you are going to end up in the grave. I knew that he was listening to me. I would talk to him and encourage him. My other colleagues used to say I was soft on crime because of what I was doing, but I could be tuff. I am a mother of two sons; just ask my sons how tuff I can be. If I feel that I have done the best that I can, and cannot do no more than that is it. This was what I was telling those kids down there.

I told them if you do not change, you are going to die. Sad to say, that is what happened to some of them eventually. The best came out of you and others in another way."

Then with a serious tone she said, "When I was reaching out to those young men through Strachan's Corner, nobody told me what to do, I was doing it from my heart. I did what I thought was best rather than giving those youngsters a police record, I tried to prevent it by letting them know if you commit crime you are going to get yourself in trouble. Then you will be confined to the Bahamas for the rest of your life, and will not see that great big world out there.

There were times in meeting I was called a baby sitter, a social worker by my colleagues. Now that we have a different leader, he looks at it the way I look at it, and he supported me in what I was doing. There were times he saw me crying, and he would comfort me and say that's okay. Commissioner Paul Farquharson was one of my biggest supporters."

Then with a tinge of anger Supt. Strachan said, "It used to hurt me, because I was trying to help somebody and they say I was babysitting. Don't tell me I am babysitting, now that I have retired now I am babysitting. So not because I was trying to reach out and work with those children, don't say I was babysitting them.
I work the Criminal Investigation Department (CID) for 22 years and I was rough in CID. I realize CID was the end result, because whenever you get to that stage you are almost finished. It is in line with the broken window theory, if you can save those youngsters before they start committing those big offenses, then they wouldn't reach CID. Crime prevention was a part of my job, I believe in going out there and trying to prevent that youngster from committing crime. He should respect other people's property."
She continued, "I would hear them say on the radio, that we need to hang them once they have been convicted for murder. I don't think that some of them should have ever reached that stage. If we had prevented them from going on death row, it would not be a discussion about hanging them."
In conclusion Supt. Strachan said, "When I hear and see young men like you and Troit, who have turned their lives around, it makes me feel good. We need to learn to love one another; there is just too much hate in this world."

I thank you for journeying with me, into the heartlands of innocence to menacing. For we have seen how youngsters evolve into monsters, and become remorseless predators.
If this book has been an eye opener for you, please write me and let me know. Better yet why don't you post your review directly on Amazon, by clicking on the buy now link on my website, I will truly appreciate it!

Please Note: To send a snail mail or an e-mail to me, concerning this book or the upcoming installments see the mailing instructions below:
Drexel D. Deal
P. O. Box CB-12063
Nassau, N. P. Bahamas

E-mail: diron.deal@gmail.com
Website: www.drexeldeal.com

Epilog
"To Be Continued."

While we have reached the end of this book, yet we've not reach the end of our journey together. This first book was just to properly identify the root problems that we face as a people, as a nation and as a region. As the late Charles Kettering puts it, the famed inventor with 186 patents to his credit. He stated *"a problem well-stated is half-solved."*

This book has not been a work of joy for me, in which so many authors refer to their first completed work. Rather this book has been a labor of pain, that has brought me to tears many times. At the same time it has given birth to my present awareness, of my important role as a father and a uncle. To know that I can shape and mold my grandchildren's and grand nieces and nephews lives tomorrow, just through my involvement in my son's nieces and nephews life today.

I know there's a lot of hurt and pain that is still balled up within me from my childhood, however, here's what I found to be interesting, the more I write about my past mistakes, the more I'm being set free. As I pour my past shame, hurts and pain out on these pages, God's healing, forgiveness and restoration is being poured into me.

At the same time something else is happening, I'm able to look back and better see the end results of not only my mistakes, but my parents and grandparents mistakes. In so doing I'm able to chart a better path, towards a brighter future for myself, my son and my nieces and nephews. Their future would be much better, not because of any material things they may possess, but rather their future would be better because of what they possess on the inside.

Each day I'm shaping and molding my son's life, by the life I live today. I'm not trying to weed out all that is bad in him, rather each day I'm doing away with what is bad within me, and in so doing my example would rub off on him. It was the popular Judge of TV's Divorce Court, Lynn Toler, who stated, *"You teach a boy how to become a man, by being one yourself."*

Through my interviews I have come to better appreciate, that we were not really fighting against each other, rather we were more or less fighting alongside each other. We might have been from different communities, and different western countries but our fight was the same. Our pain was the same; our hunger was for the same thing which was for our fathers. Sadly, too many of us died in this fight, when all we wanted was to be loved, to be accepted and embraced by our fathers. As I look back on the lives of so many of our young men whose potential were snuffed out much too early, I would've gladly sacrificed my life for all of them. I would've willingly died in their place. Instead, I'm task with the most difficult job of all, which is to tell their stories and it hurts much worse than being shot. As a people and as a nation, we have to band together and put an end to this war that is being wage against our families. If not, we would self-destruct by imploding from within.

The next book is another series of violent twist and turns, as I quickly rise to the top in the Rebellions after shooting Scrooge. This would result in a bloody and deadly internal war within the Rebellions.

Scrooge would regroup to be much stronger, before carrying out his revenge which resulted in me being shot, after dodging and running from a hail of bullets. When he revealed to me what save my life on that night, it makes the hair on the back of my neck stand up.

Yet it was from my hospital bed that I vowed not to get even, but to get rid of Scrooge and never to allow anyone I shoot again to live. I to would regroup and come back much stronger, as Scrooge and I prepare for the ultimate gun battle. The winner takes control of East Street, while the loser would rest in peace in his grave. So how does everything unfold? Who was the last man left standing?

In Book Two we would continue to present our case, and lay it on the table for a public discussion on the matter, that the fight of our lives were indeed wrapped up in our fathers.

APPENDIX

*....According to information found on Mr. Ansil Saunders' personal website—a boat maker and a bone-fishing guide on Bimini for more than 50 years—he was asked by Adam Powell to take him and a special guest out fishing. The special guest just happened to be Dr. Martin Luther King.

Mr. Saunders is proud to proclaim that he was the guide who took Dr. King out fishing. Dr. King had first visited in 1964, where he worked on his Nobel Peace Prize acceptance speech while on the island. He would also visit in 1968, where he again worked on another speech that he planned to deliver to a group of striking sanitation workers in Memphis, Tennessee, just weeks before his death. On October 5, 2012, the Bahamas Government unveiled a bust in the image of Dr. King designed and sculpted by renowned sculptor Erik Blome. The bust was placed in the mangroves on Bimini where Dr. King is said to have found peace, solace, and inspiration during his two trips.

The island of Bimini is just one of the more than 700 islands that make up the Bahamas' chain of islands.

@@@

**....The capital of the Bahamas is Nassau, which is the commercial heart beat for our entire country. Even though New Providence is only 21 miles long and 7 miles wide, which represents a mere 3% of the total landmass of the Bahamas, yet 70% of our population resides within New Providence. Everyone refers to the island of New Providence as just Nassau, which is not only the island's capital but also the capital of The Bahamas. Nassau is the city of opportunity for young adults from the outer islands. The majority of them, after completing high school, migrate to Nassau in search of gainful employment.

According to the 2010 census, the population of the Bahamas is little more than 350,000; and close to 260,000 people resides in Nassau alone. We refer to the outer islands surrounding the capital as "family islands" because every Bahamian has family members who still reside in the outer islands.

***….. It is said that the island of Eleuthera is the birthplace of the Bahamas. It was named by Captain William Sayles, who was the leader for the group of Puritans known as the Eleutheran Adventurers, in the mid-1600s. They had sailed from Bermuda in search of religious freedom. Thus, the name Eleuthera comes from the Greek words eleuthero or eleuther, which means "free" or "freedom."

Even though Long Island is said to be the most scenic of the 29 inhabited islands of The Bahamas, the island of Eleuthera has the most frequently highly ranked and awarded beaches anywhere in The Bahamas, which is due in part to the soft pink sand beach of Harbor Island.

However, it's no secret in the travel industry that The Bahamas has more beautiful beaches than all of the Caribbean destinations combined. With miles of splendid, tranquil, and naturally unspoiled powder white sand beaches, each of them is authentically different in their own way. While each of our islands is surrounded by the same turquoise and blue waters, it's the different landscape of the islands that makes each beach magnificent and beautiful to look at.

It is common knowledge that the coastal areas of every country around the world have the highest human development and traffic on earth. Yet it is often said that our beaches are visited more by the gentle sea breeze, warm sunshine, and rhythmic sea waves than by people.

When spending time on one of our outer island beaches, it can sometimes feel as if you have your own secluded tropical paradise all to yourself. There are so many undeveloped and unfrequented beaches in The Bahamas that it is not unusual for days or even weeks to pass by without seeing any sign of human traffic on them.

@@@

#....The island of Andros, where my grandmother is from, is better known among the locals by two nicknames: "The Sleeping Giant" and "The Big Yard." It is the largest island in the Bahamas, stretching some 104 miles long and some 40 miles wide. Andros is known as the bonefish capital of the world, and as having one of the oldest dive resorts in the world. It is said that when the Spanish discovered Andros, they named it Isla del Esperita Santo, the Island of the Holy Spirit, a tribute to the abundance of fresh water laced with thousands of miles of inland waterways.

Even though Andros is rich with natural resources, and is the largest island of The Bahamas, it is the most under-populated and underdeveloped of our islands. According to our 2012 census report, slightly fewer than 8,000 residents called Andros home. However, when one compares the Long Island of New York to Andros, Long Island is slightly smaller in size, being some 118 miles long and some 23 miles wide, but has a population of 7,568,304 residents, according to the 2010 U.S. census report. I guess this is why it is said, "Andros is perhaps the largest tract of unexplored and underdeveloped land in the Western hemisphere."

@@@

##.... According to the Bahamian historian H. Johnson "The Contract was a farm labor program established on March 16, 1943, by the governments of The Bahamas and the United States of America. It allowed thousands of Bahamian men and women from islands throughout the archipelago to carry out agricultural work in many American states. Bahamians cultivated and harvested a variety of crops, from tobacco in Tennessee and peaches in Georgia to corn in Minnesota, citrus in Florida, and peanuts in North Carolina. Some workers returned to The Bahamas. Others settled in communities located around the United States, particularly in the state of Florida and New York."

@@@

(i)....The mail boat is an inherent part of the Bahamian culture, and is the largest domestic shipping network in The Bahamas. The mail boat system, of course, got its name from the fact that these boats were responsible for carrying the mail to the many islands. Over the years, this system has developed into a major shipping industry that transports tons of goods from the city of Nassau to the family islands on a weekly basis. It is vital to the Out Islands to get food, and building supplies.

Designated mail boats still carry the government mail as well as any other government cargo. The system is of such importance that it captures a spot on the morning news, which is referred to as the 'Shipping Report'.

The system of mail boats in The Bahamas is a true net; it binds the country together. From Nassau, the mail boats go to every major island, with mostly cargo, but do take the adventuresome passenger.

The above information came from the websites: www.briland.com, and www.bahamas4u.com.

@@@

+…. In an article entitled "What is Bahamian Culture," Adrian Gibson, a noted Bahamian scholar and writer, stated, "One original aspect of Bahamian culture is the Asue, which is a custom that has survived the test of time and allows many Bahamians to form cooperatives to contribute and accumulate cash. Since slaves were banned from using banks, they formed Asue's—with trustworthy persons organizing everything—to save and borrow money. Today, Bahamians participating in this continue to anxiously await their 'draw.'"

++….According to the Junkanoo Corporation of New Providence (JCNP), which is the governing/organizing body for Junkanoo in Nassau. The following information came from their website, [jcnp.net]: "The roots of Junkanoo are to be found in the continent of Africa. The most popular theory surrounding the name (originally referred to as John Canoe) is that John Canoe was an African trader on the West African Coast during the era of slavery. Whatever the origin of the name, the celebration began with the slaves who were transported across the Atlantic. Under British law, slaves in British colonies were given three days' holiday at Christmas. Junkanoo has been documented in the former British territories of Jamaica, Belize, and North and South Carolina (in the US), but only in the Bahamas has Junkanoo grown into such an elaborate festival, one of which all Bahamians are justly proud.

"Legend has it that the slaves attempted to decorate themselves by sticking materials to be found in their environment, such as paper and feathers, onto their clothes. The custom of sticking paper has evolved over the years into a fine art. Nowadays, the finely cut crepe paper is pasted onto cardboard shapes in the most intricate designs, using every color in the spectrum. Costumes may be as tall as fifteen feet, and are danced for the entire parade. The music is also historically based, and is still centered around the traditional cowbells (which were originally used because of their availability on the plantations), and the goatskin drum, which is a staple African instrument. The traditional horn of Junkanoo was a conch shell, and today we also use a variety of whistles and other horns.

"Over the years, the Junkanoo Parades have increased in size, which has led to more organization. Barricades and a circular route were introduced in the 1970s, and bleachers in the 1980s. So to have the costumes evolve into the spectacular works of art that we see today, the costumes have always reflected the availability of materials in the society, and so from the feathers and scraps of the plantation, the costumes grew through a variety of materials: plant life, straw work, sponge, newspaper, tissue paper, and finally to the crepe paper of today.

The participants in this uniquely Bahamian festival come from all walks of life, and are all ages. The organized groups, which compete for cash prizes, spend at least six months of the year producing the elaborate costumes. Junkanoo participants may parade as individuals, or as part of a group, in adult and juvenile categories. Adult groups may number between 3-500 members. Many persons opt to parade for fun, and are called 'Scrap.'

"Junkanoo, the major cultural festival of the Bahamas, is a magnificent celebration of life and freedom. It is celebrated in two spectacular parades on Boxing Day, December 26, and New Year's Day, January 1 of each year, from 1:00 a.m. to 9:00 a.m. on Bay Street in downtown Nassau. Breath-taking costumes made from cardboard, wire, and finely cut crepe paper, are paraded to the unique sounds of pulsating goatskin drums, cowbells, horns, and whistles. The festival attracts large crowds of Bahamians and visitors, and has become a spectacle of color and celebration. For Bahamians, it is the highpoint of the season: eight exhilarating hours in the early morning, when the nation's main street is transformed into a sea of sight and sound that amazes, astounds, and enthralls all who view it.

"Junkanoo parades are also held in most of the Family Islands of The Bahamas, but do not approach the elaborate scale of the parade in Nassau. Junkanoo is a unique cultural phenomenon that is a 'must' activity for everyone in The Bahamas at Christmas time."

www.ingramcontent.com/pod-product-compliance
Lightning Source LLC
Chambersburg PA
CBHW060459090426
42735CB00011B/2037